ENTREPRENEURSHIP AND SUSTAINABLE DEVELOPMENT IN AFRICA

SAGE was founded in 1965 by Sara Miller McCune to support the dissemination of usable knowledge by publishing innovative and high-quality research and teaching content. Today, we publish over 900 journals, including those of more than 400 learned societies, more than 800 new books per year, and a growing range of library products including archives, data, case studies, reports, and video. SAGE remains majority-owned by our founder, and after Sara's lifetime will become owned by a charitable trust that secures our continued independence.

Los Angeles | London | New Delhi | Singapore | Washington DC | Melbourne.

Paschal Anosike

ENTREPRENEURSHIP AND SUSTAINABLE DEVELOPMENT IN AFRICA

$SAGE

Los Angeles | London | New Delhi
Singapore | Washington DC | Melbourne

SAGE Publications Ltd
1 Oliver's Yard
55 City Road
London EC1Y 1SP

SAGE Publications Inc.
2455 Teller Road
Thousand Oaks, California 91320

SAGE Publications India Pvt Ltd
B 1/I 1 Mohan Cooperative Industrial Area
Mathura Road
New Delhi 110 044

SAGE Publications Asia-Pacific Pte Ltd
3 Church Street
#10-04 Samsung Hub
Singapore 049483

Library of Congress Control Number: 2021946203

British Library Cataloguing in Publication data

A catalogue record for this book is available from the British Library

Editor: Matthew Waters
Assistant editor: Jasleen Kaur
Senior project editor: Chris Marke
Project management: TNQ Technologies
Cover design: Francis Kenney
Typeset by: TNQ Technologies
Printed in the UK

ISBN 978-1-5264-6939-7
ISBN 978-1-5264-6938-0 (pbk)

At SAGE we take sustainability seriously. Most of our products are printed in the UK using FSC papers and boards. When we print overseas we ensure sustainable papers are used as measured by the PREPS grading system. We undertake an annual audit to monitor our sustainability.

In loving memories of my Dad – who first took me to school…

And

my little brother D'boy – whose love is unyielding.

SUMMARY OF CONTENTS

CONTENTS

PRAISE FOR THE BOOK

'This book provides a timely update of the topic of sustainable development in an African context. The African continent remains characterised by inequality, poverty, unemployment and significant societal challenges. Despite several African nations experiencing significant economic growth, the significant challenges of climate change and the Covid-19 crisis offer significant immediate challenges that require transformational change. This book offers a fresh perspective of how these challenges can be met and provides an excellent overview of a potential roadmap to a more prosperous African nation. I would highly recommend this book for policy makers, academics and the business community.'

Paul Jones, Professor of Entrepreneurship and
Innovation, Swansea University, UK

'An impassioned assessment of the development travails and opportunities of the African continent. Paschal Anosike writes lucidly, with the persuasiveness of a scholar who has spent considerable time reflecting on these issues. This book is a must-have for every African or Africanist development scholar, policymaker, entrepreneur, and other stakeholders and investors in the African project.'

Oka Obono, Professor of Population Studies and Chair
Population Studies Unit, University of Ibadan, Nigeria

'If you are going to read one book to understand contemporary Africa in terms of its socio-economic trajectory, I strongly recommend this lucid and frank detour exploring pressing issues facing the African continent. The author writes with palpable connection to the African experience, covering the positives and negatives of development from the stagnating institutional forces to the entrepreneurial energy and optimism of African youth. The book charts issues as they unravel within the decimating impact of Covid-19 and picks up on the possibilities of leap frogging through the adoption of emerging Industry 4.0 technology. A must read if you want to come to grips with Africa today.'

Pervaiz K. Ahmed, Professor of Management and Director,
Institute of Global Strategy and Competitiveness,
Sunway University, Malaysia

'This book cannot come at a better time than this. In his book, Paschal Anosike meticulously dissects the complexities of the African continent and offers sustainable solutions for everyone concerned with building the 'Africa We Want'. His views on building strong foundations for entrepreneurship and sustainable development through reform and investment in quality education and entrepreneurship training for young people are unparalleled. A must read for everyone who takes an interest in building a prosperous future for Africa.'

Matt Kuppers, Independent Policy Expert and Executive Board Member, European Institute of Innovation and Technology (EIT)

'The central role of developing entrepreneurship and employability skills for the sustainable development of Africa cannot be overemphasized, especially during the post Covid-19 era. This book is designed for academics, scholars, development partners and policy makers, and provides an incisive study on these contemporary issues facing the continent, with an ever-increasing population.'

Professor Abel Idowu Olayinka, Vice-Chancellor (2015–2020), University of Ibadan, Nigeria

ABOUT THE AUTHOR

Paschal Anosike (FRSA) is Associate Professor of Entrepreneurship and Innovation and the Founding Director of the Centre for African Entrepreneurship and Leadership (CAEL) at the University of Wolverhampton. He is also the Convener, Forum for Innovation in African Universities (FIAU) Global Annual Meeting. Paschal is heavily engaged in creating and implementing full-range systems of entrepreneurship and innovation with a sub-Saharan African focus.

He is published at the top-tier of authoritative scientific rankings and has spoken widely on these topics, including several keynotes.

He advises the African Union Commission (AUC) and the London-based global think-tank – the Legatum Institute (LI) – through which he helped to pioneer the publication and launch of the Africa Prosperity Index (API) at the World Economic Forum on Africa. Previously, he advised The Commonwealth/UNCTAD, UNDP, British Council and GIZ – the German Development Agency.

PREFACE

We live in a worrying new world order in which Africa represents the most striking symbol of global inequality and post-colonial failure. In addition to being a key economic concern, inequality represents the greatest societal challenge of the twenty-first century. The COVID-19 pandemic has no doubt given a sharper edge to the seriousness of this challenge. I was struck by the socio-economic effect of the pandemic on young Africans, particularly in terms of curtailed access to education and employment at a crucial stage in their life's development. But even before the pandemic, what concerned me the most was the troubling state of the wider social and economic development challenges in Africa, amid a fast-moving globalising world in which our lives are governed almost entirely by advances of the Fourth Industrial Revolution (4IR). So in writing this book my intention is to stimulate a much-needed serious discussion about tackling inequality in Africa through an emphasis on entrepreneurship and human capital development. Thereby, pave the way for policies and actions that can bring about inclusive economic growth and sustainable development in the region.

4IR technological advances, such as artificial intelligence (AI) and machine learning, internet of things (IoT), augmented reality, blockchain, robotics, quantum computing, open data and genetic engineering, have created immense opportunities, revolutionised the way in which we live and work, thereby widened the chasm of inequality especially between the Global South and the Global North. Like the Third Industrial Revolution which used electronics, computers and new forms of telecommunication to shape our lives and enhance income, the 4IR is building on these advances to further improve our quality of life and income levels through a digital revolution. Today, digital technologies have made it possible and easier for new products and services to increase the efficiency that converges the pleasure of our working and personal lives.

From accessing news and information to the way we study, learn and work and such simple activities like buying a product, making a payment, ordering a taxi or a takeaway and watching a movie – any of these can now be done both efficiently and conveniently from the comfort of our own homes and on-the-go by using mobile devices. For me, it seems surreal to talk about 4.0 technologies and their impact on our work and personal lives when in fact I am aware that majority of my relatives in Africa have not yet transitioned fully into the Third Industrial Revolution world. For instance, technological advances made it possible for me to continue to provide uninterrupted education to my MBA students throughout the COVID-19 lockdown. Whereas in Africa only a handful of mainly private universities had or were able to launch the technological firepower to keep classes open and students engaged. For the majority of African universities, their students, and there are millions of them, were locked out of education for as long as the lockdown in their countries lasted. The consequence is that the African students' population, far greater than in any other region, may have suffered a decade setback in their social and cognitive development as a result of the COVID-19 lockdown. Unless Africa overhauls its entire educational systems by addressing the issues of equality in access, affordability, quality and relevance to labour market needs, many graduates of African universities may never be able to compete on an even term with their global counterparts.

In fact, there is a mismatch between the skills attainment of highly educated and trained graduates in Africa, and the skills needed to obtain and succeed in employment in today's knowledge economy. Perhaps, this situation explains why only about 3 percent, or less, of an estimated 11 million graduates produced in Africa every year obtain formal jobs after school. The rest are either unemployed, underemployed or poor. As a result, sub-Saharan Africa faces three layers of compounding socio-economic challenges of high youth unemployment, low human capital and lack of productivity needed to achieve inclusive growth and boost shared prosperity. These issues have ramifications for employment, productivity and sustainable economic development in the region. Also, Africa is still dealing with the past severe consequences of some of the deadliest political, economic and social upheavals including conflicts, famines, poverty and natural resource plunder ever witnessed in human history. These historical problems, coupled with the wider contemporary issues of population growth, urbanisation and inadequate infrastructure, mass unemployment, brain drain and food security are compounded by rapid changes in global affairs in relation to gender equality, environmental and climatic shocks.

The cumulative social and economic effects of these problems have serious implications for meeting the sustainable development goals (SDGs) target by 2030. Perhaps, I am more pessimistic, than optimistic, about resolving these challenges, especially the rising poverty and inequality in the region. This is because the same people who got Africa into its present social and economic mess are still holding political and economic power and are still pursuing broadly similar policies. It sounds hopeless. Yet, ironically, I share the optimism of a more prosperous future for Africa. It began the twentieth century as the least populated and urbanised continent. But it has gone through an unprecedented demographic transition since then, doubling its share of the world's population in a century. In 2050, the UN predicts that 24% of the world population will be in Africa, and by 2100 *The Lancet* estimates that Africa's population will increase further by additional 35%, putting countries, such as, Nigeria into the G20 league. This is because Africa's population growth is averaging 2.5% annually while the rest of the world, particularly in Europe and North America, is ageing and receding in population growth by almost equivalent percentage, if not more.

With its growing young population, coupled with being home to seven out of the ten fastest growing economies in the world, it seems Africa holds the key to the future of the global economy. As such, there is much to be optimistic about, particularly in terms of the benefits that come with demographic dividend. But demographic dividend can only be achieved if African governments get their acts together by creating opportunities that increase life chances for young people. Asian countries know that Africa holds huge demographic and economic potentials, which could have implications for the future of the world economy. This is most apparent in the way in which China, amid accusations of 'a debt-trap diplomacy', has sought to maintain a controversial strategic leverage over the region's natural resources through bilateral partnership with acquiescent African countries. Whether such partnerships have been in the best interest of Africa and Africans is debatable. Bilateral, and even multilateral partnerships with outsiders have hardly ever been sufficient to address Africa's social and economic problems at home. For Africa, immediate problems, such as, poverty and insecurity of lives and property, which occur because of growing urbanisation and mass youth unemployment, constitute an even greater threat to the region's economic prosperity and ability to curtail the prevalence of brain drain. If not curtailed immediately, brain drain is the singular most serious threat to economic prosperity and sustainable development in Africa. Because brain drain grows out of other social, economic and political problems that lead to forced migration of mostly young talents, it is hidden away and rarely ever the focus of policy priority. Although most of the emigration by Africans, about 55 percent, is happening within Africa, African immigrants abroad (historically in Europe and North America, and more recently in Asia and the Middle East) in all kinds of professions including academia, medicine, arts, science and engineering are hard to estimate. It will require many more years of reversal to regain, if at all possible, the loss of tangible assets and the human capital cost which Africa has suffered because of the mass movement abroad of its mostly young talents.

Analysis of publicly available data shows that the human capital cost of qualified medical practitioners alone emigrating from countries, such as Ethiopia, Kenya, Malawi, Nigeria and South Africa to destinations in Europe and North America in 2011 was about $2.17 billion. Whereas the financial savings and benefits (from not having trained the recruited doctors) to the destination countries including Australia, Canada, United Kingdom and the United States for recruiting qualified and trained medical practitioners who are African immigrants was about $2.7 billion the same year. If the same figures were used to compute a roughly conservative cumulative human capital loss to these African countries over a nine-year period to 2020, the loss in financial assets will more than quadruple to about $19.5 billion in 2020 with destination countries of these African professionals probably achieving slightly more in financial gains in the same year. This figure is far more than half of Nigeria's (Africa's largest economy) 2020 national budget of $34.6 billion, and makes the 2020/2021 national budget of about $2.8 billion in Malawi pale into insignificance.

Whether these rough estimations are precise or not is beside the point. The reality is that the social and economic costs of brain drain to Africa is staggering. The real cumulative costs may never be accurately measured or even known. For this reason, there is a need to fully understand the underlying factors, such as, poor human development, weak institutions and poor natural resources governance, as well as the demographic challenges including lack of opportunity for decent income, which give rise to brain drain and their implications for socio-economic growth and sustainable development in the region. My point in raising these rather uncomfortable realities is that there may be even greater consequences for the region if its people fails to act now. Thus, for a start, my underlying motivation is to use this book as a medium to show how Africa can begin to address some of these critical challenges through entrepreneurship and human capital development. Thereby, begin to alter the life chance of its growing youth population in a genuinely fundamental way. From this motivation arises the three main goals of this book.

The first goal traces the development challenges facing Africa by showing how they hinder economic progress in the twenty-first century. The second goal seeks to lay bare the institutional contexts of these challenges and how to address them by building and maintaining inclusive political, social and economic institutions by taking advantage of 4IR opportunities. The third goal evolved while writing this book and relates to the overlapping nature of the first and second goals within the contexts of the COVID-19 crisis. It is in these specific contexts that *Entrepreneurship and Sustainable Development in Africa* offers a new way of understanding and addressing the social, economic and even political challenges facing Africa in the twenty-first century. By introducing new ideas and actionable policy steps that situate these challenges within the frameworks of African Union's Agenda 2063 – *Africa's economic transformation blueprint* and the United Nations SDGs, this book delimits these challenges which until now have been largely theory-bound in existing literature.

In Chapter 1, the book unmasks the debilitating legacy of colonial and post-colonial failure in development effort and shows how this failure has created a conflicting social and economic reality for many Africans. We know, for instance, that African governments that are dependent on foreign aid are not only notoriously less accountable to their citizens, but they are also less interested in pursuing serious political and economic reforms to boost shared economic prosperity in their own countries. By unmasking such conflict, the book offers new insights into how high economic growth and human development can be realised without the burden of development assistance and aid from rich donor countries. Chapter 2 extends the thorny issues of Africa's economic growth and human development by shedding a new light on the narrative of poverty, particularly the distortive effects of proxies, such as, poverty line and purchasing power parity (PPP). By redirecting attention on the governance and institutional failures that are the root causes of poverty, poor human capital and low human development outcomes, it delineates the limitations in the use and delegation of these proxies to target pro-poor schemes in Africa. The chapter proposes new ways of tackling these failures, especially by ensuring there is equitable access in education and health care.

In Chapter 3, the emphasis shifted towards the wider institutional contexts that govern Africa's natural resources and their allocation, and how these contexts give rise to incidences of 'resource curse' and 'State fragility'. It draws from my own research and experience to demonstrate that stunted socio-economic growth and human capital development in Africa is down to poor institutional arrangements and their associated dysfunction, including corruption, governance failure, rent-seeking and plunder. It exemplifies this dysfunction by providing multi-country cases of how the detrimental effects of governance failure have led to economic deprivation. It thus proposes remedies based on insights from governance practices in natural-resource rich countries that enjoy economic prosperity and stability. Chapter 4 extends the negative effects of Africa's weak institutional context from the perspective of the demographic challenges and their implications for human capital development and employment creation. It plots the linkages between Africa's rising youth population, unemployment, youth bulge, political violence and emigration and provides the pathways by which African countries can navigate these challenges to achieve demographic dividend through investment in educational and training initiatives that adequately prepare and equip their young populations with employability skills and livelihood opportunity in a fast globalising knowledge-based economy.

Alongside these, Chapter 5 examines the merits and demerits of various educational and training initiatives, especially technical vocational education (TVET) used by African governments to provide young people with employability skills. Within this, an attempt is made to show and evidence how entrepreneurship education can address the main concerns of human capital formation and the development of a more sophisticated and productive African workforce ready to tackle the challenge of unemployment. To address the region's youth unemployment crisis, Chapter 6 introduces the reader to the author's conceptual framing of an entrepreneurship education ecosystem. This includes the critical knowledge and skills institutional gaps and entrepreneurial attributes that individuals, particularly students, must possess to succeed as early-stage entrepreneurs. It also charts the neglected issues related to the pedagogy, contextual drivers and barriers to using entrepreneurship education to develop human capital and entrepreneurial competencies of young people. By showing how entrepreneurship education can function effectively as an integral part of the general education system, it proposes a framework that most African countries can adopt to provide their young people with livelihood opportunities - thereby reduce the negative effects of institutional dysfunction.

Chapter 7 discussed how to address the specifics of institutional dysfunction that gives rise to informality and the informal sector. Although the informal sector is a central pillar of Africa's economic success story over the past decades, governments and development partners remain at a loss about how best to manage and support economic actors in the informal sector ecosystem. By using fresh evidence to advance the debate about the legality and the illegality of economic activities in the informal sector, the book provides a comprehensive analysis of Africa's informal economy and offers measures to raise the creativity and incentivise positive behaviour among the key players, thereby bringing them into the tax net. Through synthesis of the key issues raised in the previous chapters, the concluding chapter forges a clearer focus for future researchers and policy experts. Thus, based on many years of my close and active work with key stakeholders including with governments and young people in Africa, this book is a call to action to tackle inequality. The ideas in this book will help policy makers, governments, inter-governmental and third-sector organisations, and will also better educate students, teachers, and researchers desperate for new ways of understanding the steps Africa must take to retrace its steps and better position itself as a prosperous region as it emerges from the devastating effect of the COVID-19 crisis.

PARADOX OF A RISING AFRICA

1

If you talk to economists, development and policy experts about Africa's potential as the new global economic frontier, you will probably hear two contrasting narratives. The first is optimistic. It suggests that if Africa could accelerate and maintain structural economic and political reforms, then it could replicate China's unparalleled economic success of the last 50 years. The second is less so. It predicts a situation in which the current pace of Africa's economic progress is likely to stall. From all indications, there is some merit in both viewpoints. Unfortunately, because the region's often sit-tight political leaders tend to pursue broadly similar nearsighted policies that got Africa in the worse economic condition, there is a disproportionately high risk of social unrest and political instability that may hinder the pace of economic progress in the region. In any case, incontrovertibly, Africa's socioeconomic environment in the decades before the millennium is a sharp contrast to the reality of a region that we see today.

1.1 AFRICA AT TURN OF THE MILLENNIUM

More than in any other region, Africa has witnessed an unprecedented period of social and economic transformation in the period leading to and after the millennium. But several interconnected factors are responsible for Africa's remarkable social and economic turnaround following the millennium. Among others, the shockwaves of the dotcom bubble, (2000–2001) and more recently the 2008 global financial crisis, saw the global economy significantly driven by economic activities in the Emerging Markets and Developing Economies (EMDE) led by Asia and Africa.[1] Growth across Africa, particularly in the sub-Saharan African (SSA) region, averaged between 5 percent and 11 percent from year 2000 to 2016.[2] Analysis by McKinsey also showed that the region's spending from 2000 to 2015, led by Nigeria, Egypt and South Africa, was buoyant at $4.0 trillion.

It outstripped spending in India, Brazil and more than doubled spending in Russia over the same period. By 2025, business and consumer spending are projected to reach $5.6 trillion.[3] However, Africa's predicted spending may be slowed down by

---

[1]IMF (2018)
[2]World Bank (2019)
[3]McKinsey (2016)

fragile economic recovery due to significant job losses, high unemployment, extreme poverty and the slow pace of the COVID-19 vaccination programme. Limited availability and slow uptake of COVID-19 vaccination are likely to result to increased transmissibility of variants of the diseases, thereby slow down the pace of economic activity as the region enter the recovery phase in the fight against the pandemic. Because of these inter-connected factors, Africa's advanced economies, such as, Nigeria and South Africa, are forecast to experience negative economic growth of −3.4 percent and −5.8 percent, respectively, before the region sees an average of 2.8 percent sub-regional economic rebound by the end of 2021, and 3.3 percent by 2022.[4]

Another factor that might have boosted the pace of Africa's economic growth after the millennium was migrants' remittances. The surge in international migration from Africa in the period following the millennium brought with it record number of remittances to the region. Between 2005 and 2009 alone, migrant remittances (a.k.a. Western Union Transfer) to SSA increased exponentially by more than 50 percent to $66.2 billion led by Nigeria and Egypt. Both countries saw inflows of between $22.0 billion and $20.00 billion (2017 figures), respectively.[5] Migrant remittances have been and remain an important catalyst for economic development in many African countries. They help to provide immediate startup capital for Africa's booming micro-, small- and medium-sized business sector, which creates about 80 percent of the region's employment. Even with the recent decline in remittances by as high as 20 percent (more than $100 billion) to low- and middle-income countries because of the economic fallout of the COVID-19 pandemic,[6] migrant remittances still account for a significant share of the GDP of many African countries including Liberia (27 percent), the Gambia (21 percent) and the Comoros (21 percent).

Apart from migrant remittances, other factors, such as, macro- and micro-economic reforms, fiscal discipline, economic liberalisation and a comparably stable political climate, have led to enduring trade partnerships with many countries outside Africa. These partnerships have provided inward investments and created new jobs and business opportunities that have helped to accelerate the region's economic growth. Traditionally, while Europe and the United States have been the dominant commercial trading partners in Africa, the increased relations in recent years between Africa and China have no doubt revived the momentum of economic activities in Africa. China's economic ties, negotiated mainly through trade, project financing and low interest commercial loans, have undoubtedly helped to address some of Africa's backlog of infrastructural challenges, especially in the transportation and energy sectors.

Between 2000 and 2014 alone, China had given more than $86 billion in low-interest commercial loans to several African governments and government-owned organisations for infrastructural investments amid accusations 'debt-trap-diplomacy in Africa' by Western governments keen to reset their bilateral and multilateral partnership with Africa. As a result, by early part of the twenty-first century, Chinese Outward Direct Investment (ODI) of $26.0 billion to Africa had significantly surpassed its ODI to the United States, which stood at $22.0 billion in 2015.[7] Also, despite the recent global

---

[4]IMF (2020)
[5]World Bank (2021)
[6]World Bank (2020)
[7]Chen, Dollar and Tang (2015)

outrage over alleged racism towards Africans resident in China, which became more prevalent as Chinese authorities battled to contain the COVID-19 pandemic,[8] Sino-Africa relations remain strong and very deep. All diplomatic and trade relations between Africa and China are coordinated under a tightly controlled but very effective political lobby group known as the Forum on China–Africa Cooperation (FOCAC).

Established by China in October 2000, FOCAC is the powerful diplomatic channel through which Beijing's top leadership reaffirms its commitment to Sino-Africa relations. China's development and economic cooperation including investment plans, which has risen from $5 billion in 2006 to $60 billion in 2015, is usually announced during the triennial leaders' FOCAC summit. According to China's Foreign Minister, Wang Yi, this year's summit, which will be held in Dakar, Senegal, will centre on three priority areas of COVID-19 vaccine cooperation, economic recovery and transformative development.

Perhaps, such political gestures not only demonstrate China's unflinching determination to deploy the necessary tools to respond to both emerging and historical challenges Africa faces. But also it shows that the country's primary goal, among others, is to use every opportunity to reassert a dominant narrative that seeks to advance a 'shared future' for China–Africa cooperation through financial commitment. Although China's financial commitment to Africa has been tempered in recent years due to the global economic slowdown, bilateral financial commitment is still being funnelled to friendly African countries through a complicated mix of grants, special funds and concessional loans. Such high-level bilateral arrangement has meant that many African countries, knowingly or unknowingly, have in turn become heavily indebted to China. With a financial commitment accounting for more than 14.0 percent of Africa's (excluding South Africa) total debt stock, China is now the largest creditor in Africa.[9]

Thus, even as China forges ahead with its ambitious but polarizing multibillion dollar 'Belt and Road' Initiative, something to which participating African countries including Djibouti, Egypt, Ethiopia, Nigeria and Uganda often look to with pride, there is no denying that its presence in Africa is being felt across the world. If anything, amid intensified competition with Europe and the United States, China's increasing bilateralism in Africa has paved the way for a long list of new entrants scrambling for Africa's vast natural wealth. Notably, in 2007, as a response to China's growing political and economic influence in the region the European Union established the new Africa–EU Strategic Partnership aimed to transition into a win-win bilateral partnership with Africa.

Also, in January 2020, the United Kingdom launched and hosted the UK-Africa Investment Summit. The summit was widely seen as the UK's post-BREXIT gesture towards African leaders aimed at introducing a new era of a 'win-win partnership' with Africa. Prior to that, the Russia–Africa summit in Sochi – during which about $12.5 billion deal was agreed including international students' scholarships targeted at Nigeria, Egypt, Ethiopia, Ghana, Ivory Coast, Rwanda and South Africa – was intended to give Russian entities increased leverage over Africa's vast oil and mineral reserves. With direct investments in vocational centres across SSA, India is also deepening its trade relations with Africa in technology transfer. If managed effectively, technological advancement has the potential to accelerate innovation and socio-economic development, thereby increase Africa's global competitiveness.

[8]Pilling and Wong (2020)
[9]International Monetary Fund (2020)

Also, despite growing tensions over a 'neo-Ottoman revival', Turkey's 'Open to Africa policy', considered the most substantive outgrowth of Ankara's ambitious interest in Africa since the cold war, is aimed to substantially increase Turkey's commercial and diplomatic ties and influence in SSA, particularly in the Horn of Africa including Ethiopia, Somalia, Eritrea, and Djibouti.[10] Equally, as new entrants to Africa's geopolitical space amid the tension in the Gulf led by Saudi Arabia, United Arab Emirates and Qatar are ramping up their diplomatic ties and investments in infrastructure, energy, tourism, agriculture and security affairs in Africa. The full impact and socioeconomic benefits of this deepening and expanding diverse interests on Africa are yet not entirely clear.

However, among the key players, there is clearly a common and increased economic gesture and diplomatic convergence towards the mutual benefits that could arise from Africa's trade integration and economic liberalisation under the landmark African Continental Free Trade Agreement (AfCFTA). Ratified by all the 55 member countries of the African Union (AU) except Eswatini, it is possible that the key regional players across Asia, Europe and North America are positioning for a strategic advantage over a massive future trade in Africa estimated to be worth $4.2 trillion by 2023.[11] Yet, even with this positive outlook, Africa faces very serious, and in some cases debilitating social and economic challenges that cannot be swept aside.

1.2 AFRICA'S ECONOMIC TURNAROUND – ILLUSION OR REALITY?

There is a lot at stake for Africa in terms of the pace of economic progress and regional competitiveness. Although Africa accounts for about 17 percent of the global population, yet as a region it contributes only about 3 percent of the global GDP. Because of infrastructural challenges, low productivity and slow technology adoption, Africa's manufacturing and agricultural sectors are heavily underutilised and underserved. Unlike in Asia and Europe, Africa still imports one-third of its essential foods and beverages, with poverty on the rise.

The region is home to nearly one-third of the global population living in extreme poverty. This poor populations are concentrated in Nigeria, Africa's richest economy and the most populous. Productivity and performance in SSA's corporate sector lag behind global benchmark and competition. Due to lack of investor confidence, there is not yet a single fully Africa-owned organisation in the Fortune 500 companies. Fortune 500 companies in the region mainly operate through proxies, mostly located in South Africa. In fact, nearly half the large companies in Africa are either foreign-based multinationals or State-owned entities. Moreover, most State-owned entities that play dominant roles in the socioeconomic lives of many Africans including in energy, communication and transportation sectors are poorly run and consequently inefficient.

In addition, the region is no stranger to underdevelopment and suffering at the hands of outsiders. It has been 'ravaged by slavers, colonisers, exploited by world

---

[10]Vertin (2019)

[11]McKinsey (2010)

powers during the Cold War and devastated by post-colonial conflicts. These social, economic and political phenomena have left the region with a legacy of relentless volatility, fragility, horrific violence and widespread poverty'.

Alongside these problems are other serious social and economic challenges that pose a threat to Africa's potential as a rising global economic frontier. They include corruption, poor human capacity, weak and failing institutions and lack of regional integration. In addition to these structural and historical socio-economic challenges are a new set of emerging challenges, such as, climate change effects, demographic shifts and rising inequalities. If Africa is to succeed in emerging as a truly next economic frontier after China, then African leaders must address these historical and emerging challenges in a genuinely fundamental way. To do so, it entails they must at least embrace and actively pursue the AU's Agenda 2063,[12] which sets out the blueprint for Africa's social, economic and political transformation.

With mass unemployment, especially among youths, there is much work left to be done to tackle the issue of extreme poverty. Unemployment and poverty have implications for the persistent conflict and political violence that we see in the region today. To compound matters, Africa's big economies are not economically self-sustaining. Many of them, including Egypt, Ethiopia, Kenya and Nigeria, rely heavily on official development assistance (ODA) (a.k.a. foreign aid) as a significant share of their revenue source to support investments in critical sectors including defence, education, health and public sector pay.

Over a three-year period between 2013 and 2016, OECD records show that official aid to Ethiopia alone averaged more than $3.6 billion per annum. This is followed by Egypt, which received an average of $2.7 billion, while Nigeria and Kenya received more than $2.4 billion each. Besides heavy reliance on foreign aid, there is a looming debt crisis in Africa. The gains made in 2006 under the Heavily Indebted Poor Countries Initiative (HIPC) and the Multilateral Debt Relief Initiative (MDRI) programmes piloted by the World Bank, International Monetary Fund (IMF) and the African Development Fund to lower the unsustainable debt burden of mostly poor African countries have diminished in both economic value and impact.

By the end of 2006, the 33 African countries that were eligible for a debt relief of about $80 billion under the HIPC-MDRI schemes are today still struggling to accelerate progress towards meeting the Millennium Development Goals (MDGs) and the Sustainable Development Goals (SDGs). To compound matters, as of 2017, about one-third of SSA countries that benefitted from debt relief programmes under the HIPC and MDRI have been classified as being 'either in or at a high risk of debt distress'.[13] Although the current situation in the region is comparably far from the conditions prior to and during the HIPC/MDRI period, it raises questions about the sustainability of SSA's increasing debt portfolio, and whether the region is conducive to foreign direct investments (FDI)?

Lack of conditions for inward investment and overdependence on foreign aid constitute the most serious threats to Africa's economic progress. Despite these challenges,

---

[12]African Union (2015). AU's Agenda 2063 sets out a clear vision for Africa's future development based on the building the foundations for economic, social and political inclusion and the pathways to achieve 'The Africa We Want'.
[13]Coulibaly et al. (2019)

aid is seen as important and promoted as essential to Africa's economic development and progress. However, many experts with a background in history, politics and economics have been puzzled by why Africa has not yet transitioned economically, socially and even politically as other regions where aid programmes have been introduced.

For instance, South Korea went from an aid-dependent economy to acquire a first-world economic status in just under four decades. It achieved this through a combination of their internal governments' efforts and commitment to democratic and market reforms, and by creating the conditions for enterprise to thrive without foreign aid as a share of their revenue source and income. Thus, because many African countries that receive the largest share of the ODA budget today remain the most politically and economically fragile, the underlying rationale and effectiveness of aid flows to Africa warrants further detailed examination.

1.3 FOREIGN AID FLOWS AND DETERMINANTS

Generally speaking, the effectiveness of aid is often assessed by the extent to which the given aid has helped the recipient country to achieve a positive and long-term socioeconomic benefit even after the aid had stopped or considerably reduced.[14] Because foreign aid is widely seen as a foreign policy instrument of rich donor countries, both its existence and value remain a highly controversial subject. Particularly between those who view aid as a fulfilment of an obligation of few rich nations towards poor countries, and those who believe that aid is neither in the interest of donors nor recipient countries.

Notwithstanding, in a post-war global economy, rich donor countries are notoriously very good at pursuing 'a variety of their own political self-motives and interests when giving aid to other countries'. Because of this, foreign aid flow raises a particularly thorny problem of transparency, not just in Africa but also across the world. Thus, to address the moral question about the effectiveness and lack of transparency in aid flows, rich donor countries have converged under the umbrella of the Development Assistance Committee (DAC), run by the Organisation for Economic Co-operation and Development (OECD). The DAC established a code of practice, which provides easily accessible annual reports about the foreign aid obligations of the 30 strong OECD member countries including the European Institutions and the United States.

Despite calls by critics, DAC reports have always failed to provide the underlying political motives for members' aid commitments to aid recipient countries. To make matters worse, the political dynamics of aid programmes distinguished between *need-driven aid* (based on an unbiased assessment of the recipient country's needs and deprivation) and *interest-driven aid* (based on donors' concerns with matters of their own national interest such as values, export trade and home security) make it almost impossible to accurately establish the true value and impact of foreign aid on the social and economic development priorities of recipient countries, particularly in SSA.[15]

---

[14]Carlsson et al. (1997)
[15]Alesina and Dollar (2000)

However, on the face of it, by subordinating their social and economic fortunes to the political expediencies of donor countries, it seems the governments of many aid-recipient African countries are disproportionately disadvantaged by the dynamics and determinants of foreign aid programme. As an extension of the donor country's foreign policy priorities, aid has a way of influencing political and socioeconomic outcomes in aid-recipient countries. For instance, we know that there is very little appetite, if at all, on the part of African political leaders who rely on foreign aid to introduce serious democratic reforms. As such, such adverse influence erodes aid effectiveness which consequently make in difficult to usher in the political and economic stability needed to lift many of their poor citizens out of poverty.[16] Although, in recent times the flow of foreign aid to Africa has been declining in real terms, accelerated by the 2008 global recession and more recently by the economic effects of COVID-19 pandemic, aid commitments to the region continue to largely operate through 'leverage' and 'conditionality'.[17]

In most cases, aid giving is determined by layers of other complicated factors including 'need', 'merit' and 'self-interest', which fall within the donors' prerogative. Coupled with these factors are the compounding influences of other factors, such as donor ideology, whereby left-wing donor countries, such as Sweden, are known to favour increased aid, often bilaterally, to lower income countries where government rent-seeking is high.[18] Other key determinants of foreign aid flow stem from a desire by rich donor countries to maintain colonial and geopolitical alliances with aid recipient African countries.

Following the eras of the Cold War and colonialism, when foreign Western powers in Europe and the United States were fractured into different spheres of geo-political influence, foreign aid has become 'the new weapon of choice' used to maintain hegemony of global economic and political affairs.[19] For instance, while, during and after colonialism, Britain and France used aid to maintain strategic geopolitical strongholds in Africa, for the United States and the former USSR, aid became 'the key tool in a fierce contest to turn the world either capitalist or communist'.[20] Similarly, Sweden presents a strikingly although less harmful post-war example of strategic use of foreign aid to maintain social, political and economic influence in aid recipient countries.

As a rich Nordic country and the 'darling of the Third World in aid giving', Sweden has an enviable record as the only one of six DAC member donor countries to have met the United Nations 0.7 percent of GDP recommended target in aid assistance to developing countries. It also has a long-standing commitment to disbursing its foreign aid on purely favourable bilateral terms. OECD records show that in 2015, Sweden provided $7.1 billion in net foreign aid representing 1.4 percent of its GNI and a 38.6 percent increase in real terms from the previous year. However, this impressive record masks Sweden's ambition to export, through aid giving, its foreign policy principles of egalitarianism, peace and equality, which it views rather ideologically as national values.

To underscore the importance of its ambition, in 2014, a staggering 70 percent of Swedish ODA programmes, determined and administered by the Swedish

---

[16]Brech and Potrafke (2014)
[17]Kersting and Kilby (2014)
[18]Svensson (2000, p. 437)
[19]Acht, Mahmoud and Thiele (2015, p. 1)
[20]Moyo (2009, p. 14)

International Development Cooperation Agency (SIDA), were selectively targeted at poor and fragile African countries. This unbeaten record earned Sweden a unique status in the aid community as 'the jewel in the crown' of aid giving to conflict-torn Africa. This is not surprising. Much of Swedish aid has always been targeted at politically and economically fragile countries, such as Mozambique ($128 million), Democratic Republic of the Congo ($73 million), Somalia ($71 million) and South Sudan ($62 million) – with Afghanistan receiving $133 million in 2016 alone, the highest non-African country recipient of Swedish aid.[21]

However, with the persistent political conflict and poverty, lower GDP per capita, debt burden and dwindling national fortunes in these aid-recipient African countries, it is obvious that Swedish aid has not paid off and may probably not pay off even in the long term. These examples raise the wider question of the effectiveness of foreign aid as a sustainable model for economic development. Unlike in post-war Europe under the European Recovery Programme (ERP) launched in 1948 and lasted for about four years to 1951, there is no clear roadmap as to when ODA to Africa would end. Because the ERP, otherwise known as Marshall Plan, had a time limit, it was credited to have significantly contributed to restoring the foundations of the economic success we see today in Western Europe.

Most of the countries including Germany that benefitted from the aid scheme have regained their national self-esteem under a new vision of shared prosperity, which has helped to shape their global economic status. The fact that there was no large-scale economic recovery programme in Africa like the Marshall Plan, particularly after colonisation, which halted all aspects of Africa's social, economic and political life is puzzling. Despite this, the key question has to be whether donor aid to Africa will help to accelerate or hinder the pace of economic progress in the region?

1.4 DOES AID PAY OFF IN THE LONG RUN

As a post-war phenomenon, foreign aid in the form of humanitarian assistance following a period of severe and prolonged conflict or a natural disaster may help to restore social and economic stability in a recipient country. Apart from Marshall Plan launched in the aftermath of the Second World War, a more recent case in which the argument for foreign aid could be pertinent, even necessary, is the December 2004 Indian Ocean Tsunami. About 280,000 people lost their lives and more than 2 million others across 46 countries were made homeless. The deluge of horror justified the swift global response of an unprecedented $6.25 billion in foreign aid. The Indian Ocean Tsunami aid came mostly from private donations, which were channelled through a central United Nation's relief fund to assist recovery efforts in the tsunami-affected countries.

Since then, the closest use of foreign aid to target a similar carnage came after the January 2010 earthquake that struck the Caribbean Island of Haiti. The disaster killed more than 223,000 residents including 17 percent of Haitian government officials, 102 UN staffs and forced more than 2 million people from their homes.[22]

---

[21]OECD (2016)
[22]Gronewold (2011)

In that context, the use of nearly $23 billion of aid received in global response under the UN aid appeal was necessary and justified.[23] Yet, even under both circumstances the possibility that foreign aid could be derailed, misdirected and mistargeted looms large. Particularly in situations in which the recipient country lacks the institutions for proper aid governance and the capacity and systems including the human and non-human apparatuses to effectively police and prioritise the aid effort.

For instance, in Haiti, funding was divided in two categories – humanitarian aid and recovery aid. The latter was earmarked for long-term financing for reconstruction and development, while the former was dedicated to immediate relief efforts including construction of temporary shelters and supply of medical help for victims. Although actual figures are difficult to come by, available statistics from the office of the Special Envoy on Haiti show that nongovernmental organisations (NGOs) and private contractors (intermediaries) had received nearly $2.3 billion humanitarian aid raised for the Haiti quake appeal. Somewhere between 15 percent and 21 percent of the recovery funding was channelled through the Haitian government for relief effort.

Yet, several years on, Haitians are 'disillusioned with the overall lack of progress and with the lack of transparency in the use of the aid resources'.[24] The problem is that Haiti's aid relief had been mired in a complex web of financial scandals, faltering promises and lack of accountability. For instance, many years after the disaster, only a handful of homes have been completed with the millions of dollars raised for the LAMIKA housing project in Campeche, Port-au-Prince, overseen by the Red Cross.[25] Internal confidential documents obtained by ProPublica, the US-based independent and non-profit investigative news organisation, showed that in some cases aid agencies were themselves completely unaware of how the millions of aid money donated and channelled through them had been spent.[26]

International aid agencies, such as Red Cross and Oxfam GB – rather than the local aid agencies – raised far more money during the Haiti's aid campaign than any other charitable organisation. But corruption, apathy, bloated bureaucracy, bad management and allegations of systemic impropriety, particularly in the widely known case of Oxfam GB, were found to have marred relief efforts in Haiti.[27] Although such scandals are uncommon within the aid community, public knowledge of these scandals, however, came with colossal consequences. Thousands of regular donors abandoned their financial and nonfinancial commitments to aid agencies amid public backlash over their exploitative behaviour in poor vulnerable countries.

Also, leadership crisis including poor staffing, lack of indigenous capacity and non-use of local personnel to effectively coordinate the aid relief efforts compounded matters. These crises meant that some international aid agencies were forced to outsource their work to third-party foreign NGOs or to predominantly expats community, who themselves lacked knowledge and insight into local dynamics, thereby leading to all sorts of other issues as a result of language barriers. Because of these problems, most of Haiti's aid relief budget ended up disproportionately as expensive

---

[23]United Nations Office of the Special Envoy to Haiti
[24]Ramachandran and Walz (2012)
[25]Elliot and Sullivan (2015)
[26]Elliot (2015)
[27]BBC (2019)

overheads and management costs to the detriment of ordinary Haitians who desperate needed help.

The Haiti case is not isolated. Following the 2004 Indian Ocean tsunami, the $7.7 billion of aid that was directed towards infrastructural reconstruction in the worst hit coastal Indonesian province of Aceh created new layers of inequalities that alienated communities. Although Aceh's physical transformation was obvious, given there were tens of thousands of newly built homes, long stretches of new roads, schools and health centres in addition to seaports and airports with landing strips. This physical transformation, however, obscured the deep-rooted problems of economic decay and fragility in the region, which made long-term social and economic recovery for many Acehnese much harder and elusive.[28]

Ten years on, a 2014 assessment of Aceh's tsunami-aid relief effort by Lilianne Fan, a Research Fellow at the London-based Overseas Development Institute (ODI), depicted an ironic picture of 'ghost villages', as many have abandoned their rural communities in search of livelihoods elsewhere. Although Haiti and Aceh's catastrophe provides a rare but important insight into situations in which aid may be necessary, aid nonetheless is insufficient to bring about economic transformation. Long after the aid efforts, Aceh and Haiti still suffer from high unemployment and economic stagnation. In Aceh, for instance, many of the tsunami survivors including youths and children who became breadwinners following the disaster have abandoned their aid-built homes and migrated to other big cities within and outside Indonesia in pursuit of more sustainable livelihood opportunities.

The mass exodus is perhaps an illustration of Aceh's unfinished post-aid reconstruction recovery. Aceh remains among the poorest provinces with 18 percent of the population considered poor, significantly higher than the national average of 10.86 percent that live below Indonesia's poverty line of about $25 per month. Aceh's post-aid reconstruction has a knock-on effect on other social ladders. The province still has the highest school drop-out rate of 26 percent, and between 2013 and 2014, it recorded the highest number of secondary school failures in Indonesia.

By any logic, it is true that aid cannot be blamed for all of Aceh, Haiti and indeed Africa's socio-economic, even political problems. But as Lilianne observed, some critical questions needed answers. There are questions about whether the prioritisation of physical infrastructures and reconstruction over Aceh's weakened institutions – due to over a 30-year conflict and several decades of isolation and underdevelopment – was more appropriate. Should sufficient aid have been targeted at creating strong and inclusive institutions to encourage education and training in knowledge and skills for entrepreneurship? Could more aid have been shifted towards developing critical human capacities for sustainable livelihoods alongside the physical transformation? These critical but unanswered questions no doubt, will resonate strongly with Africa's long-running aid project.

---

[28]Fan (2014)

1.5 HAS AID ALWAYS BEEN GOOD FOR AFRICA? BOTSWANA'S CASE

Although the share of ODA allocated to Africa by rich donor countries has been declining real terms since 2008, reducing by 1.7 percent to $49.9 billion in 2016 alone,[29] it is important to recognise that not all aid programme is problematic. When aid is targeted at a specific social needs and economic priorities of the recipient country, it can be an effective catalyst for social and economic mobility in the recipient country. For instance, a foreign aid programme directed at reducing diarrhoea mortality in children under five years of age in a recipient country could be used as the basis of increasing public awareness, justifying increased government budget and expenditure as well as research targeting the leading causes of diarrhoea in that recipient country.[30]

Aid programmes targeted at medical research, funding to develop critical vaccines to tackle diseases and outbreaks could also be effective and scalable. Equally, in many ways, social and economic development programmes anchored on aid can prove counterproductive if not effectively administered with the immediate and long-term needs of a recipient country in mind. Within the development and donor communities, Botswana's experience with foreign aid since its 1966 independence from Britain has always been held up as a good model of how foreign aid to Africa could provide the foundations for economic success. Often cited as an excellent example, aid was portrayed to have facilitated the effective use of Botswana's mineral wealth (Diamonds) to support investments in human and physical infrastructures as well as to build strong political institutions.

Today, the credibility attributed to this narrative by the donor community has ensured Botswana's political stability, which has helped to guarantee its international reputation as a stable and peaceful country. As among Africa's upper middle income countries, it would probably come as no surprise that Botswana enjoys an enviable status, alongside major Western countries, such as Denmark and New Zealand, in both the Good Governance and the Corruption Perception Indices. As a country, it is also recognised as among the top third of countries globally for Ease of Doing Business (EODB). However, since the millennium, Botswana has been on a downward slope in practically every indicator of economic stability – although comparably to other African countries, it still enjoys political stability.

Severely restricted by trade imbalance with neighbouring South Africa, Botswana's slipping stature is in large part caused by its inability to deal with similar social and economic challenges facing other resource-rich and resource-dependent African countries with a history of aid dependence. For instance, just like Nigeria with its abundant crude oil reserves, Botswana is struggling to deal with both the historical problems of corruption and poverty and the contemporary socioeconomic consequences of urbanisation and spiralling youth unemployment.

[29]OECD.org (2018)
[30]Pickbourn and Ndikumana (2019)

The European Centre for Development Policy Management (ECDPM), an independent think tank, recently observed that the rate of youth unemployment in Botswana was significantly higher than the 13.3 percent (2016–2017) average for SSA, despite being held up as a country where foreign aid has been an effective instrument of economic and political stability.[31] To compound matters, Botswana's youth unemployment has continued to rise, peaking at 37.52 percent in 2019.[32] This is similar to the average youth unemployment in the Southern African and Development Community (SADC) region led by South Africa, which in 2019 recorded more than 50 percent youth unemployment.

Also, like many other African countries that are graduating students faster than their labour markets can absorb because of systemic socioeconomic challenges, Botswana suffers from skills mismatch between labour market demands and the skills possessed by many of its own young graduates. In addition, 21.9 percent of its 2.2 million population live with the acquired immunodeficiency syndrome (AIDS), which means that Botswana ranks second globally as the country with the most HIV/AIDS prevalence. The challenge of high youth unemployment, coupled with high HIV/AIDS prevalence, poses a serious threat to Botswana's social, economic and political future.

Globally, and regionally, these challenges, along with trade imbalance with neighbouring South Africa, are likely to further diminish Botswana's faltering national competitiveness. However, many analysts including from the World Bank believe that Botswana can address these challenges by diversifying its diamond-dependent economy, foster a strong spirit and culture of entrepreneurship and strengthen existing social and political institutions through greater public accountability. Botswana's case perhaps offers yet another glimpse of why aid is in fact the metaphorical 'big elephant in the room' of Africa's economic progress. Aid has neither enhanced economic nor political progress, if anything, it has been found to have harmed political progress and disrupted the quality of democratic governance and institutions in Africa.[33]

1.6 THE PROBLEM WITH AFRICA'S AID

Just as aid can help to restore economic planning especially during a period of unexpected severe economic shock, it can equally hinder economic progress, such as, when donors use aid as a tool to serve their own strategic self-interests and geopolitical motives. A situation in which aid flow focuses on trade-related motives or is motivated by a donor's strategic economic interests, rather than the recipient country's real economic needs and priorities, then aid is very unlikely to facilitate socioeconomic progress in the recipient country. As a vocal critic of aid giving to Africa, Dambisa Moyo has argued convincingly that what Africa needed in a post-colonial era was to be 'weaned off its aid addiction'.

Moyo's vocal stance on aid to Africa perhaps stems from a shared frustration with the lack of socioeconomic progress in the region despite several decades of aid

---

[31]Pharatlhatlhe and Byiers (2019)
[32]Statista.com (2020)
[33]Schraeder et al. (1998)

giving. For her, continuous aid flow to Africa without proper accountability has had a damaging 'crowding-out effect on the inflow of FDI', 'discouraged private sector participation and investment in the economic development process', 'encouraged corruption', 'induced conflict and inflation' and 'choked off the export sector' while 'depressing the growth of a strong middle-class population able to hold governments to account'.[34] Even without Moyo's strident indictment of the aid sector as a hindrance to Africa's economic progress, there is no denying the fact that aid giving has come at a serious political and consequently economic cost to Africa, especially state-to-state aid.

In Africa, donors have a tendency to allocate aid primarily in response to donor-led demands for reforms, such as democratic reforms. Somehow, such demands allow them to influence the political affairs of a recipient country without serious or even commensurate economic benefits.

Through cronyism and rent seeking, cunning aid-recipient African governments have often consented to such donor-led demands, but without any real commitment to democratic and economic reforms. This is because African political leaders have a way of circumventing the threat of aid withdrawal for a lack of political reforms or economic progress tied to donor-led demand for reforms. Thus, by implication, it means that foreign aid somehow plays an influential role in the formation of elected African governments that show lack of respect and accountability to their citizens. Equally, we know that African governments that receive large chunks of foreign aid rarely explore other sustainable forms of internal revenue-generating mechanisms including effective taxation as a source of State revenue; therefore, they tend to be less accountable to their citizens.[35]

As a result, they have weaker incentives to build and nurture strong public and democratic institutions, as well as low incentive to build efficient socioeconomic structures to deliver good and reliable public services, particularly in education and health. Through breeding corruption and misgovernance, state-to-state aid plays a direct and indirect role in the building and sustenance of structures that stifle the development and nurturance of strong institutions needed to ensure proper political reforms and effective economic planning. In the long run, this ironic situation, coupled with the lack of political will to pursue serious social and economic reforms, harms the effectiveness of the political process and economic institutions that are essential to creativity, innovation and sustainability, which offer the foundations for sustainable development.

From this analysis, it seems that African countries that are highly dependent on foreign aid seem to be more prone to weak institutional arrangements (discussed in the next chapter), which undermines the presence and effectiveness of high human development, democratic process and consequently economic growth. Of this situation, Ethiopia presents a particularly striking example in that it has cumulatively received the most foreign aid in Africa. Yet, for decades, it has remained one of the most politically volatile and economically fragile countries in the world.

---

[34]Moyo (2009)
[35]Moss et al. (2008)

1.7 ETHIOPIA AND FOREIGN AID

Ethiopia, Africa's second most populous country with more than 115 million people, is at war with itself. Even before the recent political feud between Mr Abiy Ahmed (the country's Prime Minister and Nobel Prize Winner) and the Tigray People's Liberation Front (TPLF), the country has struggled with daunting social, economic and political challenges that have led to ethnic violence and allegations of ethnic cleansing that has the potential of tearing the country apart and destabilising the entire 'Horn of Africa'. As a country, Ethiopia has a far more long-standing intricate relationship with foreign aid than any other African country. It is the largest non-war recipient of foreign aid globally. For several decades, a significant proportion of Ethiopia's annual budget has come from international aid and financing agencies including the World Bank and the IMF. Although it is difficult to determine precisely how much of Ethiopia's annual national budget (about $12.8 billion in 2019) is supplemented by foreign aid, Oakland Institute, a California-based independent policy think tank, however, reported that foreign aid has previously represented between 50 percent and 60 percent of Ethiopia's national budget.

Despite vast amounts of aid support, year on year, Ethiopia's government has returned a deficit budget averaging −3.25 percent of GDP from 1990 to 2017, with a record low of −8.90 percent of GDP in 2000 after it peaked at 6.60 percent of GDP in 2003. Also, official government figures show a budget deficit of −3.5 percent of GDP in 2018, with the government's debt currently at 59 percent of the country's GDP.[36] A country declares a budget deficit when its government spends more money than it has or can generate through financial prudence, fiscal discipline, trade, taxes and export-led investments. This contrasts with when a country can leverage its budget surplus, accrued through export-led economic policies and financial prudence, to reinvest in other areas of domestic benefit, such as human capital, infrastructure, education and health without the burden of huge and mounting external debts.

Besides Egypt, which receives annual military aid of about $1.2 billion from the US government to protect the latter's geopolitical interest in the Middle East and in the 'Horn' of Africa, Ethiopia ranks fifth on the World's Atlas map for countries that rely on foreign aid to run its economy. This is not surprising. From 1991 to 2016, Ethiopia has received more than $56 billion from various international aid channels to support critical sectors including defence, education, health, infrastructure and public sector pay.[37] Just like donor countries in Europe, the US foreign aid programme, mostly administered through the United States Agency for International Development (USAID), is entangled in a complex web of political, humanitarian and development assistance that somehow inexorably ties the recipient country to US foreign policy. Almost 95 percent of US foreign aid to Ethiopia, amounting to nearly $1 billion in 2016 alone, was economic aid.

Similarly, out of the five largest ODA recipient countries in Africa, Ethiopia received more than $4.1 billion in 2017. This represents by far the biggest chunk of ODA given to an African country in that year. Thus, making Ethiopia the third largest ODA aid-recipient country behind Afghanistan ($4.4 billion) and Syria ($5.9 billion) – two

---

[36]Maasho (2018)
[37]Farah, Onder and Ayhan (2018)

countries that are on the brink of economic disintegration because of protracted political unrest and conflict. Additionally, since the early 1990s, Ethiopia has received more than $3.1 billion from the International Development Association (IDA) in form of grants and concessional loans, including most recently $1.2 billion in form of a grant and a credit to support its ambitious agenda to attain a middle-income country status by 2035.

So far, the country has received about 8.0 percent per capita from IDA, thereby making it the largest and number one IDA borrower globally.[38] As part of the World Bank Group, IDA funds are peculiar in that they carry little to no interest charges. The World Bank relies on several eligibility criteria including the recipient country's risk of debt distress (i.e., a high probability of debt default) and level of GNI per capita to qualify a country's eligibility for IDA assistance. So, by implication, Ethiopia's top spot on the IDA's borrowers' list and concerns over debt distress have made the country Africa's aid haven.

Because of its debt burden and inability to repay debts, in 2018, China was forced to cancel all loan interest payments amounting to nearly $123 million on the accumulated $12.1 billion it has provided to Ethiopia through State policy banks since the 1970s. With a falling per capita income, and threat of political disintegration triggered by the Tigray separatist campaign in the north, standard of living in Ethiopia has for a long time been among the lowest in Africa. Consequently, and because of lack of opportunities in education, in labour market and in the health sector, the country has persistently ranked low on the human development index (HDI).[39] Ethiopia's dependence on foreign aid hampers institutional reforms, particularly in the areas of introducing and implementing serious democratic reforms needed to drive the economy and hold the country together through a more inclusive political representation.

Over dependence on foreign aid is incompatible with political independence and economic progress. Aid dependence creates political inertia and economic stagnation; together, they hinder national prosperity in African countries.[40] It seems from all indication that Ethiopia's fragile economic and sociopolitical landscape represents an epitome of the poor legacy of an aid-dependent economy.

1.8 ETHIOPIA'S POLITICAL AND ECONOMIC CONTEXTS

Politically, like other aid-recipient African countries, Ethiopia presents a complex and deteriorating political mix. It suffers from entrenched ethnic politics, which leads to frequent politically motivated armed resistance from the Oromias – the country's largest population. Ethiopia's ethnic conflicts arose from a legacy of unequal political representation, which has hindered any meaningful economic progress in the country. Even after the *Dergue* regime (1974–1991), which oversaw one of the worst

---

[38]IDA/worldbank.org (2018 accessed via:https://ida.worldbank.org. Washington D.C.)
[39]Kochhar (2015)
[40]Bräutigam and Knack (2004)

human rights atrocities in the country's history, Ethiopia's political scene is still dominated and fractured by one-party politics.

With credible reports of political kidnappings, state-sponsored killings, arbitrary arrests by security forces and torture, the Human Rights Watch publicly observed that 'serious abuses in Ethiopia did not end with the Dergue'.[41] The ruling Ethiopian People's Revolutionary Democratic Front (EPRDF) has for so long controlled the parliament. One-party dominance of the political process makes democratic reforms almost impossible. Even after many years of relinquishing political power, the country's political institutions are still heavily controlled by powerful former high-ranking military officials outside the government. However, the economic implications of the country's political fragility, perhaps, have forced the current reformist Prime Minister to embark on a radical political reforms and economic liberalisation.

To drive home his ambitious commitment to political reforms, he recently detained senior officials and also terminated the multibillion dollar government contracts awarded to the powerful State-owned enterprise, Metals and Engineering Corporation (METEC), whose economic activities dominate the economy. METEC is seen by many as a tool of political patronage in a country in which the State largely controls virtually all aspects of business, economic and social life. Established in 2010, and run by the military, METEC is Ethiopia's largest industrial conglomerate with about 98 companies across different sectors including manufacturing of military equipment and hardware.

The company was contracted to build sugar and fertiliser plants as part of the country's agricultural reforms programme, which has since been terminated under Abiy. In addition, the company's $5 billion contract to install turbines for the controversial Grand Ethiopian Renaissance Dam (GERD) was revoked because of corruption and poor performance. As the focal point of Ethiopia's national economic strategy under Growth and Transformation Plan (GTP), GERD is the largest hydroelectric dam in Africa expected to generate 6,450 megawatts of electricity to replace Ethiopia's struggling energy sector.[42]

Economically speaking, Ethiopia has not been in a good shape for a long time. Its main economic policy priority is poverty reduction. Most of the country's gains on poverty reduction have come on the backdrop of its commitment to the MDG targets through implementation of pro-poor policies under its GTP agenda. Although it has seen a robust gain in poverty reduction since 2000 when 56 percent of the population were surviving on less than $1.25 a day, majority of Ethiopians are still poor and mainly rural.[43] Underlying Ethiopia's economic development vision under GTP is an ambition to transform into a lower middle-income country by 2035 as part of its SDGs commitment.

Having broadly maintained an average annual growth of 10.8 percent between 2004 and 2017 compared to a regional average of 5.4 percent, Ethiopia in many ways embodies the true paradox of Africa's widely praised economic success since the

---

[41]Human Rights Watch (2020)
[42]World Bank (2018); from the sustainable energy for all (SE4ALL) global tracking database led by the World Bank, International Energy Agency and the Energy Sector Management Assistance Program.
[43]World Bank (2018)

millennium. It is both the fastest growing economy in Africa and one of the fastest in the world. Yet it remains one of the world's poorest countries with about 29.6 percent of the population living in extreme poverty.

Apart from poverty, the country is prone to frequent outbreaks of drought and famine, which brings further hardship to poor smallholder farmers that make up the majority of Ethiopia's agro-based economy. Drought devastates farm crops and agricultural produce. Consequently, it wipes off household income, thereby causing increased poverty and starvation for Ethiopia's mainly rural farming households.[44] The fact that drought and famine still pose a serious threat to Ethiopia's economy despite many decades of aid supplement is an uncomfortable irony of the reality of economic life in Ethiopia.[45]

Recognizing that this agro-based problem is an embarrassment, the government has worked with some aid agencies to recently establish the Ethiopian Agricultural Transformation Agency (ATA). However, with a sliding GDP per capita income of $783, significantly below SSA's average of $1553.8,[46] the extent to which ATA is financially ready and viable to scale up the agricultural reforms Ethiopia requires to prosper is unclear. ATA receives budgetary support from the Ethiopian government and from a mix of development agencies and aid donors, which are known to have previously reneged on their financial commitments.

Because of its reliance on foreign aid and given a protracted low ranking (173 out of 189 countries) on the HDI scale, it is difficult to see how Ethiopia can achieve its ambition of becoming a middle-income country by 2035. To succeed, it must create and embrace an alternative economic pathway towards sustainable development that is independent of aid.

1.9 TOWARDS SUSTAINABLE DEVELOPMENT IN ETHIOPIA

Aggregated data from the World Bank, Transparency International and the Freedom House for the period 1991 to 2016 showed that foreign aid has had no substantial economic development impact on Ethiopia including on its GDP growth, although aid was believed to have contributed to the country's increased FDI over the same period.[47] Similarly, after analysing the effect of many decades of bilateral and multi-lateral aid efforts towards poverty reduction in Africa, William Easterly, an American economist concluded in his highly acclaimed book – *The White Man's Burden* – that Western aid is not the answer to economic prosperity in Africa.[48] Such a conclusion does not come as a surprise. For decades, we have known that foreign aid has been the most singular source of economic dependence that adversely affects proper economic

---

[44]Schemm (2017)
[45]Farah, Onder and Ayhan (2018)
[46]IMF (2018)
[47]Farah, Onder and Ayhan (2018)
[48]Easterly (2006)

planning and consequently economic progress in many politically independent African countries.

Yet, different African governments have continued to pursue and embrace a policy of aid-dependent economic model. Thus, if Ethiopia is serious about realizing its ambition to become a middle-income country by 2035, then it must face up to the challenge of achieving economic independence in the same way that it fought and won political independence. To achieve this, it must decouple itself from foreign aid by showing that political independence goes hand in glove with economic independence, thereby pave the way for the rest of other aid-dependent African countries. Economic independence is the conduit through which politically independent or sovereign nations have always shaped and achieved their national ambition and priorities through the pursuit of inclusive social and economic policies that are beneficial to their own citizens.

Economically independent countries are better able to develop much stronger resilience to guarantee better economic outcomes for individuals, thereby raise their citizens' economic well-being and overall national competitiveness.[49] To improve economic outcomes for its citizens, especially the rural poor, the Ethiopian government must consider a number of policy options and programmes beyond decoupling the country from foreign aid. Firstly, it must eliminate the deep-rooted socioeconomic barriers to social freedom and economic mobility by closing the growing inequality gap through solid political reforms.

Secondly, it must seriously pursue and implement a programme of economic diversification. To achieve this, the country needs to move away from its dependence on highly subsistence agro-rural-based economy by developing other promising sectors, such as, manufacturing and services, particularly in the areas of information communication and telecommunication (ICT) and banking, which hold huge economic potential and benefits. But the benefits of economic diversification cannot be realised or even guaranteed without strong institutions and improved investments in human development, such as in education and healthcare. Both are essential to high productivity and high income per capita essential to economic progress and stability in a diversified economy. Government-backed economic empowerment initiatives integrated with private sector involvement through economic diversification and liberalisation are therefore vital.

Thirdly, it is difficult to diversify the economy in a successful manner without a strong reliable political system that governs economic activity. Thus, economic diversification and economic liberalisation must go hand in hand and supported by serious political reforms aimed at incentivising private sector involvement in the country's economic development process. Economic diversification and liberalisation with private sector participation, particularly in both non-agricultural and the agricultural sectors, will bring several immediate and long-term benefits. First, it will encourage and accelerate firm entry and growth, in addition to supporting self-employment, especially in the services sector.

Within Ethiopia's fledgling services sector including telecommunications, tourism and banking are massive opportunities for innovation and job creation. Yet, for some reason, these sectors are still heavily underutilised because they are controlled and

---

[49]Ghai (1973)

monopolised by government-owned enterprises. Service provision in these sectors is limited, very inefficient and erratic. For instance, the mobile telecommunication sector is monopolised by the state-owned Ethio-Telecom, formerly Ethiopian Telecommunications Corporation, leading to lack of trust in its independence and ability to protect and preserve individual privacy. Lack of trust between the authorities and consumers also means that free subscription services offered by social networking platforms, such as Facebook, WhatsApp and Viber, are out of the reach of many ordinary Ethiopians. These platforms are often seen by the government as tools used by the opposition to organise internal insurrection and political violence. Therefore, their use is rationed, highly monitored by the State security operatives and often seized upon by the government to intrude into and police people's private lives. Internet services in Ethiopia are notoriously unreliable and non-existent in some areas outside the capital, Addis Ababa. This means that there is scope to increase efficiency, underutilisation and consequently engineer mass consumption and benefits of the internet.

Thus, the services sector could benefit from accelerated economic liberalisation through a combination of policy and regulatory framework that attracts and incentivises private sector involvement. The private sector will build and enhance human capacity, service quality through recapitalisation and modernisation of the sector. Particularly, the financial services sector will benefit through product innovation as well as through the internationalisation of financial services provision, thereby raising the sector and the country's national competitiveness. Furthermore, economic diversification and liberalisation would be widely felt in the agricultural and manufacturing sectors. For instance, through economic diversification and liberalisation, Ethiopia could benefit from an export-led model that has the potential to position it as Africa's regional hub for China's export style manufacturing. Potentially, with a strong manufacturing base and export-led sectors, Ethiopia could increase its export-led earnings and tax revenue, reduce its dependence on foreign aid, thereby improve its regional influence and global competitiveness.

Also, liberalisation of the manufacturing and export sectors no doubt presents a strong and immediate viable alternative to aid in terms of State revenue needed for domestic investments. Another area that could benefit from manufacturing and export-led reforms is the country's coffee sector. Coffee is probably the largest traded global commodity after oil. Although Ethiopia is among the top coffee-producing countries globally, it has not yet fully optimised the export and the revenue potential from its coffee sector. As a coffee exporting country, it ranked bottom three only ahead of Indonesia and Mexico based on 60-kilo sacks exported in December 2017.

Local coffee producers face significant obstacles, such as weak domestic supply chain management including traceability, coupled with an uphill task in attempting to break the barriers to international supply chain networks that feed and control the global coffee market. Unlike other top coffee-producing countries especially Brazil, Vietnam and Colombia which ranked as the three largest global exporters, Ethiopia is forced to consumes nearly 50 percent of the coffee that it produces locally.[50] While, in

---

[50]Sissay (2017)

contrast, Brazil only consumes 11 percent of its coffee, Vietnam consumes only 10 percent and Colombia about 9 percent.[51]

Secondly, a particularly important area of investment is in resilient infrastructures to support improved and mechanised agriculture to guarantee food security. Because Ethiopia is particularly vulnerable to natural disasters, and because rain-fed agriculture is the country's main source of external revenue, a resilient agricultural infrastructure with a sophisticated natural disaster risk management system will empower and protect poor smallholder farmers from the devastating consequences of drought and famine. Although, with improved awareness, better prediction and the advent of more effective response mechanisms, famine is now very different from the mid-1980s when it ravaged Ethiopia. But the threat from drought and the attendant famine remains real and likely to cause severe food insecurity and poverty.

Lack of enhanced resilience to weather-related economic shocks increases the social impact of food insecurity, poverty and inequality, which threaten people's overall happiness and well-being.[52] Put in perspective, the agricultural sector accounts for about 45 percent of Ethiopia's GDP, almost 90 percent of exports and 85 percent of employment.[53] The centrality of agriculture in the country's economic lifeline also means that majority of Ethiopians, some 12.8 million by United Nations estimation, are mainly smallholder farmers.[54] By implication, this significant workforce population rely on the agricultural sector for their livelihoods mainly through subsistence farming.

For this reason, some have suggested that 'a judiciously provided foreign aid can be of immense help' in tackling Ethiopia's high risk of exposure to natural disasters.[55] Perhaps, aid agencies can support programmes that promote transfer of knowledge and technological skills acquisition through the combined use of international and localised best practices in natural disaster risk management. In this regard, however, to consider only aid in isolation of local needs and priorities will be inadequate and misjudged. Thus, as part of a comprehensive natural disaster risk management scheme, aid agencies could work with the government, higher education sector, agricultural research institutes and the private sector in a range of areas, such as technology transfers, research and development, education, training and skills development to inject a new life into the country's agricultural and agrobusiness sectors.

Because of poor access to education and training, which results in poor agility in creativity and technological adoption of enhanced farming and agrobusiness practices, most Ethiopian farmers suffer from economic hardship and marginalisation due to the aftereffect of natural disasters including high pricing of agricultural commodities. Ideally, high food pricing should increase income for smallholder farmers to either reinvest or acquire assets for protection against economic and climatic conditions.

---

[51]Lewin et al. (2004)
[52]Devereux (2009)
[53]World Bank (2018)
[54]UNDP (2018)
[55]Mellor and Gavian (1987, p. 1)

But because the economic activities of Ethiopia's farming community are mainly controlled by third parties who negotiate produce quality and pricing, rural farmers lack control of their economic fate across the value chain.[56] Thereby, they are often swindled out of the possibility of having increased income. Thus, as a third measure, prioritising investment in education and entrepreneurial training for rural smallholder farmers will empower them to negotiate direct access and trade with buyers and competitors.[57] But also, education and entrepreneurial training will enable them to create and sustain alternative income sources for financial independence through entrepreneurship.

With the right education and training, farmers can develop increased skills, knowledge and experience in small enterprise management as well as the enthusiasm, sophistication and the technical know-how needed for integrated farming including risk management of natural disasters. Education and entrepreneurial skills acquisition are critical components for increased productivity in agricultural and agrobusiness value chains. Increased productivity guarantees surplus food production, access to markets and household food security that naturally comes with alternative income sources, particularly during climatic shocks. Alternative income source for smallholder farmers is particularly critical in the wider context of the empirical evidence[58] that shows the occurrence of a climate shock, such as drought or low rainfall, is usually not sufficient by itself to cause famine, starvation and death.

Also, evidence shows that the 'experience and impact of famine vary considerably across households according to their income sources and asset base', with relatively richer households, that is, top third of households with an average annual income of $100 per capita, coping better than the bottom poor, that is, those households with an annual income of $42 per capita.[59] Fourthly, food insecurity remains a serious problem in Ethiopia where nearly 8.0 million people including children are currently in need of food assistance.[60] Consequently, increasing investments in market-led initiatives, such as entrepreneurship development to aid alternative employment, could help Ethiopia to develop the critical internal resilience to natural disasters and their negative effects on famine and food insecurity.

Food insecurity leads to other social problems, such as gender-based inequality including increased sexual vulnerability among women who risk exposure to HIV infection as a result of dependence on multiple male providers. Prevalence of gender-based inequalities in Ethiopia (and other African countries) whereby 'women are compelled to engage in transactional sex or to remain in abusive relationships due to dependence on a male provider has been linked with risky sexual behaviour with increased exposure to HIV/AIDS'.[61] Diverse income opportunities, particularly for smallholder female famers and workers in the agricultural sector, could increase household food security, thereby empowering women to become more self-sufficient.

---

[56]Tefera et al. (2019)
[57]Tefera et al. (2020)
[58]Zmolek (1990)
[59]Webb, von Braun and Yohannes (1994, p.1)
[60]World Food Programme (2018)
[61]Miller et al. (2011)

In conclusion, economic diversification and liberalisation, a natural disaster resilience infrastructure and individual empowerment schemes through entrepreneurship education and training must not at all come at a cost of increased government control. Individuals must be allowed and encouraged to exercise the freedom to make informed entrepreneurial choices to secure financial independence to benefit their families and the wider society. In other words, appropriate policies, actions and interventions directed at building robust economic and political institutions must converge to strengthen people's innate ability to remedy a variety of causes of famines, thereby dismantling the hierarchy and legacy of aid through an emphasis on human capital and entrepreneurship.

After all, the fact that ODA donor partners have no real sense or even a clear vision of how much more aid would be needed to reproduce in Africa, the model of economic stability and freedoms that have been achieved in Asia, Europe and North America cast a shadow over the underlying motives of aid-giving as a remedy for poor economic planning. This lack of vision is in stark conflict with economic recovery under the Marshall Plan in Europe after the war. Perhaps, there is a lesson here for Ethiopia, and indeed the rest of Africa. It is only by the proper functioning of the broader political, economic and social institutions that countries can effectively deal with their own economic problems, thereby achieve the goal of self-sufficiency.

However, this goal cannot be an aid's prerogative. Ultimately, what is required is the policy praxis and granularity, far beyond aid, to bring it into action through sensible government policies and action targeting the real foundations of human development and economic growth.

BIBLIOGRAPHY

Acht, M., Mahmoud, T., & Thiele, R. (2015). Corrupt governments do not receive more state-to-state aid: Governance and the delivery of foreign aid through non-state actors. *Journal of Development Economics*, 114, 20–33.

African Union Commission (2015). *Agenda 2063: The Africa we want*. Addidas Abiba: African Union Commission. Retrieved from https://www.un.org/en/africa/osaa/pdf/au/agenda2063.pdf. Accessed on 8 May 2019.

Alesina, A., & Dollar, D. (2000). Who gives foreign aid to whom and why? *Journal of Economic Growth*, 5(1), 33–63.

Bräutigam, D., & Knack, S. (2004). Foreign aid, institutions, and governance in Sub-Saharan Africa. *Economic Development and Cultural Change*, 52(2), 255–285.

Brech, V., & Potrafke, N. (2014). Donor ideology and types of foreign aid. *Journal of Comparative Economics*, 42, 61–75.

British Broadcasting Corporation (2019). Oxfam criticised over Haiti sex claims. Retrieved from https://www.bbc.co.uk/news/uk-48593401. Accessed on 18 June 2019.

Carlsson, J., Somolekae, G., & van de Walle, N. (1997). *Foreign aid in Africa: Learning from country experiences*. Upsalla: Nordiska Afrikainstitutet. Retrieved from http://www.diva-portal.org/smash/get/diva2:272899/FULLTEXT01.pdf. Accessed on 6 June 2018.

Chen, W., Dollar, D., &Tang, H. (2015). *Why is China investing in Africa? Evidence from the firm level*. Washington, DC: Brookings Institute. Retrieved from https://www.brookings.edu/wp-content/uploads/2016/06/Why-is-China-investing-in-Africa.pdf. Accessed on 8 October 2018.

Coulibaly, B., Gandhi, D., & Senbet, L. (2019). *Looming debt crisis in Africa: Myth or reality?* Washington, DC: Brookings Institution. Retrieved from https://www.brookings.edu/blog/africa-in-focus/2019/04/05/looming-debt-crisis-in-africa-myth-or-reality/? Accessed on 8 May 2019.

Devereux, S. (2009). Why does famine persist in Africa? *Food and Security*, 1(1), 25–35.

Easterly, W. (2006). *The White Man's burden*. Oxford: Oxford University Press.

Elliot, J. (2015). Confidential documents: Red Cross itself may not know how millions donated for Haiti were spent. New York, NY: ProPublica. Retrieved from https://www.propublica.org/article/confidential-documents-red-cross-millions-donated-haiti. Accessed on 12 March 2019.

Elliot, J. & Sullivan, L. (2015). How the Red Cross raised half a billion dollars for Haiti and built six homes, New York, NY: ProPublica. Retrieved from https://www.propublica.org/article/how-the-red-cross-raised-half-a-billion-dollars-for-haiti-and-built-6-homes. Accessed on 12 March 2019.

Fan, L. (2014). Aceh's unfinished recovery. London: Overseas Development Institute. Retrieved from http://www.irinnews.org/report/100972/acehs-unfinished-recovery. Accessed on 12 March 2019.

Farah, A., Onder, M., & Ayhan, E. (2018). How foreign aid affect developing countries: The case study of Ethiopia. *Avrasya Etüdler*, 21(53), 7–38.

Ghai, D. P. (1973). Concepts and strategies of economic independence. *The Journal of Modern African Studies*, 11(1), 21–42.

Gronewold, N. (2011). Earthquake-relief officials in Haiti hoping 2011 brings better results. *New York Times*, Retrieved from https://archive.nytimes.com/www.nytimes.com/gwire/2011/01/13/13greenwire-earthquake-relief-officials-in-haiti-hoping-20-65989.html. Accessed on 12 March 2019.

Human Rights Watch (2020). To heal, Ethiopia needs to confront its violent past. Retrieved from https://www.hrw.org/news/2020/05/28/heal-ethiopia-needs-confront-its-violent-past. Accessed on 29 May 2020.

IDA/Worldbank.org (2018). Financing. Retrieved from http://ida.worldbank.org/financing/ida-financing. Accessed on 12 April 2019.

International Monetary Fund (2018). World Economic Outlook. Retrieved from www.imf.org/en/Publications/WEO/Issues/2018/09/24/world-economic-outlook-october-2018. Accessed on 10 October 2018.

International Monetary Fund (2020). *The evolution of public debt vulnerabilities in lower income economies*. IMF Policy Paper No. 20/33. Washington, DC: International Monetary Fund.

Kersting, E., & Kilby, C. (2014). Aid and democracy redux. *European Economic Review*, 67, 125–143.

Kochhar, R. (2015, July). A global middle class is more promise than reality: From 2001 to 2011, Nearly 700 million step out of poverty, but most only barely. Washington, DC: Pew Research Centre. Retrieved from http://www.pewresearch.org/wp-content/uploads/sites/2/2015/08/Global-Middle-Class-Report_8-12-15-final.pdf

Lewin, B., Giovannucci, D., & Varangis, P. (2004). Coffee markets: New paradigms in global supply chain. *Agricultural and rural development discussion paper*. Washington, DC: World Bank. Retrieved from http://documents.worldbank.org/curated/en/899311468167958765/pdf/283000REVISED0Coffee1Markets01PUBLIC1.pdf. Accessed on 18 September 2018.

Maasho, A. (2018). Update 1 – Ethiopia PM says China will restructure railway loan. Reuters. Retrieved from https://uk.reuters.com/article/ethiopia-china-loan/update-1-ethiopia-pm-says-china-will-restructure-railway-loan-idUKL5N1VS4IW. Accessed on 8 September 2018.

McKinsey (2010). Lions on the move: the progress and potential of African economies. Retrieved from www.mckinsey.com/featured-insights/middle-east-and-africa/lions-on-the-move. Accessed on 8 October 2018.

McKinsey (2016). Lions on the move II: Realizing the potential of Africa's economies. Retrieved from www.mckinsey.com/featured-insights/middle-east-and-africa/lions-on-the-move-realizing-the-potential-of-africas-economies. Accessed on 8 October 2018.

Mellor, J., & Gavian, S. (1987). Famine: Causes, prevention, and relief. *Science*, 235(4788), 539–545.

Miller, C., Bangsberg, D., Tuller, D., Senkungu, J., Kawuma, A., Frongillo, E., & Weiser, S. (2011). Food insecurity and sexual risks in an HIV endemic community in Uganda. *AIDS and Behavior*, 15(7), 1512–1519.

Moss, T., Pettersson, G., & van de Walle, N. (2008). An aid-institution paradox? A review essay on aid dependency and state building in sub-Saharan Africa. In W. Easterly (Ed.), *Reinventing foreign aid*. Cambridge, MA: MIT Press.

Moyo, D. (2009). *Dead Aid: Why aid is not working and how there is a better way for Africa*, New York, NY: Farrar, Straus and Giroux.

Organisation for Economic Cooperation and Development (2016). *Development co-operation report 2016: The sustainable development goals as business opportunities*. Paris: OECD Publishing. Retrieved from https://read.oecd-ilibrary.org/development/development-co-operation-report-2016_dcr-2016-en#page1. Accessed on 12 March 2019.

Organisation for Economic Cooperation and Development (2018). Development aid at a glance – statistics by region. Retrieved from www.oecd.org/dac/financing-sustainable-development/development-finance-data/Africa-Development-Aid-at-a-Glance-2018.pdf. Accessed on 12 March 2019.

Pharatlhatlhe, K., & Byiers, B. (2019). Youth unemployment and role of regional organisations: The case of the Southern African Development Community (SADC). *Political Economy Dynamics of Regional Organisations in Africa (PEDRO)*. Discussion Paper No. 252. European Centre for Development Policy Management (ECDPM). Retrieved from https://ecdpm.org/wp-content/uploads/DP-252-Youth-unemployment-and-the-role-of-regional-organisations.pdf. Accessed on 6 June 2019.

Pickbourn, L., & Ndikumana, L. (2019). Does health aid reduce infant and child mortality from diarrhoea in Sub-Saharan Africa. *Journal of Development Studies*, 55(10), 2212–2231.

Pilling, D., & Wong, S. (2020). China-Africa relations rocked by alleged racism over Covid-19. *Financial Times*. Retrieved from https://www.ft.com/content/48f199b0-9054-4ab6-aaad-a326163c9285. Accessed on 20 March 2020.

Ramachandran, V. & Walz, J. (2012). *Haiti: Where has all the money gone?* Policy Paper 004. Washington, DC: Centre for Global Development. Retrieved from https://www.cgdev.org/sites/default/files/1426185_file_Ramachandran_Walz_haiti_FINAL_0.pdf. Accessed on 12 March 2019.

Schemm, P. (2017), Ethiopia is facing a killer drought. But it's going almost unnoticed. *The Washington Post*. Retrieved from https://www.washingtonpost.com/news/worldviews/wp/2017/05/01/ethiopia-is-facing-a-killer-drought-but-its-going-almost-unnoticed/?noredirect=on&utm_term=.c6fa45d01030. Accessed on 8 August 2018.

Schraeder, P., Hook, S., & Taylor, B. (1998). Clarifying the foreign aid puzzle: A comparison of American, Japanese, French, and Swedish aid flows. *World Politics*, 50, 294–323.

Sissay, A. (2017). *Breaking the green curse: Ethiopia's journey towards exporting roasted coffee*. Ethiopia Business Review. Addis Ababa: Champions Communications.

Statista.com (2020). Botswana: Youth unemployment rate from 1999–2019. Retrieved from https://www.statista.com/statistics/811692/youth-unemployment-rate-in-botswana/. Accessed on 5 March 2020.

Svensson, J. (2000). Foreign aid and rent-seeking. *Journal of International Economics*, 51, 437–461.

Tefera, D. A., Bijman, J., & Slingerland, M. (2020). Multinationals and modernisation of domestic value chains in Africa: Case studies from Ethiopia. *Journal of Development Studies*, 56(3), 596–612.

Tefera, D. A., Bijman, J., & Slingerland, M. (2019). Quality improvement in African food supply chains: Determinants of farmer performance. *The European Journal of Development Research*, 32, 152–175.

United Nations Development Programme (2018). From seed to market, transforming agriculture in Ethiopia. Retrieved from http://www.undp.org/content/undp/en/home/ourwork/ourstories/from-seed-to-market–transforming-agriculture-in-ethiopia.html. Accessed on 18 September 2018.

United Nations Office of the Special Envoy to Haiti. General information on the status of international assistance to Haiti. Retrieved from http://www.lessonsfromhaiti.org/lessons-from-haiti/international-assistance/. Accessed on 12 March 2019.

Vertin, Z. (2019). *Turkey and the new scramble for Africa: Ottoman designs or unfounded fears?* Washington, DC: Brookings Institution. Retrieved from https://www.brookings.edu/research/turkey-and-the-new-scramble-for-africa-ottoman-designs-or-unfounded-fears/. Accessed on 18 June 2019.

Webb, P., von Braun, J., & Yohannes, Y. (1994). Famine in Ethiopia: Policy implications of coping failure at national and household levels. *Food and Nutrition Bulletin*, 15(1), 1–2.

World Bank (2018). Global Economic Prospects – The turning of the tide? Retrieved from www.worldbank.org/en/publication/global-economic-prospects. Accessed on 10 October 2018.

World Bank (2018). The World Bank in Ethiopia. Retrieved from https://www.worldbank.org/en/country/ethiopia/overview. Accessed on 17 April 2019.

World Bank (2019). The World Bank in sub-Saharan Africa. Retrieved from http://pubdocs.worldbank.org/en/506341557323188659/Global-Economic-Prospects-June-2019-Analysis-SSA.pdf. Accessed on 5 February 2020.

World Bank (2020). World Bank predicts sharpest decline of remittances in recent history. Retrieved from https://www.worldbank.org/en/news/press-release/2020/04/22/world-bank-predicts-sharpest-decline-of-remittances-in-recent-history. Accessed on 9 July 2020.

World Bank (2021). Global Economic Prospects, Sub-Sahaan Africa. Retrieved from https://thedocs.worldbank.org/en/doc/600223300a3685fe68016a484ee867fb-0350012021/related/Global-Economic-Prospects-June-2021-Analysis-SSA.pdf. Accessed on September 2021.

World Food Programme (2018). *Ethiopia Food Security Outlook June 2018–2019*. Retrieved from https://reliefweb.int/sites/reliefweb.int/files/resources/ETHIOPIA_Food_Security_Outlook_June2018_final_0.pdf. Accessed on 18 September 2018.

Zmolek, M. (1990). Aid agencies, NGOs and institutionalisation of famine. *Economic and Political Weekly*, 25(1), 37–48.

ECONOMIC GROWTH AND HUMAN DEVELOPMENT

2

Human development is measured by three distinct but interrelated indicators. These include people's standard of living – *measured in gross national income (GNI) per capita*; level of knowledge – *measured in exposure to and quality of education* and long and healthy life – *measured in life expectancy at birth*. Together, these indicators constitute the human development index (HDI). People's level of education can have either a favourable or unfavourable effect on their income and standard of living. This in turn affects their quality of life and ability to contribute to nation building through participation in an economic activity. Thus, education not only influences income, but it also affects whether one is employed or unemployed, and consequently one's overall sense of self-worth and well-being.

Arguably, there is symmetry in how the institutional dynamics of how these HDI indicators operate within nations to produce different social and economic outcomes for individuals, depending on the opportunities and choices available to them. Presumably, much would depend on the priorities of various countries and how they choose to use and distribute their national income, including how much is spent on education and public health and the total distribution of household income between the poor and the non-poor. Unfortunately, the dynamics and determinants of income distribution within and across countries are very complex and unpredictable. This complexity is heightened by changes to the political process and the socioeconomic challenges that affect each country at different stages of its development cycle.

Notwithstanding, when there is a high level of poverty in a country, either because of low or poorly managed per capita income, then government and household expenditures on human development are likely to suffer. Equally, when a country or a household has a low level of poverty, there is likely to be a high expenditure on those activities that enhance human development with such corresponding positive outcomes in poverty levels.[1] As it is, at least in development discourse, the idea of human development owed its early intellectual impetus to the basic human needs approach under the 'new growth agenda' of the International Labour Organisation and the World Bank and the Capabilities Approach propounded by the new growth economist Amartya Sen.

---

[1]Ranis et al. (2000)

Sen defined human development from the contemporary viewpoint of 'enlarging people's choices in a way that enables them to lead longer, heathier and fulfilled lives'.[2]

Historically, before the new growth agenda, the classical theory dominated the discourse about economic growth and human development. In the classical era there was more emphasis on physical factors of wealth, labour and technology. The idea of human capital, acquired through formal education, training and experience, was rarely ever considered as important. The emphasis on physical wealth was reflected in the policy missteps of powerful international financing organisations, such as the World Bank. Before their newfound focus on human capital, they encouraged many governments in developing countries, especially in Africa, to prioritise investments in infrastructures, such as roads and bridges by providing conditional loans that limited their spending in education and health priorities.

The emphasis on physical factors of production was purely motivated by a desire for quick returns on investments. The outcome of this emphasis was seen in the annual incremental margins in gross national product (GNP) and GNI per capita than on how efficient educational and health institutions could improve people's overall well-being. Also, for too long, the emphasis on physical factors provided nations with the impetus to mainly define and justify their pursuit of economic growth based almost entirely on narrow measures of GNP.

GNP contributes to human development and economic growth primarily through government expenditure and household behaviour. For instance, high level of investment in education is likely to affect people's income level and ability to make positive and healthy choices for themselves and their families. These choices allow them to lead productive and comfortable lives. In turn, productive and comfortable lives are likely to positively affect their levels of productivity, and ultimately their impact on their country's socioeconomic well-being. Unfortunately, debates about classical theories of economic development, dominated by capitalist and socialist philosophies of Adam Smith and Karl Marx, were tainted by bias towards the accumulation and distribution of physical resources and monetary gains.

This bias meant that the beneficial effects of education and healthy life on human productivity and economic growth were widely ignored. In addition, environmental considerations and rising inequalities within and across nations were left on the sidelines. By the early to mid-1970s, while many developed and industrialised countries had experienced high rates of economic growth based on gross domestic product (GDP) and high per capita income, those in developing countries languished in poverty and diseases due to social and economic problems including poor health and lack of access to quality education. The rising socioeconomic gap between developed and developing countries was strongly felt by many observers who believed that the accumulation of monetary gains and physical capital by nations was inadequate to catalyse the process of achieving high human development and economic growth.[3]

With these observations, which sought to correct the shortcomings of the classical period, the emphasis began to shift more towards how non-monetary priorities, such as education – as a component of human capital, and quality of life – as a component of health and nutritional support including cleaner environment, as well as how the

---

[2]Sen (1999)
[3]Anand and Sen (2000)

infrastructures that sustain these non-monetary priorities can be utilised effectively to improve peoples' productivity. Thereby, reduce the gap between poor and rich countries. Access to these non-monetary priorities, namely, education and good quality of life, was widely seen as the catalyst to socioeconomic benefits of productive life to which everyone must be entitled, regardless of background and geography.

This broader human development perspective, initially defined in the partially successful Millennium Development Goals (MDGs) agenda and subsequently embedded in the Sustainable Development Goals (SDGs) framework, seems to have provided a more holistic basis to pursue a set of universal principles to achieve high human development targets and economic outcomes across nations. Although the SDGs recognise access to quality education, decent standard of living and healthcare as key development priorities across the world, for Africa, however, the main question has to be whether or not there is a serious argument for investing in the institutions that support and sustain these priorities. To answer this question, one must turn to the idea of the institutional analysis of human development and economic growth. But, first, what do we mean by institutions?

2.1 INSTITUTIONS

Institutions govern the established or prevailing 'rules of the game' within any society. They enable shared patterns of thought, expectation and behaviour by imposing form and consistency on human activity. By so doing, they influence and regulate the political, social and economic dynamics that are vital to human development outcomes and economic growth. The presence of rules implies that the social, economic and political effects of institutions, whether formal or informal, manifest through shared structures with a society. Shared societal structures could stretch from democratic norms and values, language, religion, family, laws and regulations, which enhance or constrain individual freedoms and the rights to education and healthcare.

However, these structures evolve and change overtime. As they evolve, they play a central role in binding together the expectations and systems that regulate economic outcomes within the society.[4] Formal institutions involve the explicit, often universal, and transferable rules, such as constitutions, laws, by-laws, edicts, charters and regulations that encompass elements such as property rights and contracts.[5] By contrast, informal institutions comprise of tacit values, attitudes and norms of a society, which are enacted and reified through social conventions and interpersonal relationships.[6] Formal and informal institutions are not entirely separate nor independent of each other. The structures within formal institutions can be indirectly influenced by informal institutional structures through official pronouncements and actions by the State.[7]

In other words, the structures within formal and informal institutions may act interdependently to define and steer the direction of economic growth and human development either towards success or failure. Although connected, formal and

---

[4]Hodgson (2006, p. 2)
[5]North (1990)
[6]Fukuyama (2000)
[7]Welter and Smallbone (2011)

informal institutional structures vary across countries and from one region to another within a country depending on historical antecedents and geography. By the same token, human development and economic growth are mutually inclusive. They are governed by the interplay between formal and informal institutions within nations.

As more fully explained in Chapter 7, this interplay forms an essential part of an 'institutional matrix',[8] whereby social and economic institutions act together to shape the political process and outcomes.[9] But for some reason, very little is known from the perspective of sub-Saharan Africa (SSA) about how institutional arrangements affect human development and economic outcomes. Apart from insufficient theoretical explanation of the institutional factors that shape and govern the human development and economic growth of a country, there is a very limited body of evidence from which to systematically analyse the cross-country differences and comparisons of institutional arrangements and their implications for human development and economic growth.

2.2 INSTITUTIONS, HUMAN DEVELOPMENT AND ECONOMIC GROWTH

It is only in the last few years has debate shifted towards the idea that new aspects of institutions, such as formal education and health, are as important, if not more for human development and economic growth than physical factors of trade and technology acquisition. With this shift comes the emphasis on which kinds of institutions play the most vital role in human development. Not many would dispute the fact that the stability of educational and health institutions has an important social and economic function that affects human development and economic outcomes. Patterns and levels of poverty, as well as whether a country experiences social, economic and political stability or equilibrium, are invariably affected by institutional arrangements through access (or lack thereof) to quality education and healthcare.

Thus, because countries develop differently and exist under different kinds of social, political and economic conditions depending on the effectiveness of their institutions and institutional arrangements, there would be variations to the human development and economic outcomes that they produce. As such, the question then, as others[10] have asked, is why do some countries experience social, economic and political stability, as a result achieve high human development and economic growth outcomes while others either go into stagnation or decline? Perhaps, from SSA perspective, a far more fundamental question relates to what main purposes are served by inclusive institutions. How do countries build and sustain inclusive institutions as well as their effectiveness to produce desirable human development and economic outcomes, such as high productivity and wealth? And what are the consequences when countries fail to build and maintain inclusive institutions?

For SSA countries, apart from curbing the prevalence of poor governance, poor educational and health outcomes that occur through institutional failure and dysfunction,

---

[8]North (1991, p. 1)
[9]Acemoglu and Robinson (2010)
[10]Acemoglu and Robinson (2008)

the answer to these questions must be determining which types of public institutions matter for human development and which are essential to sustainable economic development. Investments in education and training, and in the promotion of technological innovation in health, may lead to beneficial outcomes and perhaps even generate higher levels of economic success. With the right kind of investment and access to quality education and healthcare, individuals are far more likely to exhibit high levels of knowledge, skills and productivity, and also make healthy choices that improve their quality of life, the lives of their families, which ultimately benefits the wider society.

However, because of cross-country differences in institutional arrangements, the levels at which these benefits can be attained vary from one country to another. This variation has macro and micro-level implications on quality and levels of human capital, productivity and economic growth. At a macro level, one could hypothesise in relation to entrepreneurship development, whereby the formation of human capital relies on the quality of education within a country, which in turn influences levels of human creativity and productivity associated with entrepreneurship activity in that country.

Thus, investments in and access to quality entrepreneurship education could engender entrepreneurial knowledge and skills acquisition, which are human capital components. In turn, entrepreneurial knowledge and skills acquisition are essential to entrepreneurship and SME development, which is needed for job creation and ultimately economic growth. At a micro level, the implication of this hypothesis arises from the institutional arrangements that govern an individual's ability to create jobs as an entrepreneur. In which case, one could think in terms of the prerogative of laws and regulations that relate to the idea of 'Ease of Doing Business' (EODB) in a particular country. For example, if the institutional arrangement, that is, the business regulatory environment in relation to starting a new business and enforcing business contracts, is weak, dysfunctional or even non-existent, then, in that business environment, it is unlikely that entrepreneurs can thrive and create jobs, and ultimately such environment will stifle economic growth.

EODB 2019 measures a range of institutional factors for entrepreneurship and SME development including processes ranging from business registration, securing a building permit, property transfer, access to electricity and credit, protection of minority investors, tax payments, contracts enforcement and insolvency resolution to engaging in international trade.[11] Looking at the institutional factors related to EODB across the world, there are considerable variations across high-income developed economies of New Zealand, which ranked 86.59 percent as number one on the EOBD database, followed by Singapore (85.24 percent), Denmark (84.64 percent), Hong Kong SAR, China (84.22 percent) and the United Kingdom (82.65 percent) to low-income developing countries of Somalia, which ranked bottom at 20.04 percent, followed by Eritrea (23.07 percent), Venezuela, RB (30.61 percent), Congo Dem Republic (36.85 percent), Ethiopia (49.06 percent) and Nigeria (52.89 percent).

The effectiveness of the above institutional factors for entrepreneurship and SME development has implications for human development and economic growth outcomes. One related aspect of this hypothesis, or rather phenomenon, which has captured global attention on the importance of non-monetary components (education and health) of

---

[11]World Bank (2019)

human development and economic growth was the Human Capital Index (HCI). Launched by the World Bank in 2018 as part of their Human Capital Project, HCI was intended to encourage countries to prioritise and increase investments in education and health. It explains how differences in the institutional arrangements within a country can affect levels of productivity and human development outcomes based on the educational and healthcare priorities of that country.

Thus, it measures, or rather estimates the ratio of productivity of next generation of the labour force within each country. This is defined as the amount of human capital that a child born today can expect to attain by the end of secondary school or at 18 years of age, benchmarked against the risks of poor education and poor health that prevail in the country in which that child was born. Specifically, HCI includes three components: survival – the probability of survival to 5 years old; health – the fraction of kids not stunted and the adult survival rate and school – accounting for both access through the expected years of school and quality through assessment grades.

The underpinning logic is that countries with adequate and effective institutional requirements to prioritise, manage and sustain increased investment in education and healthcare priorities are much more likely to experience the intergenerational benefits that come with such institutional arrangement. As such, a country in which a child born today can expect to achieve full education and full health will score the highest value of 1 on the HCI index.[12] Correspondingly, there is bound to be an opposite effect under a condition of institutional deficiency or lack. Although these measures marked a clear fundamental policy shift in the development priorities of the World Bank, it is impossible, however, to achieve or experience a consistent HCI measure across countries.

As explained before, the variation to institutional arrangements within and across countries will have implications for social and economic outcomes for individuals. Given that there are comparably substantial variations to the EODB and HCI scales across countries, perhaps, there are far more important lessons for African countries. Firstly, it is possible that countries which are either poorly governed with dysfunctional institutional arrangement, or in which the institutional arrangements are weak and fragile, may experience low values on both their EODB and the HCI scales. For instance, Singapore which has the highest HCI score of 0.88 followed by Hong Kong SAR, China, which has an HCI of 0.82 – both countries ranked very high on their EODB scores at 85.24 and 84.22, respectively.

By contrast, countries with low EODB scores correspondingly ranked low on their HCI scales. Take the cases of Ethiopia and Nigeria – the two most populous African countries which have EODB score of 49.06 percent and 52.89 percent and HCI scores of 0.38 and 0.34, respectively. Secondly, seen in a different light, it may not always be the case that a country's economic performance and human development outcome is merely because of their fragile institutional arrangements and weak institutional governance mechanisms. As relevant as these factors may be, there could be other unaccounted factors that explain either their low or high EODB and HCI scores.

Because of this possibility, some have argued that social, economic and political institutions in Africa are dysfunctional not merely because they are inefficient or poorly governed, but because the intended purpose of these institutions and their

---

[12]World Bank (2019)

arrangements may be at odds with what is needed to achieve high human development and economic growth outcomes.[13] After all, New Zealand, Singapore, Hong Kong and the United Kingdom, which scored high on their EODB and HCI scales, historically differ substantially from Somalia, Eritrea, Congo Democratic Republic, Ethiopia and Nigeria, which scored low on their EODB and HCI scales in terms of their social, political, economic, geographic and even cultural balance.[14] Thus, these factors may be the underlying causes of the differences in their institutional arrangements and therefore bound to affect the social and economic outcomes that derive from their institutions, their arrangements and the socio-economic outcomes they produce.

In other words, for African countries, the overriding human development concern should not merely be in seeking to attain high values on EODB and HCI scales per se, important though this is. While the scales can be used as the basis to implement urgent institutional and regulatory reforms across the business, education and the health sectors, they do not on their own ensure institutional efficiency and effective governance needed for positive individual educational and health outcomes. It is only by improving people's knowledge and skills through building and maintaining efficient and inclusive institutions that countries can enjoy the benefits that come with high levels of productivity, creativity and innovation, thereby increase their human development and economic growth outcomes.

Even though these explanations and examples depict cases of institutional arrangements with relatively distinct social and economic implications, they are correlated with other social and economic constructs, such as poverty line and purchasing power parity (PPP), which are frequently used to make cross-country comparisons in relation to human development and economic growth outcomes. For several decades, poverty line and PPP have been misused as a 'one-size-fits-all' paradigm to evaluate distinct social and economic outcomes that arise from human development indicators within and across countries. Yet, there has not been any serious analysis of their distortive effects on poverty reduction initiatives targeting Africa.

2.3 THE PROBLEM WITH POVERTY LINE

Even though poverty has for so long been a major global concern, not much is yet known about why and how poverty came to be universally defined, categorised and reported using proxies, such as poverty line and PPP. Such universalistic views of poverty, as with their underlying empirics, are bound to create all sorts of problems with regards to context and geography of poverty across different regions of the world. For instance, if one were to compare people's economic conditions in Asia and Africa, perhaps one might begin to appreciate why a homogenous view of poverty is as problematic as attempting to universalise it in the first place. The rising income levels and wealth of mostly lower-middle and upper-middle income countries in East Asia and Pacific (EAP) raise questions about whether the standards of living to which

---

[13]Van Arkadie (1989)
[14]Acemoglu and Robinson (2010)

people aspire towards in those regions are much higher than the international poverty line benchmark of $1.90 per day.

Equally, the rising poverty in South Asian countries of Afghanistan, Pakistan, Bangladesh, Nepal and many African countries raises a similar question as to whether the $1.90 per day is a realistic estimation of what people need to survive in those regions. As a result, using a single unit of emphasis on income (i.e. $1.90 per day) seems a flawed approach to define, qualify and quantify poverty statistics as well as report various classifications and categorisations of the poor (and non-poor) and their distinct experiences across countries.[15] This is because such universalism in the use of proxies omits other nuanced but equally important variables that determine why certain sub-populations may be classified as poor, while also ignoring the implications of such omission for the economic lives of poor populations within and across countries.

As a complex phenomenon, it is misleading to either arbitrarily define or measure poverty purely in monetary statistics with little regard to the actual realities and choices facing the poor in different parts of the world. This complexity, perhaps, explains why poverty is categorised and understood in either absolute or relative terms. Absolute poverty relates to the total household income needed to afford basic needs including shelter, food and clothing in a particular country. Even this absolute view of poverty neither considers the broader quality of life as measured by people's changing basic needs nor the fact that individuals may have other social and cultural needs beyond shelter, food and clothing. Neither does it consider the wider effect of inequality on people's freedoms and rights.

Coupled with monetary deprivation, it is important to recognise that people may suffer from lack of access to basic education, healthcare and other critical services that are essential to individual well-being and productivity through no fault of their own.[16] These concerns are also borne out in the idea of relative poverty, defined in relation to the 'economic status of other members of the society'.[17] With the idea of relative poverty, people are considered poor if they were to fall below the prevailing or officially recognised standard of living in a particular country. It seems that these two poverty classifications are purely concerned with the economic prerogatives of people's income and consumption patterns.

They ignore the more subtle but important, sociological aspects of why people's standard of living and quality of life in one context may be markedly different from another context. People's quality of life is often affected by a variety of social and economic factors, even political process, some of which include access to education, health, employment and the prevailing cultural norms that marginalise certain population group in a way that is predominantly outside their control. Notwithstanding, poverty line, used interchangeably with poverty limit or poverty threshold, is the minimally acceptable level of household income deemed adequate for people to afford the basic standards of living in a particular country.

---

[15]In late 2015, the World Bank reclassified the international definition of poverty line (i.e. the minimum level of income deemed sufficient to survive in a particular country) to $1.90 up from $1.25 measured at 2005, adjusted for PPP.

[16]Yang (2019)

[17]UNESCO (2017)

It is the benchmark for estimating poverty indicators that are consistent with a country's specific social and economic circumstances. Thus, poverty line may differ for rural and urban areas in a specific country or for different geographic areas to reflect variations in the cost and standard of living including the differences in diet and consumption patterns. As a result, different indicators or measures of absolute and relative poverty may include and capture other items or measures, not just people's income. One measure is to define the basic things that people need (e.g. rights, freedoms, food, clothing and shelter) to be able to afford a decent living sense of self-worth and wellbeing.

Another measure could consider the income and resources available to a household and assess these against other households, those at the bottom of that scale could be considered relatively poor. This explains why countries have different measures and criteria for assessing and defining poverty for policymaking, planning and resource allocation. In the United Kingdom, for instance, poverty line is a binary construct measured in both absolute and relative terms. In terms of household income, poverty is defined as less than 60 percent of the average family income of £29,400 (2019 figure). But this benchmark is skewed towards higher income earners with a median income of £35,300.[18]

In the United States, the poverty guidelines ($25,000) set by the Department of Health and Human Services (DHHS), and the poverty threshold ($25,701) set by the US Census Bureau, are even more skewed as they offer two conflicting criteria. In any case, in general terms, the two poverty line metrics are used by the government as basis for determining policy on social programmes that target the poor. The problem with these guidelines is that they make it difficult to know precisely where and how to draw the line on poverty within and across different population groups within, between countries and across regions. Notwithstanding, it seems national poverty line reflects local perceptions of the level and composition of income and consumption patterns needed to be considered poor or non-poor in a specific context.

The perceived boundary between poor and non-poor typically rises with the average income of a particular country in relation to another country. In reality, it means that a poor household in the United Kingdom may be considered rich in Equatorial Guinea and vice versa. Based on this complex mix of situational criteria and variables, using a universal monetary value, of say $1.90, to categorise poor populations across the world may seem as an easy solution. But in reality it presents a rather dubious way of understanding the concept of poverty as a complex phenomenon, and its implications for people both within and across countries. If anything, just as the concept and the use of PPP is a default position in international trade finance, the use of poverty line in development discourse distorts the socioeconomic realities of certain population groups within and across countries.

2.4 THE PROBLEM WITH PURCHASING POWER PARITY

As one of the most explored issues on international trade finance and macroeconomics, it is not out of place to treat PPP and poverty line with the same scepticism in

---

[18]Office of National Statistics (2019)

terms of their distortive effect on definitions of poverty and experiences of the poor populations across countries. PPP exchange rates are used to determine a universal poverty line; thus, it affects poverty line definitions.[19] As such, this distortion has the potential to either underestimate or exaggerate people's socioeconomic conditions. Apart from that, the underpinning logic of PPP is inadequate, infrequently updated and therefore cannot be accurately applied or even relied upon as a measure to determine the consumption patterns of the extremely poor.[20]

Also, opinions are swayed between positive and negative implications of the short-run and the long-run distortive effect of PPP on cross-country comparisons of productivity and per capita income, which are determinants of a country's global competitiveness. The extent to which PPP has been used to distort the competitiveness of developing African countries is probably far worse than has ever been revealed in international trade and finance. To better appreciate the inherently flawed nature of PPP and its implications for designing and allocating resources to pro-poor schemes, one needs to understand its rationale and underpinning logic. Formulated by Gustav Cassel in 1916 in an attempt to develop a lasting 'classical' theory of exchange rates in international trade following the economic turmoil of the First World War, the economic theory of PPP works on the principle that 'the prize of a common basket of commodities is identical across all countries when quoted in the same currency'.[21]

In theory, and in practice, this principle relies on the law of one price (LOOP). LOOP specifies that the price of a commodity or a bundle of commodities should be equal across countries when expressed in terms of a common currency, say, the US dollar. In other words, the nominal exchange rate of two national currencies should adjust to price shocks and other frictions that affect commodities traded by both countries while keeping their real exchange rates unchanged.[22] The pricing shock is believed to be offset against perfect inter-country market arbitrage, which is central to determining exchange rates.[23] This assumption works on the logic that markets work perfectly well and that the arbitrage process will somehow lead to a market price convergence or equilibrium in international trade.

Thus, based on this assumption, it would mean that any deviation in pricing is short-lived and negligible.[24] But there are several inherent difficulties with these assumptions. First, neither the principle of market arbitrage nor market price convergence explains or accounts for the adjustment of price shocks in imperfect or incomplete markets under which majority of developing economies, and most especially African countries operate. Neither does it fully explain the losses these countries may encounter, or even accumulate, because of the effect of other frictions, for example, information flow or information asymmetry that may distort the dynamics of trade and commodity pricing, particularly in contexts in which information frictions are 'unobserved and endogenous'.[25]

---

[19]Deaton (2005)
[20]Deaton and Dupriez (2011)
[21]Baum et al. (2001)
[22]Yildirim (2017)
[23]Baum et al. (2001)
[24]Hachicha and Frikha (2014)
[25]Steinwender (2014)

Using household surveys to construct PPPs or poverty-linked indexes,[26] Mark Taylor argued that no one country including their currency can justify a 'unique' claim to be the base of comparison for any PPP-related transaction.[27] This is because the cost-of-living index works on the assumption that consumption patterns and preferences are identical in the two countries, or the currencies being compared. But we know that the cost-of-living index measures apply to individual countries and not to the averages with which PPP and poverty-linked indexes deal with. Thus, it becomes messier when one begins to think of indexes linked to specific sub-groups, such as the rich, the poor or those living close to or even below the poverty line, whatever that may be.[28]

The second problem is the assumption that consumers in all countries, but particularly those in rich and poor countries, have the same consumption patterns, preferences, tastes and affordability including in relation to public services, such as health and education regardless of their individual circumstances. Again, this assumption is problematic. For instance, it would be misguided to assume that food consumption patterns and preferences in Africa are similar to those in Western societies, or more specifically between Nigeria and the United States.[29] Because of this, there is a serious issue as to whether cost-of-living index numbers should be used as the 'gold standard' in approximating PPP exchange rates globally.

In the real world, if the LOOP-PPP principle were to be applied to Nigeria with its high concentration of poor population, then other economic variables, such as transaction costs, subsidies, trade restrictions, imperfect competition, taxation, non-traded goods, foreign exchange interventions, price indices across countries and differential composition of commodity baskets, would render the price parity condition invalid at two levels of human activity. At a macro level, for instance, Nigeria with its currency the Naira (₦) would certainly always be undervalued against the US dollars – the world's most traded currency. This scenario undermines Nigeria's global competitiveness and makes it very difficult for the country to compete on an even basis with the United States in the international commodities market or even with other countries that use the US dollars as the base for transaction.

---

[26]For fuller understanding, certain interrelated factors and confusing terms associated with poverty measurement and PPP require further explanation. The nominal effective exchange rate (NEER) is the unadjusted weighted average rate at which a country's currency exchanges for a basket of multiple foreign currencies, i.e. the number of units of domestic currency that can be exchanged or purchased for a foreign currency, whereas the real exchange rate (RER) usually measures the price of products in a foreign market in relation to the price of products in a domestic market—normally linked with the consumer price index (CPI) or wholesale price index (WPI) at a national level. CPI is an indicator of the average price a consumer will pay for a bundle of consumer goods and services (e.g. food, clothing, education, transportation), whereas WPI measures average price changes in the wholesale market. Both can be regarded as PPP or poverty-linked indexes, which provide an approximation for determining cost-of-living index—derived using household surveys/data—used in constructing internationally comparable poverty lines. Cost-of-living index incorporates the measures (i.e. price variations of good and services such as food, clothing and education purchased in the marketplace) used to determine CPI and WPI, but would further consider other environmental (e.g. energy, food, water and transportation) and governmental (laws affecting consumption of public goods including education and health) factors that affect people's consumption patterns over a period of time.
[27]Taylor (2003)
[28]Deaton and Heston (2010)
[29]Almas (2012)

At a micro level, the tendency to misclassify and lump together the 'transiently' (temporary) and the 'chronically' (long-term) poor in each case, without sufficient insight into the social, political and economic realities under which these distinct populations must co-exist and survive, raises another problem. Because of these differences, it is difficult to unilaterally apply the logic of PPP and poverty line to determine social and economic remedies for the survival of poor populations across different countries. The fact is that the complexities of the socioeconomic realities the poor face do not lend itself usefully to poverty line or PPP.[30] This unsophisticated approach to dealing with the complexities of human condition and socio-economic systems of different countries makes it harder to eliminate the root causes of poverty, just as the widening gap between rich and poor populations across the world cannot be resolved simply by resorting to a single formular as a unit of emphasis and comparison.

Thus, in shifting the emphasis away from rather narrow approaches to definition and categorisation of poverty within and across nations, it may be more helpful to isolate the particularities of the socioeconomic conditions of distinct population groups and sub-groups, and instead focus effort on eliminating the source of the worst human scourge – inequality, which is the root cause of poverty.

2.5 GLOBAL POVERTY AND ITS CAUSES

About 3.4 billion people currently live in poverty across the world. As a condition of human deprivation and distress present in all nations, poverty arises from the failure of various institutional arrangements and adverse factors that govern the political, social and economic lives of people within and across countries. If such institutional factors were reversed, it is possible that the condition of poverty could be drastically altered. The different economic cycles of the largest industrialised economies that control most of the global wealth have shown that at least absolute conditions of poverty can be drastically reduced if not eliminated. For instance, measured in annual income per capita, the United States in the seventeenth and eighteenth centuries with average GDP per capita income of $3363 in those periods was poorer than the present-day SSA with an average annual per capita income of $3987.5 including countries, such as Eswatini ($10,637.8), Ghana ($4746.7) and even conflict-torn Cameroun ($3785.1), Sudan ($4759.5) and Nigeria ($5990.9).[31]

Similarly, in the 1960s, South Korea was poor and debt-ridden and heavily relied on a weak manufacturing sector and foreign aid. In the early 1980s, with a debt-to-GDP ratio of 50 percent, South Korea was one of the most heavily indebted countries in the world only behind Mexico, Brazil and Argentina.[32] But in the decades since, following a combination of market-led reforms including strong institutions and foreign direct investment, South Korea is today among the richest countries in the world. Even with the present-day social and economic turmoil as a result of the COVID-19 pandemic, South Korea provided early exemplary global leadership in the fight against the diseases through a combination of

[30]Deaton and Case (2020)
[31]World Bank (2018)
[32]Collins (1990)

agile innovation, cutting-edge technology (test, trace and contain) and fiscal humanitarianism.[33] For instance, it is the only country that covered all COVID-19-related medical costs for both its citizens and foreigners living in the country, at least in the early onset of the pandemic.

Perhaps, more profoundly, by emerging from an aid recipient to an aid donor country through its OECD membership, South Korea has demonstrated how the social, economic and political institutional arrangements within a country could be altered and reversed to reduce poverty and create shared prosperity. But the absence of strong institutions coupled with low human development is making it very difficult for poor countries to achieve the type of socioeconomic transformation seen in South Korea in less than two decades.

Although the world has made a remarkable progress in eliminating extreme poverty, inequality, however, remains by far the single most persistent threat to global efforts to eradicate all forms of poverty in both developing and developed countries. For instance, even though the United Kingdom is the world's sixth largest economy based on nominal GDP of $2.83 trillion (2019 figures) behind Germany ($3.86 trillion) and India ($2.87 trillion), yet, 22 percent of UK households, that is, about 14.3 million, live in poverty because of inherent inequality in the systems that govern access to education, livelihood opportunities, income, housing, food security and consequently overall quality of life. Of these, 8.3 million are working age adults, 4.1 million are children and 1.9 million are of pensionable age, with 1.1 million of the total poor population living in extreme poverty.[34]

Because inequality is manifested in low pay, child poverty is more acute in single-parent households where nearly half of the children (49 percent) live in poverty compared with one in four (25 percent) in double-parent households.[35] Thus, it means that 1 in 3 children live in UK households in which the government's recommended daily healthy diet is unaffordable. The 'MakeTheUTurn campaign' for free school meals, led by the footballer, Marcus Rashford, is perhaps a poignant reminder of the severe inequalities and consequences still facing many UK households unable to feed their children, particularly during the COVID-19 lockdown when most schools were closed in a government-led effort to contain the disease.

Similarly, the US Census Bureau estimates that 38.1 million Americans, that is, 11.8 percent of the population, live in poverty, of which 16.2 percent are children.[36] The Children's Defense Fund (CDF), a children's charity, estimates that about 1 in 6 children in the United States, about 11.9 million, live in poverty, with nearly 5.9 million living in extreme poverty.[37] Although poverty affects all children from different backgrounds depending on their race, gender, parents' occupation and social status, poor children are disproportionately more prevalent in single-parent households where a dependent child presents more significant maintenance burden than in double-parent households. Emphasis on child poverty is of interest and particular

---

[33]Ahn (2020)
[34]Social Metrics Commission (2019)
[35]Barnard et al. (2018)
[36]Semega et al. (2019)
[37]Children's Defense Fund (2019)

relevance because it provides the barometer of other social and economic ladders within any society.

Besides, the future prosperity of any nation should be judged by the social and economic systems under which its children and young people must survive. Although rich developed countries have well-established institutional arrangements (e.g. the welfare system) for supporting the unemployed compared to developing countries. Yet, they have not adequately and fully addressed the root causes and the consequences of rising inequality within their societies. Also, despite the phenomenal progress to tackle poverty in Asia, nearly 500 million people mostly in Lao PDR, Timor-Leste and Papua New Guinea and rural population in affluent China, India and Malaysia are thought to be poor and insecure.[38] In Latin America and the Caribbean, an estimated 182 million people (2018 figures) live in poverty, of whom 63 million (i.e. 10.2 percent of the population) are extremely poor.[39]

Although up-to-date data are hard to find, about 29 million (2016 figures) children in the Middle East and North Africa (MENA), that is 1 in 4 children, are believed to be extremely poor without access to proper education and healthcare.[40] Poverty in MENA is made worse by the ongoing conflicts in countries like Yemen and Syria.[41] In Africa, although more people are escaping extreme poverty according to World Poverty Clock, SSA still accounts for about two-third of the world's extremely poor population.[42] Following a recent spatial data captured from satellite images involving 102 countries across the world, it emerged that SSA is the 'globally designated poverty hotspot',[43] which suggests that the poverty situation in Africa may be nuanced in relation to the nature of poverty in Asia, Europe and North America.

2.6 POVERTY IN AFRICA

The reason why poverty persists in Africa even with the region's vast natural wealth and decades of continuous foreign aid programme is too complex to understand. Particularly, SSA has the largest percentage of households that have experienced longer cycles of household and intergenerational poverty.[44] In the last decade, there is a striking irony about the two percent overall reduction in the geography of the global poor – especially, India, Southeast Asia and South American countries, where each percentage point increase in per capita income has seen a reduction in the percentage of the world's overall poor population – and the stagnation in poverty reduction in Africa. Poverty is particularly more acute among Africa's rural than urban populations.

In the previous two decades, for instance, the formerly poor populations in Africa's two most populous countries – Nigeria and Ethiopia – have merely transitioned mostly into low-income status (i.e. those on $2 per day with a significant risk of

---

[38]World Bank (2019)
[39]Economic Commission for Latin America and the Caribbean (2019)
[40]UNICEF (2017)
[41]Atamanov and Tandon (2018)
[42]World Bank (2018)
[43]Cohen et al. (2019)
[44]Hulme (2003)

slipping into poverty), increasing from 45 percent to 54 percent between 2001 and 2011.[45] Thus, the percentage of those who could be classified as either poor or on low income barely changed over that period, down by only 2 percent from 94 percent to 92 percent. If these statistics are anything to go by, then it seems poverty in Africa may have comparably increased by nearly the same rate at which global poverty may have fallen over that 10-year period. It is also the case that over the same period, poverty may have risen at the same pace by which Africa's population size may have correspondingly increased.

Perhaps, there is a correlation between rising population size and increasing poverty in Africa. Analysis by World Data Lab shows that in early 2020, about 48 percent of Nigerians, that is, nearly 96 million out of 201 million people (2019 figures) live in extreme poverty. Similarly, in Ethiopia, 25 percent of the 112 million population are extremely poor. Poverty is even worse in Democratic Republic of the Congo (the third largest by population) where 74 percent (more than 63 million people) of the population is thought to be living on less than $1.90 per day. What is a bit more surprising, perhaps even baffling, is that the poor populations in SSA are likely to grow at more than the average population growth in the region.

The reason why there is poverty in much of developing economies, especially in Africa, is because poor populations generally lack access to opportunities that quality education provides, as well as the fact that they are more likely to suffer from illness due to lack of access to quality healthcare services. Because of these factors, poor populations are more likely to have far higher fertility rates and low human development outcomes than non-poor populations. As Figure 2.1 shows, most African countries ranked mostly low on the HDI because of poor education and healthcare access. The poor are often

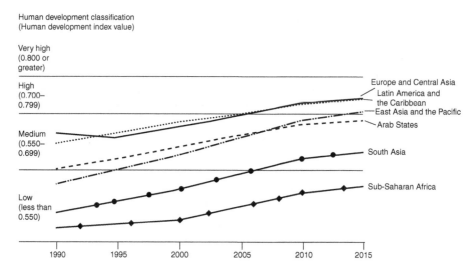

FIGURE 2.1   Regional trends in human development index values

Source: UNDP, Human Development Report (2016 accessed via:https://www.undp.org/publications/human-development-report-2016).

---

[45]Kochhar (2015)

denied access to choices in education and health, which are essential to access livelihood opportunities, earn sustainable not subsistence income and enjoy a productive and healthy life. Thus, compared to their global counterparts, Africa's poor populations face a very different set of institutional obstacles outside their control that give rise to their adverse conditions, thereby making it impossible for them to escape poverty.

Apart from lack of access to quality education and healthcare, housing is another major obstacle that prevents the poor from escaping poverty. Analysis of housing and sanitation in SSA shows that as many as 53 million urban dwellers live in city slums.[46] From the sprawling suburbs of Khayelitsha in Cape Town, South Africa and Kibera in Nairobi, Kenya, to Makoko in Lagos, Nigeria, majority of households live in ghettos, many without access to proper sanitation and electricity. Most slum dwellers tend to be economic migrants, young, jobless, and consequently more prone to crime. Without access to proper housing, sanitation and title to homes, the crammed urban poor cannot live a productive and healthy life.

Housing with a proper sanitation is essential to individual well-being and productivity, both as a 'social glue' and a source of personal financial investment. Thus, making it a good source of economic development, as investment in housing through individual ownership of property contributes to national asset accumulation. Added to this, and given its labour-intensive nature, housing construction equally provides employment and increased spending on other infrastructural projects, such as roads.[47] But to have a title to housing, or own a property, individuals must have a sustainable livelihood and stable income. Both can be acquired through access to quality education.

In addition, education plays a key role in broadening opportunities for individuals as it provides a breadth of skills needed to thrive in life, work and citizenship, thereby reversing poverty. Prospectively, if one were to consider the EODB–HCI hypothesis discussed earlier, then the consequences of lack of access to quality education as one of the main social barriers to high human development outcomes and sustainable development becomes even more striking. Compared with other regions across the world, SSA sub-region is the most off track to meeting the SDG 4.1 target: *free, equitable and quality basic education* by 2030. Over one-fifth of children aged 6–11 years old, one-third of young people aged 12–14 years old and almost 60 percent of youths aged 15–17 years old are either not in school or have dropped out of school.[48]

Children from the poorest households are more than twice likely than children from rich households to be out of school. Children without formal education are twice more likely to be in poverty than children with formal education. Without formal education, children lack the social, cognitive and the behavioural skills needed to survive in employment as adults. Also, children without formal education are far more likely to have lower earnings and income potential than children with formal education, thus twice more likely to commit crimes and engage in violence. In addition, children that are denied formal education are far more likely to have health challenges because of poor nutritional choices related to illiteracy.

In Africa, sociocultural complexities mean that mostly girls face steeper barriers to educational opportunities than boys. According to the 2018 Global Multidimensional

---

[46]Tusting et al. (2019)
[47]Mills et al. (2017)
[48]UNICEF (2017)

Poverty Index (MPI) published by the Oxford Poverty and Human Development Initiative (OPHI), lack of education and poor nutrition are the largest contributors to poverty in SSA. To assess individual-level poverty worldwide, OPHI uses three HDI dimensions to link ten indicators of acute deprivations along Education – *years of schooling and school attendance*, Health – *nutrition and child mortality* and Standard of Living – *cooking fuel, sanitation, drinking water, electricity and housing.*[49]

On the MPI scale, it emerged that Nigeria has the worst education deprivation among children of school-age group, followed by nutrition and child mortality. Whereas in health, Ethiopia emerged as the country with one of the worst conditions of health-related poverty among the global population. Thus, the worse conditions in education and healthcare deprivations in Nigeria and Ethiopia necessitate the need to examine the general state of formal education and healthcare in Africa through the lens of both countries.

2.7 EDUCATION IN NIGERIA

From basic, secondary to higher education, the education sector in many African countries appears to be in a crisis. In particular, lack of funding, poor quality education, accessibility and affordability issues are the major challenges facing the Nigerian educational sector. This has resulted to university closures due to prolonged strike action by academics and the consequent loss of talented scholars and young people through emigration and brain drain. Also, lack of security in schools is not only a major barrier to education access. But its consequences have been especially devastating for young girls in northern Nigeria wishing to acquire primary and secondary education. For instance, at the northern edge of Bornu State in northeast Nigeria sits the desperately poor and isolated remote village of Chibok. Although a predominantly Christian community, Chibok came to international limelight in April 2014 following the abduction of 276 schoolgirls from the only Government School by the Boko Haram terrorist group.

Officially known as Jamā'at Ahl as-Sunnah lid-Da'wah wa'l-Jihād, Boko Haram literally translated means 'Western education is bad'. Of the abducted schoolgirls, 112 remain in captivity. As efforts have faded to find the remaining abducted girls, Yana Galang, the grieving mother of one of the girls still in captivity has lost hope of educating her abducted daughter, Rifkatu Galang. In Yana's words: 'nobody comes to us to tell us anything about the girls'.[50] Of the many unreported similar incidents across Africa, the Chibok case is a poignant reminder of the myriad of challenges facing the wider issue of equality in access to education in Nigeria, particularly for girls. More than half of girls of primary and secondary school age are not in school. Of those that are enrolled in early or basic education, the annual dropout rate is disproportionately very high compared to boys.

Globally, Nigeria has the highest cumulative school dropout rate of 30 percent, with significant variation in dropout rate between northern and southern Nigeria.[51] Also, the gap in educational attainment between northern and southern Nigeria and

---

[49]OPHDI (2019)
[50]BBC (2019)
[51]UNICEF (2018)

the gap in the rate of admission and accessibility of education between men and women are more acute in the higher education sub-sector.[52] Barriers to educational opportunities among most people are linked to funding crisis and poverty.

The funding crisis has knock-on effects in that in many cases teachers are ill-equipped and poorly paid, and classrooms are overcrowded and dilapidated with undernourished school children who face a risk of childhood stunting. With about 11.5 percent of the country's population undernourished, Nigeria has a fair share of the global population of chronically undernourished school-age children due to food insecurity.[53] The risk factors for stunting among school-age children have been attributed to polygamy and low maternal education, which are more prevalent in Nigeria's poorest and single-parent households.[54] A mother's level of education affects her income level, which in turn influences her health choices and ability to provide the right nutritional support for her children during their school age.

But with young girls and women routinely marginalised in education and employment access in Nigeria, a significant percentage of them are illiterate and poor. This makes it much harder and far more challenging for women as mothers to support their school-age children with the right nutritional support. Good nutrition is essential to children's physical and cognitive development. As such, a reliable government-backed free school meal programme is perhaps the only way to address this challenge. Free school meal will help to increase school enrolment, retention and completion of basic education and thereby reduce the high rate of dropout among school-age children.

Unfortunately, inadequate funding and poor planning have hampered the implementation of the Nigerian government's National Home Grown School Feeding Programme (NHGSFP) launched in 2018. Despite the serious challenges in its educational sector, Nigeria's annual education budget remains among the lowest globally. In 2019, the sector received 7.05 percent (₦620.5 billion; equivalent to $162 million) of the country's annual total budget. This is significantly below UNESCO's recommendation of 15–20 percent of a country's annual budget.

2.8 ETHIOPIA HEALTH SECTOR

As a human development indicator, health is a key measure of individual well-being, productivity and quality of life. Ethiopia's global ranking on the HDI has been very low at 173/189 due to poor levels of individual and workforce productivity.[55] Unfortunately, it is in the areas of health and survival that Ethiopia struggles far more than many countries in Africa. Spiralling communicable and non-communicable diseases due to poor health infrastructure and weaknesses in the delivery of essential healthcare services hamper Ethiopia's ability to boost the productivity of its workforce population. Also, on the World Economic Forum's Global Gender Parity Index measured across four key indicators namely, educational attainment, health and

---

[52]Oludayo et al. (2019)
[53]Roser and Ritchie (2020)
[54]Senbanjo et al. (2011)
[55]UNDP (2019)

survival, economic participation and opportunity, Ethiopia ranks significantly below the world average at 115 out of 144 countries.[56]

Systemic and structural problems including acute human resource problems, inadequate budget and weak infrastructures have led to a severe shortage of qualified healthcare professionals. Although medical education is free in Ethiopia, the sector suffers from a severe brain drain among its qualified medical professionals. To compound matters, medical students and trainees, about 53 percent, have a high desire, much stronger among male trainees, to emigrate to Europe and North America after graduation.[57] The high rate of emigration among Ethiopian medical practitioners is linked with poor working environments, low workforce morale, limited career progression and low pay.

The average annual salary for a qualified physician is about ETB113,095 (Ethiopian Birr), which equates to less than $5000. As a result, the health sector workforce ratio is 0.7 per 1000 population, well below the 1.6 average threshold in Africa, and significantly below the minimum threshold of 2.3 per 1000 population recommended by the World Health Organisation (WHO) as the benchmark to provide the essential healthcare services in any country. Nearly half of healthcare expenditure comes from outside the country in form of bilateral and multilateral aid grants and loans. For instance, in 2019, Ethiopia requested nearly $237 million in foreign aid assistance from the United States to address its worsening health sector funding crisis. Of this amount, nearly $170 million was needed to combat HIV/AIDS prevalence, maternal and child health as well as malaria. With the exception of the capital, Addis Ababa, all areas of Ethiopia are malarious.

Another source of healthcare financing is from household expenditure or 'out-of-pocket expense' (which is as high as 36 percent) and government budget, which is the reigonal lowest at about 16.5 percent.[58] Even though there has been a significant increase in budgetary allocation to Ethiopia's health sector in the last decade, this increase masks the reality of overall decline in its healthcare expenditure when adjusted for inflation and population growth. Also, the per capita health expenditure over the same period only amounted to ETB268 ($12) in 2015–2016.[59] This is comparably lower than the average $98 per capita health expenditure in SSA, and well short of the 15 percent national budget threshold agreed by African countries at the Abuja Declaration, as well as the $30–$40 per head recommended by the WHO for financing essential healthcare services.

To compound matters, because of budgetary constraints, health infrastructures including public hospitals are severely underutilised because they are ill-equipped to meet the growing public healthcare needs. As a result, most Ethiopians are left with direct out-of-pocket expenses at the mercy of private healthcare providers. For many of Ethiopia's rural poor, this creates a significant financial burden and a barrier to access vital healthcare needs. Inadequate budget also means that Ethiopia is unable to build the infrastructures to meet its citizens' basic healthcare needs, such as child and maternal health, nutrition and reproductive health. With AIDS-related mortality among Ethiopians comparably high at 15,000–26,000 deaths annually,

---

[56]World Economic Forum (2017)
[57]Deressa and Azah (2012)
[58]World Health Organisation (2017)
[59]UNICEF (2017)

these services, along with other vital healthcare needs, such as antiretroviral therapy, are still out of reach for Ethiopia's predominantly rural poor population.[60]

2.9 TRANSFORMING EDUCATION – TOWARDS THE SDGs

Africa ceased the occasion of the World Economic Forum in 2000 to develop a realistic policy agenda to improve the quality and access to all levels of education based on a set of regional educational priorities aimed at meeting the challenges of 21st century education for the continent. Since then, not much can be shown by many African countries in terms of concrete sector transformation geared towards delivering the knowledge and skills young people need to access livelihood opportunities and meet labour market needs of the 21st century. But there are several way in which African governments can work with stakeholders to transform the education sector and pave the way to realise the "Education for All" commitment under the Dakar Framework for Action. At the very least, there needs to be a 5–10-year radical education funding strategy beyond UNESCO's recommended 15 percent to 20 percent of national budget or between 4 percent and 6 percent of GDP. Such a strategy is vital across the region and entails a serious and significant government commitment to expanding education opportunities for girls, increased monitoring, especially children in fragile locations affected by conflicts and wars. Girls' education would have immediate positive social and economic impact on household income across Africa. If anything, it will contribute towards guaranteeing sustainable healthy nutritional support for school-age children.

To meet its Dakar obligation, there are a few positive policy options and actions that Nigeria in particular, and indeed other African countries may consider. Firstly, it needs to invest at least 30 percent of its national budget year on year over the next 5 years to help deal with its worsening crisis in the education sector. At a higher education level, especially, funding should be earmarked to encourage and reward research and scholarship, promote an 'entrepreneurial university' concept through policies that reward academic-industry collaboration, establish a transparent system of academic promotion and reward and develop global best practice mechanisms for teaching evaluation, quality assurance and students' support.

Secondly, at a primary education level, broad-based school feeding programme that includes take home ration, targeted at girls and the marginalised, must be implemented and subsidised through the tax system. In addition to helping to increase enrolment, retention and success in the early stages of a child's education, such a programme will also help to improve human capital formation and economic growth at later stages of a child's productivity as an adult. Early child nutrition brings several socioeconomic benefits, such as good hygiene practices and good eating habits. In addition, a school feeding programme that 'aligns local consumption with local production' will guarantee stable supply chains and boost employment for local farmers. Also, a broad-based school feeding programme targeting girls and the marginalised will increase gender parity and

---

[60]UNAIDS.org (2017)

equality in access to education, thereby breaking the intergenerational cycle of poverty and hunger through human capital development.[61]

Although quality education is essential to human capital development, good health and early child nutrition are also important indicators of positive human capital outcomes. When children's health and nutrition are improved, they learn better. Also, educated and healthy children are more able to transform their educational opportunities into tangible economic benefits for their countries through increased productivity as adults. As such, scaling up national school feeding programme as part of the broader basic education strategy will be vital to achieving high human development outcomes and economic growth. For this strategy to be successful and the benefits realised, it would require increased effort and commitment in partnership with regional and global education stakeholders. Nigeria can learn from countries, such as Namibia, South Africa, Kenya and the United Kingdom, where early school feeding programmes have been effective and successful for many years.

Thirdly, the acceleration of investments in education innovation and the modernisation of the regulatory environment are essential to acquisition of future-oriented skills for human development outcomes. Thus, policies prioritising education reforms and evaluation systems along several measures will ensure that the curricula are aligned with current and future labour market needs. Emphasis on entrepreneurship education and work-based training with private sector participation will help to facilitate school-to-work transition for many young people, thereby reducing high youth unemployment. Revamping Technical and Vocational Education and Training (TVET) to align with the skills needs, priorities and employment aspirations of Africa's changing demography will also lead to immediate socioeconomic benefits and impact, particularly in terms of increased productivity and job creation.

Fourthly, the professional capacity of educators across the education value chain must be strengthened by improving the quality of their training and remuneration systems. This will lift morale and make teachers more agile and well-motivated to prepare and support pupils and students to embrace future trends in the labour market. Teachers are powerful agents of change, thus, they can help to actualise the SDGs and EFA commitments in any society. But to do so effectively, teachers must first acquire the requisite know-how through competence-based upskilling and reskilling.

Skills training will empower teachers to embrace new forms and new ways of working to ensure and sustain students' engagement, including through digital and online provision in a rapidly changing world in which the COVID-19 pandemic has further limited education access for many in Africa. Skills training will also help teachers to develop the attitude, aptitude and the attributes as well as the right mindset, commitment and motivation to influence learners – thus, help to deliver the educational commitments under the SDGs/EFA frameworks. Therefore, prioritising policy targeted at reforms, changes to employment conditions and work environments, incentives that encourage commitment to research, and Continuous Professional Development (CPD), and academic mobility will help to boost educational outcomes across the board.

Fifth, adapting to a rapidly changing world demands that education policies, resourcing and curricula be aligned with the endless opportunities offered by the

---

[61]World Food Programme (2019)

Fourth Industrial Revolution (4IR) technologies. This can be achieved through emphasis on digital literacy, fluency and STEM skills to complement changing labour market needs, particularly the future nature of work in which disruptive technologies and automation are seen as central to productivity, efficiency and effectiveness in the workplace. In addition, through academic-industry collaboration and by investing in the necessary infrastructures that facilitate increased learning and adoption of disruptive technologies, education curricula and pedagogies can be modelled in ways that meet the current and the future skills needs of the private sector in a new and disruptive economy.

Thus, governments, educators and the private sector must ensure that educational systems in Africa are agile and future-proofed to serve, prepare and enable pupils and students to take advantage of the livelihood opportunities offered by, for instance, Cloud Computing, Artificial Intelligence (AI)/Machine Intelligence, Internet of Things (IoT), Robotics, Renewable Energy and Blockchain necessary for data gathering, new business modelling and management. This will ensure that education is strategically well aligned to empower current and future generation of pupils and students including the poor and the marginalised to embrace the current and future 4IR opportunities and priorities. Also, as Africa's working population is set to increase by 2030, government must create the conditions that encourage educators to integrate innovative forms of learning, such as augmented reality to address the problem of skills mismatch, but also plug the high-skills gap between education attainment and labour market needs.

Compared to other regions of the world with a sizeable population, SSA has large proportions of workers in low-skilled jobs. Majority, especially women and young people, are either underemployed or languishing in the vulnerable informal sector, without job security. Education design and provision that consider labour market needs and 4IR opportunities will ensure that young and adult learners are more responsive and productive as they develop the skills and know-how to better react to emerging labour-market trends (e.g. automation) through an approach that rewards life long learning (LLL). Thus, this will ensure that the current and future generation of learners are able to contribute meaningfully to new and rapidly evolving sectors, such as in Fintech, FoodTech, AgriTech and Smart Cities.

2.10 TRANSFORMING HEALTHCARE – TOWARDS THE SDGs

Just as there is a strong case for increasing the budgetary allocation and monitoring in the formal education sector, there is equally a strong social and economic imperative to ramp up investment in Africa's healthcare sector. This is particularly needed from educational, infrastructural and technological viewpoints. A healthy population is far more likely to be more productive, happier and prosperous, thus, far more capable than an unhealthy population to contribute to economic growth and sustainable development. An equitable and sustainable system of financing healthcare provision through increased budgetary allocation as well as tracking and blocking wastages will help to mobilise and reinvest resources in critical areas of healthcare provision.

In addition to raising budgetary allocation to the health sector, the introduction of a national health insurance scheme could also help the marginalised poor and rural populations through reduction of burdensome out-of-pocket health expenditure. Most of the impoverished rural population are twice more likely to be denied access to vital healthcare services because of poverty. Even though health service is supposed to be free in most African countries like Ethiopia, the quality of public health services is often insufficient and of poor quality to meet local needs and complex healthcare needs. As such, to meet the growing healthcare needs of the poor population, African countries are likely to benefit through the introduction of a Universal Healthcare Coverage and strong governance mechanisms. Strengthening governance mechanisms will not only reduce corruption, track waste and leakages in the sector but also lead to improved service provision in public hospitals.

Secondly, increased regional cooperation and continental partnership involving exchange of best practices, research and innovative strategies in collaboration with the private sector will help to mobilise private sector resources and create more sustainable financing models to reduce the burden of individual healthcare financing, thereby guarantee affordable high-quality healthcare for all and reduce donor dependence in healthcare financing. Donor commitment to health reforms and financing tends to be inadequate and unpredictable. Also, they are rarely aligned with local healthcare needs and priorities.[62] This is particularly the case in Ethiopia where, for example, the USAID and the United Nations Population Fund (UNFPA) reneged on their financial commitments between 2012 and 2013.[63]

Thirdly, a move towards a patient-centred approach to healthcare provision integrated with strong referral networks, mutual accountability between providers and patients, coupled with improved working environment for healthcare professionals could have a transformative impact on the quality of patient care. In addition to helping to restore patients' dwindling confidence and trust in the public systems of healthcare delivery, it will help to reduce the sector's brain drain, particularly in Ethiopia. Thus, a significant system-level change and investment in the restructure of public healthcare delivery mechanisms to make them more robust, reliable and relevant to twenty-first-century healthcare provision is vital.

Fourthly, twenty-first-century public healthcare delivery requires human capital for exploration and the uptake of opportunities presented by the 4IR in healthcare provision. Bolder investment and commitment to programmes that encourage the use of digital and disruptive technologies to improve healthcare delivery and compensate for poor or limited physical infrastructures and lack of qualified healthcare professionals, especially in rural areas, can provide significant benefits for people of ages and background with varied healthcare needs. As use of mobile technologies is becoming increasingly more common across Africa, mobile internet can be used as a force for good in the health sector in terms of service delivery, data capture and healthcare management.

In addition, they can also be used to mobilise support and improve disaster response rates among healthcare professionals during a pandemic. Platforms and policies that encourage greater regional and increased international collaboration with healthcare experts, researchers, private sector and public authorities including the WHO in the use of disruptive technologies could strengthen the capacity to better protect against and also manage diseases outbreaks, such as the COVID-19. For these

---

[62]Shaw et al. (2015)
[63]Ethiopia Federal Ministry of Health (2014)

ideas to work and become effective, national governments must find ways of using the tax system to incentivise increased participation of technological companies to work with local healthcare providers to improve service delivery in the sector.

Some private sector companies, such as the Israeli-based MobileODT and the US-based International Business Machines Corporation (IBM), are already working with local healthcare providers and professionals in Africa to deploy AI in healthcare provision and management. For instance, AI is used to increase accuracy and widen access in the early detection and diagnosis of serious illnesses, such as cervical cancer and malaria.[64] Also, disruptive technologies can improve and widen healthcare access, such as in Rwanda where high-speed medical drones are being used to deliver blood and save lives in remote rural communities across the country.[65] Also, just like in the financial services sector where mobile technologies (e.g. M-Pesa) are being used to facilitate real-time transactions, uptake of health mobile technologies, such as mobile-tracking (mTRAC) used in Uganda to track and monitor disease patterns,[66] has the potential to revolutionise information sharing and management between healthcare professionals, health authorities and end-users. Investments in these technologies will make a significant difference in terms of increasing the quality of healthcare outcomes for individuals and ultimately contribute to improved human development outcomes and economic growth.

To sum up, while many African countries are making incremental gains towards meeting their SDGs commitments, those gains, while important, will not be sufficient to eradicate all forms of poverty by 2030. Thus, if any further beneficial outcome from the current gains is to be realised, and to meet the threshold for human development and economic growth outcomes by 2030, then African political leaders must reassess the policy norms through which they make and shape both education and healthcare priorities in their countries. At the very least, implementing some of the policy options suggested here would require a more efficient, prudent and transparent approach to use of natural resources revenues (discussed in the next chapter) and their effective governance. Effective governance of natural resource revenues will guarantee that they form part of a broader framework for investments in and maintenance of institutions that are geared towards achieving high human development and economic growth outcomes.

BIBLIOGRAPHY

Acemoglu, D., & Robinson, J. (2008). The role of institutions in growth and development, *The Commission on Growth and Development*. Working Paper No. 10, Washington, DC: World Bank Publications.

Acemoglu, D., & Robinson, J. (2010). The role of institutions in growth and development. *Review of Economics and Institutions*, 1(2), 1–33.

Ahn, M. (2020). *Combating COVID-19: Lessons from South Korea*. Washington, DC: Brookings Institution. Retrieved from https://www.brookings.edu/blog/techtank/2020/04/13/combating-covid-19-lessons-from-south-korea/. Accessed on 15 April 2020.

Almas, I. (2012). International income inequality: Measuring PPP bias by estimating Engel curves for food. *The American Economic Review*, 102(2), 1093–1117.

---

[64]Champlin et al. (2017)
[65]Fleming (2018)
[66]TRENDS (2018)

Anand, S., & Sen, A. (2000). The income component of the Human Development Index. *Journal of Human Development*, 1(1), 83–106.

Atamanov, A., & Tandon, S. (2018). Measuring regional poverty in MENA: Update and remaining challenges. World Bank Blogs. Retrieved from https://blogs.worldbank.org/arabvoices/measuring-regional-poverty-mena-update-and-remaining-challenges

Barnard, H., Collingwood, A., Leese, D., Wenham, A., Drake, B., Smith, E., & Kumar, A. (2018). *UK poverty 2018 – A comprehensive analysis of poverty trends and figures*. Report by the Joseph Rowntree Foundation, York. Retrieved from https://www.jrf.org.uk/report/uk-poverty-2018. Accessed on 4 August 2019.

Baum, C., Barkoulas, J., & Caglayan, M. (2001). Nonlinear adjustment to purchasing power parity in the post-Bretton Woods era. *Journal of International Money and Finance*, 20, 379–399.

BBC (2019). Letters from Africa: Why Chibok parents turning to TV 'miracle' pastor to find daughters. Retrieved from https://www.bbc.co.uk/news/world-africa-47910800

Champlin, C., Bell, D., & Schoken, C. (2017). AI medicine comes to Africa's rural clinics. *IEEE Spectrum*. Retrieved from https://spectrum.ieee.org/biomedical/devices/ai-medicine-comes-to-africas-rural-clinics. Accessed on 1 February 2020.

Children's Defense Fund (2019). Ending child poverty now. Retrieved from https://www.childrensdefense.org/wp-content/uploads/2019/04/Ending-Child-Poverty-2019.pdf

Cohen, J., Desai, R., & Kharas, H. (2019). *The geography of poverty hotspots*. Washington, DC: Brookings Institution. Retrieved from https://www.brookings.edu/blog/future-development/2019/09/24/the-geography-of-poverty-hotspots/

Collins, S. (1990). Lessons from Korean economic growth. *American Economic Review*, 80(2), 104–107.

Deaton, A. (2005). Measuring poverty in a growing world (or measuring growth in a poor world). *The Review of Economics and Statistics*, 87(1), 1–9.

Deaton, A., & Case, A. (2020). Rebottling the Gini: why this headline measure of inequality misses everything that matters. *Prospect Magazine*. Retrieved from https://www.prospectmagazine.co.uk/magazine/rebottling-the-gini-why-this-headline-measure-of-inequality-misses-everything-that-matters. Accessed on 3 February 2020.

Deaton, A., & Dupriez, O. (2011). Purchasing power parity exchange rates for the global poor. *American Economic Journal: Applied Economics*, 3(2), 137–166.

Deaton, A., & Heston, A. (2010). Understanding PPPs and PPP-based national accounts. *American Economic Journal: Macroeconomics*, 2(4), 1–35.

Deressa, W., & Azah, A. (2012). Attitudes of undergraduate medical students of Addis Ababa University towards medical practice and migration, Ethiopia. *BMC Medical Education*, 12(68), 1–11.

Economic Commission for Latin America and the Caribbean (2019). *Social Panorama of Latin America (LC/PUB.2019/22-P/REV1)*. Santiago: ECLAC. Retrieved from https://repositorio.cepal.org/bitstream/handle/11362/44989/1/S1901132_en.pdf

Ethiopia Federal Ministry of Health (2014). *Ethiopia's Fifth National Health Accounts: Highlight of major findings briefing notes*. Retrieved from https://www.hfgproject.org/wp-content/uploads/2014/04/Ethiopia-NHA-Findings-Briefing-Notes.pdf. Accessed on 1 February 2020.

Fleming, S. (2018). In Rwanda, high-speed drones are delivering blood to remote communities. Retrieved from https://www.weforum.org/agenda/2018/12/in-rwanda-drones-are-delivering-blood-to-remote-communities/. Accessed on 1 February 2018.

Fukuyama, F. (2000). *Social capital and the civil society*. IMF Working Paper No. 74. Washington, DC: International Monetary Fund (IMF). Retrieved from https://www.imf.org/external/pubs/ft/wp/2000/wp0074.pdf

Hachicha, N., & Frikha, W. (2014). Transaction costs and nonlinear modelling of real exchange rate deviations from purchasing power parity: Evidence from the MENA region. In D. Dufrenot,

F. Jawadi, & W. Louhichi (Eds.), *Market microstructure and nonlinear dynamics keeping financial crisis in context*, London: Springer.

Hodgson, G. (2006). What are institutions? *Journal of Economic Issues*, 40(1), 1–25.

Hulme, C. (2003). Chronic poverty and development policy: An introduction. *World Development*, 31(3), 399–402.

Kochhar, R. (2015). *A global middle class is more promise than reality*. Washington, DC: Pew Research Centre. Retrieved from https://www.pewresearch.org/global/2015/07/08/a-global-middle-class-is-more-promise-than-reality/. Accessed on 4 March 2019.

Mills, G., Herbst, J., Obasanjo, O., & Davis, D. (2017). *Making Africa work*. London: Hurst and Company.

North, D. (1990). *Institutions, institutional change and economic performance*, New York, NY: Cambridge University Press.

North, D. (1991). Institutions. *Journal of Economic Perspectives*, 5(1), 97–112.

Office of National Statistics (2019). Average household income, UK: Financial year ending 2019. Retrieved from https://www.ons.gov.uk/peoplepopulationandcommunity/personaland householdfinances/incomeandwealth/bulletins/householddisposableincomeandinequality/fina ncialyearending2019provisional. Accessed on 6 June 2019.

Oludayo, O., Popoola, S., Akanbi, C., & Atayero, A. (2019). Gender disparity in admissions into tertiary institutions: Empirical evidence from Nigerian data (2010–2015). *Data in Brief*, 22, 920–933.

Oxford Poverty and Human Development Initiative (2019), Global multidimensional poverty index. Retrieved from https://ophi.org.uk/multidimensional-poverty-index/global-mpi-2018/

Ranis, G., Stewart, F., & Ramirez, A. (2000). Economic growth and human development. *World Development*, 28(2), 197–219.

Roser, M., & Ritchie, H. (2020). *Hunger and undernourishment*. Retrieved from https://ourwor ldindata.org/hunger-and-undernourishment

Semega, J., Kollar, M., Creamer, J., & Mohanty, A. (2019). *Income and poverty in the United States: 2018*. U.S. Census Bureau, Current Population Reports, Report No. p60-266. Washington, DC: U.S. Government Printing Office. Retrieved from https://www.census.gov/ library/publications/2019/demo/p60-266.html

Sen, A. (1999). *Development as freedom*. Oxford: Oxford University Press.

Senbanjo, I., Oshikoya, K., Odusanya, O., & Njokanma, O. (2011). Prevalence of risk factors for stunting among school children and adolescents in Abeokuta, Southwest Nigeria. *Journal of Health, Population and Nutrition*, 29(4), 364–370.

Shaw, P., Wang, H., Kress, D., & Hovig, D. (2015). Donor and domestic financing of primary health care in low income countries. *Health Systems and Reform*, 1(1), 72–88.

Social Metrics Commission (2019). *Measuring poverty 2019. – A report of the Social Metrics Commission*. London: Legatum Institute. Retrieved from https://socialmetricscommission.or g.uk/wp-content/uploads/2019/07/SMC_measuring-poverty-201908_full-report.pdf

Steinwender, C. (2014). *Information frictions and the law of one price: "When the states and the kingdom became united"*, WTO Working Paper ERSD-2014-12, Economic Research and Statistics Division, World Trade Organization, Geneva. Retrieved from https://www.wto.org /english/res_e/reser_e/ersd201412_e.pdf

Taylor, M. (2003). Purchasing power parity. *Review of International Economics*, 11(3), 436–452.

Thematic Research Network on Data and Statistics (2018). Data sharing via SMS strengthens Uganda's health system. Retrieved from https://www.sdsntrends.org/research/2018/9/27/ case-study-mtrac-sms-health-uganda. Accessed on 1 February 2020.

Tusting, L.S., Bisanzio, D., Alabaster, G., Cameron, E., Cibulskis, R., Davies, M., ..., Bhatt, S. (2019). Mapping changes in housing in sub-Saharan Africa from 2000 to 2015. *Nature*, 568, 391–394.

UNAIDS.org (2017). 2017 global HIV statistics. Retrieved from https://www.unaids.org/sites/ default/files/media_asset/UNAIDS_FactSheet_en.pdf. Accessed on 4 July 2019.

UNESCO (2017). Poverty. Retrieved from http://www.unesco.org/new/en/social-and-human-sciences/themes/international-migration/glossary/poverty/#topPage. Accessed on 6 June 2019.

United Nation International Children's Emergency Fund (2017). One in four children in North Africa, Middle East live in poverty. UN News. Retrieved from https://news.un.org/en/story/2017/05/557432-one-four-children-north-africa-middle-east-live-poverty-unicef-study

United Nations Development Programme (2019). Inequalities in human development in the 21st century. Ethiopia. Retrieved from http://hdr.undp.org/sites/all/themes/hdr_theme/country-notes/ETH.pdf. Accessed on 2 January 2020.

United Nations International Children Education Emergency Fund – Nigeria (2018). The challenge: One in every five of the world's out-of-school children is in Nigeria. Retrieved from https://www.unicef.org/nigeria/education

United Nations International Children Emergency Fund (2017). Ethiopia: National health and nutrition sector budget brief: 2006–2016. Retrieved from https://www.unicef.org/esaro/UNICEF_Ethiopia_–_2017_–_Health_and_Nutrition_Budget_Brief.pdf. Accessed on 31 January 2020.

Van Arkadie, B. (1989). *The role of institutions in development (English)*. Washington, DC: The World Bank. Retrieved from http://documents.worldbank.org/curated/en/575481468740986684/The-role-of-institutions-in-development

Welter, F., & Smallbone, D. (2011). Institutional perspectives on entrepreneurial behaviour in challenging environments. *Journal of Small Business Management*, 49(1), 107–125.

World Bank (2018). *GDP Per Capita, PPP (current international $) – sub-Saharan Africa*, Washington: World Bank Publications. Retrieved from https://data.worldbank.org/indicator/NY.GDP.PCAP.PP.CD?locations=ZG. Accessed on 10 December 2018.

World Bank (2018), *Poverty and Shared Prosperity 2018: Piecing together the poverty puzzle*. Washington, DC: World Bank Publications. Retrieved from https://openknowledge.worldbank.org/bitstream/handle/10986/30418/9781464813306.pdf. Accessed on 4 March 2019.

World Bank (2018). *The human capital project*. Washington: World Bank Publications. Retrieved from https://openknowledge.worldbank.org/bitstream/handle/10986/30498/33252.pdf?sequence=5&isAllowed=y. Accessed on 10 December 2018.

World Bank (2019). *Doing business 2019 annual report, training for reform*. 16th Edition. Washington, DC: World Bank Publications.

World Bank (2019). *World Bank East Asia and Pacific Economic Update, April 2019: Managing headwinds*. Washington, DC: World Bank. Retrieved from https://openknowledge.worldbank.org/handle/10986/31500

World Economic Forum (2017). *The global gender gap report*. Retrieved from http://www3.weforum.org/docs/WEF_GGGR_2017.pdf. Accessed on 3 December 2019.

World Food Programme (2019). The impact of school feeding programmes. Retrieved from https://docs.wfp.org/api/documents/WFP-0000102338/download/?_ga=2.266480014.1203638642.1580298380-865892999.1580298380. Accessed on 29 January 2020.

World Health Organisation (2017). Primary health care systems (PRIMASYS) – Case study from Ethiopia. Retrieved from https://www.who.int/alliance-hpsr/projects/alliancehpsr_ethiopiaabridgedprimasys.pdf?ua=1. Accessed on 1 February 2020.

Yang, J. (2019). A broader view of poverty in East Asia and Pacific. Retrieved from https://blogs.worldbank.org/eastasiapacific/broader-view-poverty-east-asia-and-pacific

Yildirim, D. (2017). Empirical investigation of purchasing power parity for Turkey: Evidence from recent nonlinear unit root tests, *Central Bank Review*, 17, 39–45.

INSTITUTIONAL CONTEXTS OF RESOURCE GOVERNANCE

3

Africa has large swathes of untapped renewable and non-renewable natural resources. Among these are huge reserves of crude oil and natural gas, gold, diamonds, platinum and copper. The United Nations Environmental Agency (UNEA) estimates that Africa is home to about 12 percent of the world's oil, 8 percent of world's natural gas reserves, and 30 percent of global mineral reserves. Also, 40 percent of the world's gold and 90 percent of the global platinum are located in Africa. To put the extent of Africa's natural resource wealth into context, even the resource-poor African countries, such as, Burundi, eSwatini, Gambia, Guinea-Bissau, Mauritius and Lesotho, are presumed to have a share of the global natural resource wealth higher than the resource-rich OECD countries including Iceland with its extensive renewable energy resources.

In addition to gold and platinum, Africa is home to the world's largest reserves of cobalt and diamonds and accounts for nearly 65 percent of global tantalum production.[1] Tantalum is a rare but naturally occurring mineral component that is used in modern technologies and for capacitors found in mobile phones, computers, surgical and dental instruments. As such, just like crude oil, gold and diamonds, it is a highly priced natural commodity. Most tantalum mining occurs in Rwanda and Democratic Republic of Congo (DRC), areas known for issues related to conflict minerals. Africa's share of the global oil natural resources is only rivalled by the hydrocarbon (petroleum and gas) rich Gulf countries led by Saudi Arabia.

Along with Angola, Equatorial Guinea, Nigeria and the DRC, Gabon features frequently on the global rankings of 30 resource-rich countries globally. Although with declining oil reserves, Gabon is an upper middle-income country and Africa's fifth largest oil producer. Measured in terms of natural capital per person, Gabon with its over 2 million people may probably emerge as one of the richest countries in the world. Yet, with about 33.3 percent (2017 figures) of Gabonese people currently living in poverty,[2] it

---

[1]UNEP (2018)
[2]World Bank (2019)

is obvious that poverty presents an enormous socioeconomic challenge to natural resource-rich African countries.

In cases in Africa where there have been substantial decline in the percentage of those living below the poverty line of less $1.90 per day, none had actually grown faster than the average economic growth seen in East or South Asia. If anything, the percentage of people living in absolute poverty in natural resource-rich countries like Angola and Nigeria had actually increased. Thus, it begs the question as to why many countries in sub-Saharan Africa (SSA) with abundant natural resources are not as prosperous, both in per capita income and GDP ratio, as countries in Asia and Europe with similar natural resources. Various inter-related reasons can explain this counterintuitive state of affairs.

One of the main problems is that resource-rich African countries have not been as effective as natural resource-rich Asian and European countries at transitioning away from their resource dependence economies. Natural resource-rich countries in Asia and Europe have diversified their economies. Thus, they are better able to manage the economic volatility and shocks that come with natural commodities trading and revenue. Another reason is that, until lately, exploration activities in the extractive oil and mining sectors have been comparably modest in Africa. Consequently, the value of Africa's natural wealth has not grown proportionally with other natural resource-rich regions for more than 20 years, which stagnated Africa's per capita natural resource wealth.[3] Across resource-rich OECD countries, for instance, known sub-oil reserves amount to $114 thousand per square kilometre, whereas in Africa this ratio is at $23 thousand per square kilometre.[4]

Another compounding factor is that the human and physical capital required for exploration activities in the extractive oil and mineral sectors is lacking in Africa. Because most resource rich African countries have little to no capacity and experience of deepwater oil and natural gas production, their governments are often held hostage by multinational oil and mining companies. Poor investment in the human capacity for exploration and production in the extractive oil sector is a recipe for loss of control of global natural resource supply chain networks and revenue flow, which consequently leads to poor economic outcomes in resource-dependent economies. To compound matters, most resource-rich African countries have worsening if not depleting stock of physical and human capital, as well as weak institutions to effectively manage business activities in the extractive sector.

Apart from South Africa with its modest but comparably more advanced mining infrastructures, the capacity of physical infrastructures including energy output in most resource-rich African countries is among the lowest globally. Also, as discussed in the previous chapter, productivity and human capital as well as education and health outcomes are very low. This is due to weak resource governance and mismanagement of natural resource revenues needed for domestic investments in infrastructures and human capital. This situation hinders the capability to translate natural wealth into a powerful instrument to tackle poverty and accelerate economic development.

---

[3]Izvorki (2018)
[4]Gurría (2012)

In contrast, resource-rich countries in Asia and Europe, such as China and Norway, have leveraged the economic activities in their extractive sectors to forge greater economic diversification and integration into global trade supply chain and financial networks. Also, through a combination of fiscal discipline and economic diversification, they have been able to push for more coherent medium to long-term macroeconomic policies, fiscal balance and structural reforms coupled with strong political, economic and social institutions, than resource-rich African countries. Also, by avoiding the boom and bust cycles of resource rents volatility, debt crises and resource governance challenges common in Africa, resource-rich countries in Asia and Europe have been able to build strong human capital infrastructures that have enabled them to achieve high levels of economic development.[5]

3.1 NATURAL RESOURCE AND ECONOMIC DEVELOPMENT

Analysis of the effects of resource endowments on economic development in several African countries showed that resource-rich countries have tended to grow less rapidly than resource-scarce countries. This ironic situation could only be linked to bad macroeconomic planning on the part of resource-rich countries. However, while many economies with abundant natural resources in the global north have made a significant convergence with the pace of global economic growth through a, raft of initiatives including open trade policies, economic liberalisation and diversification, strong human capital and institutional reforms, this has not been the case with resource-rich African countries which experience far greater prevalence of resource curse and Dutch disease phenomena.

Among other institutional failures, high dependence and failure to diversify their economies have been found to be the main reasons for the prevalence of resource curse and 'Dutch disease' in resource-rich African countries.[6] Apart from bad macroeconomic planning and the prevalence of resource curse, what is perhaps more pertinent is that economic development in many resource-rich African countries has for several decades lagged behind other regions with similar abundant natural resources.

In fact, only resource-poor Rwanda and Ethiopia seemed to have experienced on average a much faster economic growth than countries in South Asia since the millennium, although both countries still have very large poor populations.[7] The origins of Africa's slow economic development have always been attributed to colonial legacy and ethnic division, which is often caused by ethno-linguistic differences, as well as conflict and geography. As intriguing and revealing as this situation may seem, there is a wider issue though about whether the prevalence of resource curse in resource-rich African countries can be attributed to other factors, such as, weak institutions and poor governance of their natural resource wealth.

---

[5]Singh (2013)
[6]Sachs and Warner (1997, p. 27)
[7]Izvorski et al. (2018)

3.2 RESOURCE CURSE AND CAUSES

Among the empirical milestones in twentieth-century development literature is the notion that the pace of socioeconomic development in countries with abundant natural resources is much slower than in countries with scarce natural resources. This notion has been and remains the central focus of the resource curse hypothesis. First mooted by Richard Auty in the early 1990s, resource curse explains the peculiar tendency of oil-rich or mineral-rich countries to underperform in economic growth and other development performance indicators as a result of various political and economic reasons in those countries.[8] It underlies the idea of the concept of 'Dutch diseases' – a situation in which a rapid increase in the exploitation of abundant natural resources paradoxically leads to a decline in other export sectors within a country with that natural resources.

Resource curse is premised on the idea that resource-rich countries are more likely to squander their resource advantage through weak and careless economic policies, whereas resource-poor countries may compensate for their resource disadvantage by advocating and adopting firmer and more prudent economic policies.[9] Thus, making the abundance of natural resources and wealth a curse, rather than a blessing for many resource-endowed countries. Judging by the myriad of challenges facing many resource-rich African countries, the negative effects of resource curse of course will vary from one country to another due to country-specific factors.

These factors include the type of natural resources within a specific country, the way in which their relative importance to that country is measured and linkages with the rest of the economy, as well as the political systems that govern the resources of that specific country.[10] Other contextual factors may include population size, political and economic history of the country, the proportion of the resources relative to GDP and the institutional arrangements that govern economic activities in each country's extractive sector. In addition, factors such as the production capacity and investment capacity and structures within a country, macro- and micro-economic policies, the rate of rent-seeking and price volatility of internationally traded commodities can influence and determine the social, economic and the political ramifications of resources curse.[11]

Generally speaking, economic activities in the extractive mineral and oil sectors are prone to price volatility. Thus, the frequently changing pricing structure of oil and mineral commodities will inevitably create unexpected but differing business cycles for any resource-dependent country. However, given the linkage between resource dependence and poor governance,[12] governments in resource-rich African countries seem to have a higher tendency to have weak institutions. Therefore, they are more prone to higher levels of rent-seeking behaviour than resource-rich countries in developed societies where institutions are strong.

Politically, rent-seeking behaviour reduces the incentive to build a strong fiscal environment, effective institutions and the alternative mechanisms to generate and

---

[8]Auty (1993)
[9]Auty (1995)
[10]Papyrakis (2017)
[11]Auty (1998)
[12]Auty (2004)

increase state revenues through efficient taxation system. Efficient tax system increases state revenue, which could be used to augment State revenue for domestic investment in other areas that can enhance human development outcomes and lead to high economic growth, such as, education and health sectors. But because governments in resource-rich developing economies that rely heavily on the extractive sector to generate large percentage of their state revenue, have weak institutional arrangements, and therefore prone to corrupt practices, they have a tendency to favour inefficient tax systems. Inefficient tax systems give rise to corruption and make governments less accountable to the governed. Making governments in those countries less accountable to their people. This awkward situation perpetuates policy complacency, excessive bureaucracy and breeds political corruption among public officials who manipulate their weak institutions to secure resource rents.[13]

Thus, taken together, high price volatility and associated economic shock, rent-seeking, complacent polices, poor resource governance and weak institutions mean that resource-dependent economies have a hard time dealing with fiscal discipline and sound resource governance principles, which are essential to guarantee inclusive economic benefits that come from natural resources earnings. With a few exceptions, such as in Norway and Canada where strong institutional and democratic norms have been used effectively to maintain fiscal discipline and government accountability through efficient natural resource governance and revenue use, many resource-based countries, especially oil-dependent countries in Africa, Central America and the Middle East have experienced economic contraction because of their weak institutions and poor natural resource governance structures.

For instance, despite its robust tax system relative to resource-dependent African countries and Central America, Russia is dealing with the economic consequences of oil-dependence and resource curse. This arises from the country's bloated bureaucracy, weak political institutions and policy complacency attributed to its oil-dependent economy. Weak institutional arrangements in resource-dependent countries lead to resource rents, political corruption, risk of expropriation and ultimately eco-nomic decay. We see this situation in Russia, but also in many resource and mineral dependent countries in Africa, Central America and the Middle East including Angola, Nigeria, Venezuela, Mexico, Iran, Saudi Arabia and the United Arab Emirates.

For example towards the last quarter of 2019, as a result of falling oil and gas revenues on the back of decreasing national productivity and increased government expenditures, Russia's fiscal surplus decreased by 3.1 percent of the GDP from 3.7 percent in the same period in 2018.[14] The effect of resource curse is perhaps particularly more striking in Venezuela, where oil price volatility has led to huge budget deficits, free fall of its non-oil GDP per capita and the eventual collapse of its currency – Bolivar. Despite boasting the largest global concentration of proven oil reserves (17.5 percent by 2018 estimation),[15] Venezuela recorded the worst economic mismanagement with a high ratio of debt to GDP under its populist Socialist leaders, formerly Hugo Chavez, and subsequently Nicolás Maduro.

---

[13]Leite and Weidmann (1999)
[14]World Bank (2020)
[15]British Petroleum (2019)

Huge budget deficit, high debt and economic mismanagement have damaged the country's fiscal infrastructure, which brought an unprecedented economic disruption that has impoverished many Venezuelans. The country's dwindling economic fortune due to declining oil prices made it very difficult to fund and sustain its socialist system of subsidies and price controls, which consequently led to the expropriation of private investments in the strategic oil sectors. These economic problems caused the 2016 hyperinflation, which culminated into the country's eventual economic collapse in 2019. Thereby, forcing nearly 5 million Venezuelans, about 15 percent of the entire population, into a refugee status in neighbouring countries.

Similarly, Angola's oil-based economy meant that development in non-oil export sectors including sugar and coffee suffered both before and after its 27 years of civil war. Oil accounts for nearly 90 percent of the country's export earnings. Revenues from oil contribute 75 percent to government's budget, and 50 percent of the country's GDP relies on the oil industry. Despite heavy post-war investments in key sectors, such as education, health and transportation through cheap Chinese loans, Angola's economy remains undiversified. With weak democratic norms and political institutions, the Angolan government is rarely accountable to its people, majority of whom are poor and illiterate. Also, falling oil prices and negative account balance, rising public debt, increased rent-seeking and corruption means that natural resource governance in Angola is among the weakest globally.

In 2019, the country ranked 146 out of 180 on the Corruption Perception Index (CPI), with corruption more prevalent in the oil sector.[16] Angola's problems are no doubt symptomatic of the wider implications of resource curse, such as, state fragility and weak resource governance, which are common in many resource-dependent African economies.

3.3 STATE FRAGILITY AND RESOURCE GOVERNANCE

It is not out of place to say that the world is gradually becoming less fragile. However, among the globally recognised fragile states, African countries, especially those along the Sahel, are over-represented on the lowest scale of the Fragile States Index (FSI) developed by the Washington-based independent and non-for-profit think tank, Fund for Peace (FFP). FFP uses the FSI index anchored on a four-point assessment scale categorised as 'cohesion', 'economic', 'political' and 'social' to track 178 countries globally to assess their risk of conflict and war at any given time. The FSI index scale constitutes 12 risk assessment indicators including, among others, group grievance, economic decline, uneven economic development, public services, brain drain, human rights and the rule of law, as well as demographic pressures and external intervention.

These indicators have implications for human security and socioeconomic development in any country. As such, they provide an insight into the various distinct but related factors that can lead to state fragility in any society, but particularly in natural resource-dependent countries. As a concept, state fragility can be linked to different

---

[16]Transparency International (2019)

combinations of various institutional dysfunctions than hinder the economic well-being and survival of individuals within a country.

These include economic decline due to persistent poverty, unstable and weak governance, poor public services, such as in education and healthcare, lack of territorial control, violent conflict and war due to political and economic repression. In these contexts, state fragility relates to the wider socioeconomic effects of resource curse on several resource-rich African countries, which can be attributed to the weak political and economic institutions that give rise to political and economic fragility in those countries. In the history of economic and development literatures, there is a widely shared belief that the persistence of state fragility in Africa – which gives rise to institutional dysfunctions, such as governance failure, political corruption and ethnic conflict – had its roots in the legacy of colonisation.[17]

Particularly, there is a widely held assumption, although rarely proven, that boundary demarcation and the process of state formation in Africa may have been designed to serve the geopolitical interests of colonising powers, and primarily modelled to facilitate trade and export of natural resources from Africa to Europe. However, the European Development Report on fragility in Africa acknowledged that the common features of state formation in SSA relied almost exclusively on the extractive nature of colonial domination, the administrative system of indirect rule which consequently led to the artificial character of modern day African States following decolonisation.[18] Thus, if this report is anything to go by, then it raises a fundamental question about the extent to which the prevalence of state fragility and conflict in resource-rich African countries might be perceived differently as entirely not of Africa's own making. If one were to consider this alternate viewpoint, then the root cause of State fragility in Africa may be seen as the negative outcome of the faulty process of State formation and demarcation of the region's landscape, engineered and perpetrated almost single-handedly by colonising powers who were more keen to facilitate trade and export of Africa's natural resources, than in the peace and security of the region.

There is no denying that the legacy of colonisation impaired Africa's political and economic progress. However, the pertinent question has to be whether or not resource curse in resource-rich but economically poor performing African countries is inherently preconditioned by this impairment? Or, whether the presence of appropriate set of sound economic policies and effective political process including effective resource governance structures could have prevented the prevalence of resource curse in these African countries. If the latter, then it is not out of place to suggest even attribute the poor economic performance and development deficits including public debt liabilities and vulnerabilities of many resource-rich African countries to the lack of effective mechanisms including fiscal discipline essential to better management of earnings or revenues from natural resources.[19] Most resource-rich African countries are at the bottom of the Resource Governance Index (RGI) used by the New York-based Natural Resource Governance Institute (NRGI) – a non-for-profit independent organisation – to monitor the transparency of country's governance over their natural resources. Apart

---

[17]Bertocchi and Guerzoni (2010, p. 4)
[18]European Report on Development (2009)
[19]Sarraf and Jiwanji (2001)

from Botswana with its large reserves of precious minerals, such as, diamonds, oil-rich but economically poor performing African countries like Nigeria and Angola equally have very weak natural resource governance systems.

Out of the 88 natural resource-rich countries assessed globally by the NRGI, Angola and Nigeria – the two biggest oil producers in Africa where oil represents 90 percent of export earnings ranked comparably very low at 42 percent and 35 percent on the RGI index, respectively. Thus, from an SSA perspective, the relationship between state fragility and resource curse might perhaps be best understood, although tentatively, through the lens of Africa's large oil producers – Nigeria and Angola. As oil-dependent economies, crude oil exportation is the main source of state revenue for both countries. In 2013, they accounted for more than 75 percent of Africa's total oil production exports.[20] As such, the socioeconomic challenges they face appear to be similar. For instance, both countries have a history of violent conflict, poor human development outcomes, weak resource governance system and majority of their populations suffer from extreme poverty. For instance, like Nigeria, Angola's HDI rank is very low at 149 out of 189 countries.

Also, analysis by the University of Oxford-based Oxford Poverty and Human Development Initiative (OPHI) found that 48 percent of Angolans (90 percent in rural areas) are multidimensionally poor. Deprivations in years of education were found to be the largest contributors to poverty in Angola, whereas in Nigeria, 47.5 percent of the population were found to be multidimensionally poor.[21] The governments of both countries promote national participation in the extractive sectors through an initiative known as the Local Content (LC), which has only shown a fledgling success. However, as Africa's largest economy and crude oil producer with proven reserves of nearly 37 million barrels, the issue of weak natural resource governance and lack of effective management of oil revenue is particularly more acute in Nigeria. Because of this, Nigeria offers a more appropriate context through which to further explore the causes and effects of resource curse in resource-rich African countries.

3.4 NIGERIA, OIL RESOURCES AND GOVERNANCE

After more than 40 years of oil exploration and export, Nigeria, unlike other oil-rich countries in Asia and Europe, has comparatively very little to show in terms of shared prosperity, high human development outcomes and economic stability from its vast oil reserves and excess earnings from oil exports. It is currently home to the largest global concentration of the extremely poor population, having overtaken India as the world's epicentre of global poverty. Rent-seeking, bribery and political corruption are rife. Like Angola, Nigeria ranks very low at 146 on the CPI scale.[22] Also, resource governance and fiscal policy challenges, coupled with lack of government account-ability, explain Nigeria's poor rating and very low ranking on the RGI scale. In an

[20]Ovadia (2014)
[21]OPHI (2019)
[22]Transparency International (2019)

attempt to help improve Nigeria's poor ratings on natural resource governance, one of its former political leaders President Olusegun Obasanjo, was forced to set up the Excess Crude Account (ECA) and adopted an oil price-based fiscal rule designed to decouple State budgetary and non-budgetary spending from oil revenue volatility.

His intention was to make Nigeria's excess oil revenue management more transparent and publicly accountable. The new fiscal rule required that additional revenues from budgeted oil prices – that is, revenues above the base amount adopted as the oil price benchmark in the budget – be paid into the ECA as national savings. It was envisaged that the ECA assets would provide the fiscal buffer to support domestic investments in infrastructures and for economic stability, especially during periods of global economic shock and oil price volatility. Just like in other oil-rich countries with similar buffer funds, such as, Norway, which invests excess oil revenue into its Government Pension Fund Global (GPFG), and Angola, which makes similar investment through its Fundo Soberano de Angola (FSDEA) programme, the fiscal policy of ECA transactions works on the principle of Sovereign Wealth Funds (SWFs).

To manage the ECA revenue inflows and transactions, the Nigeria Sovereign Investment Authority (NSIA) was established via the NSIA Act of 2011. To fulfil its mandate and to help facilitate the implementation of the new excess oil revenue fiscal rule, NSIA set up three main SWFs. The first is the Stabilisation Fund (SF) with about 20 percent funds allocation split between hedge and growth assets. Nigeria's SF acts as a short-term fiscal buffer for macroeconomic stability of government activities related to considerable excess revenues derived from oil exports.

The second SWF is a diversified portfolio of growth assets called the Future Generations Fund (FGF), and the third is the Nigeria Infrastructure Fund (NIF). The NIF has the highest allocation of 40 percent of excess oil revenue and acts entirely as the fiscal buffer for domestic investments in infrastructure. Just like Angola's FSDEA, the NSIA is a signatory to the Santiago Principles established under the umbrella of the International Forum of Sovereign Wealth Funds (IFSWF). IFSWF is a voluntary body set up and overseen by the IMF through which the bank assigns best practices for the global operations of SWFs including transparency and governance. However, at issue in the case of Nigeria is not so much the financing, but with the weaknesses of the resource governance mechanisms under which the ECA and the NSIA operate.

For instance, unlike in other oil-rich countries such as Norway, which has a similar excess oil revenue-related financing arrangement, the ECA-related inflows and outflows have very weak management portfolio including lack of legislative oversight and accountability. Lack of effective policing of financial inflows and outflows related to excess oil revenues increases the risk of financial imprudence and corruption. This risk not only undermines the fiscal policy of the ECA, but it also makes NSIA's subscription to the Santiago Principles pointless if not perverse. This is because, in Nigeria's case, when oil prices dropped in the aftermath of the 2008 global financial crisis, the surplus from ECA was diverted to prop up budgetary spending, not necessarily to stabilise and grow the economy through a fiscal stimulus.

Such a diversion of funds from ECA was purely discretionary and also conflicts with the ECA fiscal rules as well as the resource governance rules under the Santiago Principles. To compound matters, as oil price rebounded in 2010, the Nigerian government again reneged on its SWFs payment commitments, thereby leaving the ECA unreplenished before the 2014 oil price crash which eventually caused a recessionary gap in the country's economy. Faced with a rapidly weakening economy, the Nigerian government was forced to abandon its budgetary commitments by reducing expenditures and introducing austerity measures including tax rises and spending cuts. Both scenarios spelt an economic doom for ordinary Nigerians many of whom were already poor and unemployed even before the government introduced its austerity measures.

Some believe that the fiscal policy of austerity measures coupled with drastic cuts in government expenditure eventually led to Nigeria's first recession in 25 years in 2016, when the country's GDP plummeted to 1.6 percent from an average GDP of 5.7 percent between 2010 and 2014.[23] Four years after the recession, perhaps keen to explore the country's fiscal space to stabilise the economy amid the economic effects of the COVID-19 global pandemic, Nigeria's Accountant General, Ahmed Idris, in 2019 revealed to the Senate Committee on Finance that a cumulative practice of discretionary and illegal withdrawals and over-deductions have left the ECA with a depleted balance of $71.8 million from $20.01 billion recorded before the pandemic.[24] This revelation shocked both the committee and a nation already struggling to feed their families even before the pandemic.

With these experiences, it was not surprising that Nigeria's ECA ranked the lowest on the GRI scale as the most poorly governed SWFs globally. In reality, a low ranking means that the Nigerian government discloses publicly almost none of the rules or practices governing neither deposits and withdrawals nor ECA-related investments and financial dealings. Determining the success of any sovereign wealth fund is less about the finance but more about the quality of, and adherence to, the fiscal and governance rules that regulate such fund.

Effective governance is necessary in order to ensure strict controls over the fiscal rules governing ECAs, thereby preventing its misuse through discretionary withdrawals or for political patronage. Given that Nigeria's oil sector accounts for almost 90 percent of government's revenues and 80 percent of its export earnings, the revenue loss through the ECA-related transactions amounts to a lack of fiscal discipline and poor governance, perhaps may have contributed to the countries poor rankings on all globally recognised human development and economic performance indicators. Broadly, it exemplifies the wider institutional deficiency and dysfunction that hinder effective natural resource governance for proper economic planning and development, not just in Nigeria but also across other resource-rich African countries.

3.5 ECONOMIC COST OF INSTITUTIONAL DEFICIENCY

Institutional deficiency is associated with weak and dysfunctional political institutions more prominent in natural resource abundant countries in the global south. As a feature of state fragility, institutional deficiency leads to other inter-related social and economic problems including governance failure. As explained in the previous chapter,

---

[23]Izvorski et al. (2018)
[24]Ayado (2020)

governance failure hinders the efficiency and effective functioning of the institutional structures (e.g. laws, rules and regulations) that regulate human activity including implementation of resource governance principles vital to economic development.

Institutional deficiency does not imply the absence of institutional structures. Rather, it relates to the persistence and pervasiveness of weaknesses and failures within the institutional environment that limit the proper functioning of institutional structures. Over time, such weaknesses and failures lead to institutional dysfunctionality, which in turn undermines the credibility of such structures or the apparatuses (e.g. fiscal rules) of resource governance and socio-economic growth in that environment.

Proper institutional functioning ensures that a layer of equilibrium is built into a country's social, economic and political systems. As explained in Chapter 2, when the credibility of the institutional environment is undermined then individuals, and most especially entrepreneurs, only succeed through political ties and cronyism, rather than through knowledge, creativity and innovation. When this is the case, the institutional environment is weakened and no longer in the service of the wider public, but rather a few individuals with corrupt political ties. Thus, in any society, such a condition can neither support human capital formation nor spur entrepreneurship activity essential to job creation and economic development.

Besides undermining the credibility of the institutional environment, institutional deficiency also limits access to knowledge acquisition and knowledge transfer through lack of investment in education and human capital development. The absence of education and human capital hinders the development of entrepreneurial skills and productivity, which are essential to creativity and innovation in any business environment. There is a linkage between the institutional arrangements, the business environment and regional development. This view is grounded in the notion that 'institutions not only shape but also are shaped by the environment'.[25]

Implications for this linkage is seen in the way the political, social and the economic lives of countries are shaped, organised and influenced by their institutional environment. Also, institutional deficiency hinders the ability of resource-rich countries to develop equilibrium across the social, economic and political spectra essential to improving the economic conditions of poor populations.[26] Social, economic and political equilibrium is achieved when institutional structures function in an inclusive manner.

Prominent institutional theorists regard the idea of inclusiveness in how institutions function as the essential part of an effective 'institutional matrix',[27] whereby strong social and economic institutions are seen as the outcome of a strong political process.[28] Unfortunately, social and economic institutional arrangements in Nigeria are not yet inclusive because of its weak political process. The lack of strong political process is seen as the root source of the country's widespread corruption and weak legal systems frequently associated with poor and developing countries.[29] It is

---

[25]Rodriguez-pose (2013)
[26]Acemoglu and Robinson (2010)
[27]North (1991, p. 1)
[28]Acemoglu and Robinson (2010)
[29]Keefer and Knack (1997)

probably for these reasons that President Olusegun Obasanjo, pledged in 1999 to halt the rapid 'decline in the deterioration of all institutions following decades of decay and corruption.'

3.6 ECONOMIC COST OF CORRUPTION IN RESOURCE GOVERNANCE

The interwoven nature of resource governance and corruption is the root cause of economic sabotage and poor economic outcomes in many resource-dependent African countries. It hampers human capital development and chokes off the ingredients of economic development. With a corrupt system of resource governance, it becomes much more harder to tackle the resource curse phenomenon or even improve economic outcomes for the poor. Generally, corruption has the tendency to benefit a few, while having a devastating socioeconomic effect on the wider population and the society. The adverse impact of corruption on any society is mostly felt by the poor. With its weak resource governance mechanism, the adverse effects of corruption on poor populations is more visible and perhaps most apparent in oil-rich Nigeria.

Summarising the impact of corruption on Nigeria's poor populations, Nuhu Ribadu, the former head of the Economic and Financial Crimes Commission (EFCC), Nigeria's anti-corruption watchdog observes: 'Nigeria is synonymous with sophisticated fraud and endemic corruption. It weighs on the poor more than any subgroup. This is because the poor are the least able to absorb the cost of corruption and depend most on the public services in education and health that corruption actually destroys'.[30] Writing under the auspices of the Washington-based non-for-profit Centre for Global Development (CGD), Ribadu's reflections illustrates the pervasiveness and the wider institutional context of the effect of corruption in oil-rich Nigeria.

Efforts by various Nigerian governments to tackle corruption have always been viewed with cautious optimism. This is not without basis. The inability of EFCC to prosecute past and serving corrupt public officials raises questions about whether the agency is autonomous, or just a mere political tool used by serving governments to hound its critics and deter opposition. Since it was established in 2002 as an anti-corruption agency through a Federal Act to investigate and prosecute all economic and financial crimes ranging from advanced fee fraud scam (also known as 419), money laundering and political corruption across Nigeria, the ability of the agency to effectively tackle corruption in the country has been severely hampered by institutional failures. These include budgetary constraints, inefficient judiciary, incompetent personnel and lack of the political will and commitment to ensure that EFCC is free from external influences.[31]

These institutional constraints are linked with the weak and authoritarian nature of Nigeria's political system, which allows public officials to exploit the country's

---

[30]Ribadu (2010, p. 6)
[31]Umar et al. (2018)

institutional weaknesses including human rights violations.[32] With notable exceptions, such as Norway and Botswana, governments in most resource-rich and resource-dependent countries have a tendency to become authoritarian. We see evidence of authoritarianism, which in SSA manifests in form of flawed and hybrid democracy, in countries, such as DRC (formerly Republic of Zaire), Egypt, Nigeria, Gabon, Sudan, Tanzania and South Africa. As a common problem which undermines due process and weakens the credibility of state institutions, authoritarianism and corruption are intertwined and a feature of resource-dependent countries.[33]

The crippling pattern of corrupt interference in the work of Nigeria's EFCC not only speaks volume, it also illustrates the scale of the difficulty in tackling corruption, particularly in Nigeria's oil sector where it is most pervasive. Through a host of practices in oil license procurement, undisclosed royalties, capital flight and tax sheltering, political corruption is particularly endemic in Nigeria's extractive oil and gas sectors. For instance, a major oil deal involving the US-based ExxonMobil and the Nigerian government led to a high-profile corruption scandal investigation by the EFCC.[34] That is not all. Evidence have shown that the business activities of most multinational oil companies operating widely in Africa cause corruption, slow socio-economic development, lead to political conflict[35] and prolong violent conflicts and wars.[36]

In particular, the economic costs of corruption in Nigeria's oil sector are compounded by environmental degradation of the agricultural sector including farmland, fishing, forestry and destruction of the aquatic ecosystem and consequently resource curse, which leads to loss of livelihoods.

3.7 TACKLING RESOURCE CURSE

Resource curse has been linked with weak or lack of effective resource governance and bad economic policies in resource-dependent countries. To tackle these problem, many economists and development experts believe that there is a need for resource-rich countries to develop and implement a suite of strong governance mechanisms and principles that ensure the political, social and economic institutions in their own countries are legitimate, transparent, fair and above all inclusive.[37] Justification for this view has been repeatedly supported with a specific resource-rich country case – Norway. As an oil-rich country, Norway has a commanding influence in the global oil and gas sectors. It controls Johan Svendrup in the North Sea, which is one of the largest oil-fields discoveries (2011 figures) in the world where most of the country's oil production takes place.

The country is both Western Europe's largest producer of petroleum liquids and among the world's top natural gas exporters. As at 2018, Norway holds oil reserves of

---

[32]Human Rights Watch (2011)
[33]Wantchekon (2002)
[34]Global Witness (2016)
[35]Yates (2012)
[36]Di John (2007)
[37]Lockwood et al. (2010)

about 8.6 billion barrels, an increase from 6.8 billion barrels in 2010.[38] For several decades until the 1990s, Norway lagged behind other Nordic countries measured in terms of the aggregate value of GDP per capita. But after the discovery of oil in the early 1970s, Norway reached parity and forged ahead most Nordic countries including Sweden and Denmark. At $82,500 (2019 figures), Norway's GDP per capita income is the highest and by far surpasses that of the most influential Nordic economy – Sweden, which in 2019 has a GDP per capita of $54,100. Norway emerged from a struggling economy to achieve an enviable global status as one of the most politically and economically stable countries in the world. Economic and political stability has been and remains one of the country's exportable intangible assets.

On the fragile State index (FSI) scale used by Funds for Peace to assess the vulnerability of countries to collapse and disintegration due to social, political and economic problems, Norway has consistently ranked high as one of the most stable countries to live in. In 2020, the country ranked highest at 178th on the FSI measures out of 178 countries assessed, up from 144th in 2006.[39] Economic stability is one of nine equally weighted attributes used to measure people's quality of life. This includes citizens' perceptions about a wide variety of socioeconomic outcomes essential to happiness ranging from access to food and housing, quality of education and healthcare, employment and job security as well as individual freedoms.

Also, the annual economic report by the Nordic Council of Ministers showed that compared to its Nordic neighbours, Norway has 1.7 percent of the population aged 18+ years most likely to be recipients of State benefit or income support. This is the lowest only behind Iceland at 1.0 percent and much lower than Finland and Denmark at 3.5 percent and 2.4 percent, respectively.

Unemployment among the Norwegian workforce (aged 15 years–64 years) is low at about 3.8 percent compared to Sweden and the European Union, which has about 6.5 percent and 7.8 percent (2018 figures) unemployment rates among their economically active workforce, respectively. Also, youth unemployment is relatively low at 10.35 percent compared to 18.30 percent in Sweden.[40]

Unlike most countries, Norway currently spends 5.6 percent of its GDP on education. Since oil discovery in the country, it has also incrementally invested in its healthcare sector, moving from 3.63 percent of GDP in 1970 to 10.5 percent of GDP in 2019. Its percentage of GDP investment in health is among the highest globally. Also, the country boasts the highest percentage of nurses and midwives per head in Europe. Because of this, it has maintained its lead in productivity across all the essential oil and non-oil sectors over most OECD countries and across the world.[41] Norway achieved this remarkable socioeconomic record by developing and implementing good macroeconomic policies, trustworthy and inclusive institutions including a strong judiciary, well-functioning democracy with long-standing social and democratic norms[42], not through political corruption, cronyism, plunder and authoritarianism.

---

[38]Statista (2020)
[39]Fund for Peace (2020)
[40]Nordic Council of Ministers (2018)
[41]Gal and Witheridge (2019)
[42]Larsen (2006)

In addition, Norway developed and has maintained a sensible and robust natural resource management system that integrated natural resource-based industries with the rest of the economy through institutional linkages. Overtime, its oil-related institutions have been developed and nurtured to maturity in a sustainably diversified manner to withstand the economic cycles of 'boom and bust' that come with high price volatility in oil commodities markets. Oil and gas production constitutes about 20 percent of Norway's economy with hydropower, forestry, fisheries and mineral production as other important sectors.

Also, the transparent and disciplined use of its natural resource fund through maintenance Government Pension Fund Global, similar to Nigeria's ECA, has helped the country to maintain a solid fiscal buffer. This buffer enables the country to make domestic public investments in infrastructures as well as to support budgetary expenditure year on year including during periods of low price volatility in the international oil markets. In addition, a robust resource governance framework and transparent use of natural resource funds has helped to guarantee Norway's ability to maintain economic stability as well as support fiscal stimulus for economic recovery during global economic shocks, such as, during the 2008 global recession and through the economic criss linked to COVID-19 pandemic.[43]

3.8 RESOURCE-RICH AFRICAN COUNTRIES: MOVING FORWARD

There is no reason why resource-rich African countries cannot achieve similarly profound levels of economic success and stability seen in Norway. This is achievable by tackling the institutional dysfunctionalities that give rise to resource curse and hinder economic growth. The problem is that governments in resource-rich African countries have overtime failed to introduce and maintain credible and efficient political institutions needed to achieve economic stability. This is compounded by lack of transparent resource governance strategies to effectively manage revenues from natural resources in a way that benefits the wider society.

Inefficient institutions and fragile political arrangements also converge to impair the ability of resource-rich African countries to develop and implement sound macro-economic policies and transparent resource governance strategies for sustainable development. Thus, governments of resource-rich and resource-dependent countries in Africa must consider four immediate policy priorities if they are serious about achieving the levels of natural resource governance success and consequently economic stability seen in Norway.

Firstly, integrating their natural resource-based economy with the rest of the economy through economic diversification is vital. In turn, this will attract investments to open up other industrial sectors, such as agriculture, manufacturing and services, thereby spur entrepreneurship and job creation that naturally come with economic diversification and liberalisation. A diversified economy increases the State's revenue base, which in turn expands the fiscal space to pursue other socioeconomic initiatives

---

[43]Cappelen and Mjoset (2009)

on a scale that would have been difficult under a monotonous economy. For this to succeed, there needs to be the strong political will to create the strong institutions and economic conditions under which entrepreneurship and industrialisation can thrive simultaneously.

Alongside, there is a need to invest in education and health infrastructures in a sustainable manner. This will guarantee the development spillovers in high human productivity and in the long run the socioeconomic benefits of human development.[44] For instance, scholarship schemes targeting education, knowledge and skills in the geology of natural resource exploration and production, emphasis on academic–industry collaboration and mandatory technology transfer programmes from foreign multinational oil companies have all been found to provide improved local capacity, job creation and increased income per capita that are essential to economic stability in resource-rich and resource-dependent economies.[45] Without such investments and improved human development, resource-dependent African countries may not fully recover from the current inertia of political and economic stagnation that come with resource curse and the Dutch diseases.

The second policy priority must be in the areas of effective management and governance of resource revenues. This is crucial. Revenues from natural resources, just like foreign aid, tend to be vulnerable to squander through political corruption and cronyism. For this reason, the institutional frameworks for the governance of natural resource funds should be strengthened with clear and publicly available fiscal rules. Central to this is ensuring that the fiscal rules that govern investments and risk management of natural resource funds are aligned with internationally recognised SWFs principles, such as those championed by the IMF through the International Working Group of Sovereign Wealth Funds (IWGSWF).

This will inject fiscal discipline in the natural resource governance system while improving public confidence in governments' approach to natural resource funds utilisation. Although there may be differences in how countries choose to strengthen their resource governance systems depending on their institutional arrangements, market dynamics and the socioeconomic priorities of each country. However, to increase transparency and accountability as well as raise international confidence in the governance processes of natural resource funds management, there must be at least a legislative oversight. There are several other reasons why a legislative oversight is vital, particularly in resource-dependent African countries.

For many years, countries like Nigeria and Angola with national savings in form of SWFs from excess revenues from crude oil exports have been dragging their feet in terms of ensuring fiscal discipline, transparency and accountability in management of such funds. For instance, even though oil was first discovered in Nigeria (1956) before Norway, it took more than 50 years to establish natural resource governance systems, such as Excess Crude Account (ECA) and an Act that established the NSIA to manage the ECA revenue inflows and transactions. Moreover, because the governance risks of natural resource fund flows are high, legislative oversight will ensure that decisions about resource funds financial flows are not arbitrary, but are made and implemented within a certain national legislative fiscal formular.

---

[44]Tiba and Frikha (2019)
[45]Adne and Lars (2009)

A national legislative formular for managing excess oil revenue flows is important given that presidential decrees or executive order is often the approach employed by many resource-rich African countries to deplete their natural resource funds or SWFs. This approach often leaves room for an unbridled illegality and corruption in how flows are managed including arbitrary deductions. Arbitrary deductions are a recipe for depletion of excess revenue from crude oil transactions, thus, making it very difficult to use the savings from such funds to support much-needed economic development through domestic investments in key infrastructures, as well as to stabilise the economy through fiscal stimulus during global economic shocks. In addition, a legislative oversight will ensure the provision of a publicly available annual report on natural resource funds' assets and transactions. This practice aligns with the criteria set out by the National Resource Governance Institute regarding transparency and governance of natural resource funds.

Related to published accounts, a legislative oversight will ensure a thorough periodic review and regular audit of transactions related to such funds. These practices, in addition to providing reassurance to the public that the government is not reckless and bypassing the fiscal formular, they will help the government to fulfil its obligations in relation to the legally mandated deposits and expenditures for such funds. Lack of fiscal discipline and transparency were cited as the main reasons behind the recent depletion of Nigeria's ECA within a relatively short span. As important as the NSIA is, without a legislative oversight of the ECA-related transactions, then ECA will remain the conduit that facilitates chronic corruption instead of economic development.

Countries that have strong resource governance systems, with legislative oversight, are better able to separate resource income from expenditure and reduce public debt liability as well as the potential risk of crowding out the private sector, while protecting public budgets from natural resource revenue fluctuations. Also, effective governance mechanisms provide the fiscal space to maintain economic stability through the introduction of stimulus packages during periods of global shocks, thereby supporting recovery efforts in the short to long term.

For instance, the ongoing COVID-19 pandemic is more than just a global public health emergency, it is a crisis that has brought unprecedented economic consequences for the global economy including rapid increase in unemployment. With declining forecasts in the oil commodities markets as a result of general surplus in the industry brought about by the pandemic, oil-dependent countries with little economic diversification and weak resource governance strategy are perhaps the hardest hit with the economic shock arising from the pandemic. However, countries, such as Norway, that entered the crisis with strong natural resource governance principles and fiscal responsibility through savings in SWFs or low public debt stock during the oil boom, have a better fiscal space to adjust and stimulate their recovery efforts.

These views are borne out in a recent analysis by NRDI as presented in Table 3.1, which shows that since the COVID-19 pandemic, oil-dependent countries in Africa, particularly Algeria, Angola and Nigeria, with abysmally low SWFs asset values are in a much worse economic condition than Norway, which has a healthy SWF assets.[46] Unlike Angola and Nigeria which are unable to adjust and stimulate recovery, Norway

---

[46]Bauer and Mihalyi (2020)

TABLE 3.1 Sovereign wealth fund asset values and GDP since COVID-19 began

	Sovereign wealth fund assets (Percentage of GDP) (2019 or latest)	Gross debt (Percentage of GDP) (2019 or latest)	Country default spreads (January 2020)	Manufacturers' exports (Percentage of merchandise exports) (2018 or latest)	Breakeven price of oil production (USD/bbl) (2019)
Algeria	0%	46%	5.4%	4%	73.20
Angola	2%	95%	7.1%	1%	32.28
Azerbaijan	92%	20%	2.5%	3%	18.72
Ecuador	0%	49%	5.4%	6%	34.82
Iran	14%	31%	5.4%	20%	11.88
Kazakhstan	34%	21%	1.8%	13%	52.37
Malaysia	9%	56%	1.0%	70%	24.31
Nigeria	1%	30%	5.4%	4%	29.23
Norway	224%	40%	0.0%	17%	17.81
Qatar	175%	53%	0.5%	11%	12.18
Russia	7%	16%	1.8%	21%	37.30
Saudi Arabia	63%	23%	0.6%	16%	12.76
Venezuela	0%	182%	15.0%	2%	63.19

Source: Natural Resource Governance Institute (NRGI) (April 2020).

has committed substantial stimulus package to support both immediate and long-term economic recovery during the pandemic. Thus, based on these perspectives, a combination of fiscal buffers and fiscal rules has shown themselves as a reliably robust framework for tackling not just resource curse and the Dutch diseases in natural resource-dependent African economies, but also a necessary ingredient to stabilise and support their recovery efforts during periods of global economic shocks. It is by following these policies and by ensuring consistency in their implementation can resource-dependent African countries emerge strong, boost shared prosperity and support their citizens during a period of global economic downturn.

Thirdly, the socioeconomic benefits of economic diversification and strong fiscal environment will be hard to realise in resource dependent countries without a robust regulatory environment to support and monitor economic activities in their extractive sector. Without a strong regulatory environment, it will be difficult to curb corruption, maintain fiscal discipline and reduce ecological disaster and violent conflict, which often go hand in glove with state fragility and economic sabotage in resource-rich countries. Globally, it seems there is a lack of appetite and the political will to effectively regulate the extractive oil business sector. The law passed by the United States Congress empowering the Securities and Exchange Commission (SEC) to regulate and compel, under Dodd–Frank Act, US-listed oil and mining companies to disclose payments to foreign governments was repealed in 2017.

Thus, African leaders in resource-rich countries can lead the way by taking the initiative, through increased sub-regional and intercontinental cooperation, to introduce the necessary legislation to ensure that the business activities of multinational oil companies in Africa are undertaken in a mutually beneficial and more environmentally sustainable manner. This will also ensure that the sector's activities benefit all stakeholders, particularly those in communities in which oil exploration takes place. At the heart of these policy proposals is a firm belief that it is only by transitioning their economies away from oil or mineral dependence, building robust natural resource management system with appropriate safeguards through legislative oversight can natural resource-endowed African countries achieve the levels of economic prosperity and inclusive society that has eluded them for so long.

By achieving an inclusive society, resource-rich African countries will begin to guarantee the current and future generations a stake in the economic benefits of their natural resources. Drawing a parallel between inclusive society and economic prosperity in *Why Nations Fail*, Daron Acemoglu and James Robinson argue that societies which create the economic and the political conditions for a level playing field and that encourage investment in skills are more conducive to economic growth than societies that are structured to extract natural resources by the few, and that fail to provide the incentive for economic activity.[47] This is not to suggest that extractive institutions do not lend themselves to economic growth in resource-rich countries.

However, under conditions of excessive natural resource extraction by the few, economic growth cannot be sustained, as there is lack of innovation and creativity needed to disrupt the economic *status quo*, thereby, bring about positive change in the economy. In conclusion, natural resources are limited in size and have a life span. If

---

[47]Acemoglu and Robinson (2010)

large enough, the sector can easily crowd out other important sectors of the economy, thus leading to Dutch diseases since most natural resources are vulnerable to market and price volatility. For instance, plummeting oil prices would mean that the main source of revenues for oil-dependent countries would always be prone to crash, thereby leaving them with a very limited fiscal space for domestic investment, economic stimulus and ultimately recovery during falling oil prices and other phenomena that have the potential to disrupt the global economic order.

For African countries rich in natural resource, especially oil, it becomes important to use their oil wealth in a much more efficient and effective manner to tackle the challenges of rising unemployment, which would always worsen during and following any global economic shock. These observations, perhaps, provide the most potent reason for African governments with natural resources to implement robust resource governance mechanisms in their countries. The need to address the problem of high unemployment, particularly among African youths hit hardest by the COVID-19 pandemic, is a shared and desperate demographic challenge facing both resource-rich and resource-poor African countries. Thus, the demographic challenges of youth unemployment facing Africa, not just resource-rich African countries, are worth exploring.

BIBLIOGRAPHY

Acemoglu, D., & Robinson, J. (2010). The role of institutions in growth and development. *Review of Economics and Institutions*, 1(2), 1–33.

Adne, C., & Lars, M. (2009). *Can Norway be a role model for natural resource abundant countries?* WIDER Research Paper, No. 2009/23, *The United Nations University World Institute for Development Economics Research (UNU-WIDER), Helsinki.*

Auty, R. (1993). *Sustaining development in mineral economies: The resource curse thesis.* London: Routledge.

Auty, R. (1995). Economic development and the resource curse thesis. In O. Morrissey, & F. Stewart (Eds.), *Economic and Political Reform in Developing Countries.* London: Palgrave.

Auty, R. (1998). *Resource abundance and economic development: Improving performance of resource-rich countries. The United Nations University World Institute for Development Economics Research, Helsinki.*

Auty, R. (2004). *Patterns of rent-extraction and deployment in development countries: Implications for governance, economic policy and performance.* In: *Paper prepared for the poverty reduction and economic management unit seminar, World Bank.*

Ayado, S. (2020). Nigeria's excess crude account depletes to $71.813m. *Business Day*. Retrieved from https://businessday.ng/business-economy/article/nigerias-excess-crude-account-depletes-to-71-813m/. Accessed on 21 May 2020.

Bauer, A., & Mihalyi, D. (2020). *Coronavirus, the oil crash and economies: How can governments of oil-dependent countries respond? Natural Resource Governance Institute, Blog.* Retrieved from https://resourcegovernance.org/blog/coronavirus-oil-crash-economies-how-governments-respond. Accessed on 31 May 2020.

Bertocchi, G., & Guerzoni, A. (2010). Growth, history, or institutions: What explains state fragility in sub-Saharan Africa? *Journal of Peace Research*, 49(6), 769–783.

British Petroleum. (2019). *BP statistical review of World energy 2019* (68th ed.). Retrieved from https://www.bp.com/content/dam/bp/business-sites/en/global/corporate/pdfs/energy-economics/statistical-review/bp-stats-review-2019-oil.pdf. Accessed on 11 April 2020.

Cappelen, A., & Mjoset, L. (2009). *Can Norway be a role model for natural resource abundant countries?* WIDER Research Paper, No. 2009/23, ISBN 978-92-9230-192-7, *The United Nations University World Institute for Development Economics Research (UNU-WIDER)*, Helsinki.

Di John, J. (2007). Oil abundant and violent political conflict: a critical assessment. *The Journal of Development Studies*, 43(6), 961–986.

European Report on Development. (2009). *Overcoming fragility in Africa – forging a new European approach. Robert Schuman Centre for Advanced Studies, European University Institute: San Domenico di Fiesole.*

Fund for Peace. (2020). *Fragile states index, country data and trends – Finland.* Retrieved from https://fragilestatesindex.org/country-data/. Accessed on 10 May 2020.

Gal, P., & Witheridge, W. (2019). *Productivity and innovation at the industry level: What role for integration in global value chains?* OECD Productivity Working Papers, 2019/19, Paris: OECD Publishing.

Global Witness. (2016). *Probe into murky ExxonMobil deal shows why strong U.S. transparency rules are needed for oil companies.* Retrieved from https://www.globalwitness.org/en/press-releases/probe-murky-exxonmobil-deal-shows-why-strong-us-transparency-rules-are-needed-oil-companies/. Accessed on 21 May 2020.

Gurría, A. (2012). *Harnessing Africa's resources for sustainable and inclusive growth.* In: *12th International Economic Forum on Africa, OECD Headquarters.* Retrieved from https://www.oecd.org/about/secretary-general/harnessingafricasresourcesforsustainableandinclusivegrowth.htm. Accessed on 12 June 2019.

Hammond, J. (2011). The resource curse and oil revenues in Angola and Venezuela. *Science and Society*, 75(3), 348–378.

Human Rights Watch. (2011). *Corruption on trial? The record of Nigeria's Economic and Financial Crimes Commission.* New York, NY: Human Rights Watch. Retrieved from https://www.hrw.org/sites/default/files/reports/nigeria0811WebToPost.pdf. Accessed on 20 May 2020.

Izvorski, I. (2018). *Resource-rich Africa can boost growth to reduce poverty.* Retrieved from https://www.brookings.edu/blog/future-development/2018/09/25/resource-rich-africa-can-boost-growth-to-reduce-poverty/. Accessed on 2 March 2019.

Izvorski, I., Coulibaly, S., & Doumbia, D. (2018). *Reinvigorating growth in resource-rich sub-Saharan Africa.* Washington, DC: World Bank Publications. Retrieved from http://documents.worldbank.org/curated/en/617451536237967588/pdf/5-9-2018-17-9-2-SSAGrowthforweb.pdf. Accessed on 12 June 2019.

Keefer, P., & Knack, S. (1997). Why don't poor countries catch up? A cross-national test of an institutional explanation. *Economic Inquiry*, 35, 590–602.

Larsen, E. R. (2006). Escaping the resource curse and the Dutch diseases?: When and why Norway caught up with and forged ahead of its neighbours. *The American Journal of Economics and Sociology*, 65(3), 605–640.

Leite, C., & Weidmann, J. (1999). *Does mother nature corrupt? Natural resource, corruption, and economic growth.* IMF Working Papers No. 99/85. Retrieved from https://www.imf.org/en/Publications/WP/Issues/2016/12/30/Does-Mother-Nature-Corrupt-Natural-Resources-Corruption-and-Economic-Growth-3126. Accessed on 5 April 2020.

Lockwood, M., Davidson, J., Curtis, A., Stratford, E., & Griffith, R. (2010). Governance principles for natural resource management. *Society and Natural Resources*, 23(10), 986–1001.

Nordic Council of Ministers. (2018). *Nordic statistics 2018.* Retrieved from https://norden.diva-portal.org/smash/get/diva2:1257993/FULLTEXT01.pdf. Accessed on 21 May 2020.

North, D. (1991). Institutions. *Journal of Economic Perspectives*, 5(1), 97–112.

Ovadia, J. S. (2014). Local content and natural resource governance: The cases of Angola and Nigeria. *The Extractive Industries Society*, 1(2), 137–146.

Oxford Poverty and Human Development Initiative. (2019). *"Angola country briefing", multidimensional poverty index data bank.* Oxford Poverty and Human Development

Initiative, University of Oxford. Retrieved from https://ophi.org.uk/wp-content/uploads/CB_AGO_2019_2.pdf. Accessed on 25 May 2020.

Papyrakis, E. (2017). The resource curse – what have we learned from two decades of intensive research: Introduction to the special issue. *The Journal of Development Studies*, 53(2), 175–185.

Ribadu, N. (2010). *Show me the money – leveraging anti-money laundering tools to fight corruption in Nigeria. An Insider Story*. Washington, DC: Centre for Global Development. Retrieved from https://www.cgdev.org/sites/default/files/1424712_file_Ribadu_web_FINAL.pdf. Accessed on 20 May 2020.

Rodriguez-pose, A. (2013). Do institutions matter for regional development? *Regional Studies*, 47(7), 1034–1047.

Sachs, J., & Warner, A. (1997). Sources of slow economic growth in African economies. *Journal of African Economies*, 6(3), 335–376.

Sarraf, M., & Jiwanji, M. (2001). *Beating the resource curse – the case of Botswana*. Environmental Department Papers, Environmental Economic Series, Paper No. 1, The World Bank Group, Washington, DC: World Bank Publications.

Singh, A. (2013). *Conference on harnessing natural resource wealth for inclusive growth and economic growth*. In: *International Monetary Fund, Dili*. Retrieved from https://www.imf.org/en/News/Articles/2015/09/28/04/53/sp091813. Accessed on 12 June 2019.

Statista. (2020). *Proved oil reserves in Norway 1995-2018*. Retrieved from https://www.statista.com/statistics/447353/proved-oil-reserves-norway/. Accessed on 15 May 2020.

Tiba, S., & Frikha, M. (2019). The controversy of the resource curse and the environment in the SDGs background: The African context. *Resources Policy*, 62, 437–452.

Transparency International. (2019). *Corruption around the World in 2019*. Retrieved from https://www.transparency.org/en/countries/nigeria. Accessed on 20 May 2020.

Transparency International. (2019). *Corruption perceptions index 2019*. Retrieved from https://www.transparency.org/cpi2019. Accessed on 12 April 2020.

Umar, I., Samsudin, R. S., & Mohamed, M. (2018). Ascertaining the effectiveness of Economic and Financial Crimes Commission (EFCC) in tackling corruptions in Nigeria. *Journal of Financial Crime*, 25(3), 658–668.

United Nations Environment Programme. (2018). *Our work in Africa*. Retrieved from https://www.unenvironment.org/regions/africa/our-work-africa. Accessed on 5 May 2020.

Wantchekon, L. (2002). Why do resource abundant countries have authoritarian governments? *Journal of African Finance and Economic Development*, 5(2), 57–77.

World Bank. (2019). *The World Bank in Gabon*. Retrieved from https://www.worldbank.org/en/country/gabon/overview. Accessed on 2 March 2019.

World Bank. (2020). *Russia monthly economic developments, January 2020*. The World Bank. Retrieved from http://pubdocs.worldbank.org/en/591171581001563683/RMED-Jan2020.pdf. Accessed on 9 April 2020.

Yates, D. (2012). *The scramble for African oil: oppression, corruption and war for control of Africa's natural resources*. London: Pluto Press.

DEMOGRAPHIC DIVIDEND AND CHALLENGES

4

It would be incomplete to discuss Africa's demographic trends and related challenges without first looking at the wider context of what it means to be a young person in our twenty-first-century world ravaged by the economic impacts of COVID-19 pandemic. With nearly 1 in 5 young people made jobless, and more than 500 million pushed deeper into poverty and possibly starvation, the effect of the COVID-19 economic crisis particularly on young people has been systematic, deep and disproportionate.[1] The cumulative negative effects of the crisis have given a new edge to the long-lasting negative consequences of young people's marginalisation in access to education, health, employment and political leadership. Most troubling is the fact that many young people now face a far greater risk of being left much further behind in education and economic opportunities during a crucial stage in their life's development as a result of the impact of COVID-19 economic crisis.[2]

In Africa, especially, the scale of job losses and economic hardship threatens the progress made over the last two decades towards achieving demographic dividend. Yet, as most people have become more focused on survival and family in response to the crisis, young people have in many ways risen to the challenge of equally finding answers to other existential challenges facing humanity. From participating in the world's first 'COVID-19 challenge trials', in which healthy young volunteers are deliberately infected with the virus to hasten vaccine development, to raising awareness of the negative effects of rising social and economic inequalities, young people have seized the moment to confront the wider global challenges of our time.

Through purpose, activism, innovation and entrepreneurialism, the youth population is dismantling and overthrowing systems of social injustices and economic dysfunctionalities that predate and unfortunately have been exacerbated by the pandemic. For instance, by amplifying their frustration with the political *status quo* through mass movements for tougher action on global issues, such as inequality – as seen in the *Black Lives Matter* movement led by Alicia Garza, Patrisse Cullors and Opal Tometi, and climate change as seen in the *Fridays for Future* activism led by the Swedish Greta

---

[1]International Labour Organisation (2020)
[2]United Nations Department of Economic and Social Affairs (2020, p. 1)

Thunberg, it seems young people are at the forefront of the global push for both social and economic change in response to the economic devastation of the pandemic.

What is even more profound is not just the complexion of these movements, but their underlying cause and purpose. If anything, they have given us a scathingly different, but relevant, insight into the complexity of the insecurities facing many young people across the world. Not just in poor developing countries, but also in more affluent developed societies of the global North. Prior to the onset of the COVID-19 pandemic, young people, especially in Africa, were twice more likely than older adults to be unemployed or to be in precarious informal sector employment with poor working arrangements. As new entrants to the labour market, young workers are twice more likely than adults to be susceptible to underemployment, exploitation and job loss. But the employment conditions for young people in Africa are much more stark. As workers, they often lack adequate social and economic protections that come with secured employment.

Because of this, they are often excluded from the full employment rights and career progression opportunities for which they prepared themselves in training and education. Therefore, they are far more vulnerable to global economic shocks, such as the COVID-19 pandemic, than their global counterparts. Not only because of unmet educational attainment, joblessness, hunger and poverty, but also because of food insecurity, driven mainly by a variety of factors including climate-related economic shocks as well as conflicts. In particular, countries in the Sahel region, the Horn of Africa and Southern Africa have all seen an increased number of food insecure youth populations exacerbated by these factors, particularly conflict.

In East Africa, the tensions and inter-ethnic conflicts in Ethiopia, Somalia and South Sudan are turning large numbers of young people into refugees and internally displaced peoples (IDP) with food insecurity. In northern Nigeria where many young people are affected by the ongoing Boko Haram terrorist conflict has resulted to an increased number of IDPs and undernourished youth populations, as many as more than 25 million as of 2018.[3] Combined with conflict, the threat to livelihoods and household incomes has been exacerbated by the COVID-19 economic crisis, thereby leading to increased undernourishment and food insecurity in these fragile regions. There has been yet little research understanding of malnutrition as a co-morbidity of COVID-19. However, people with weakened immune system as a result of undernourishment are known to be at a much greater risk of a range of illnesses. As a consequence, they are twice more likely to be severely affected by the virus.[4]

As COVID-19 related economic crisis wears on, the threat of food insecurity and loss of income leads to other social vices that particularly affect a sub-group of vulnerable young female population who are dependent on a male provider. This sub-group is now at a much higher risk of domestic abuse and violence due to national lockdowns to contain the diseases. In fact, the United Nations found that the COVID-19 curfews and lockdowns may have created an ugly 'shadow pandemic' in households in which there is increased male violence against young women and girls.[5] Couple with this are the institutionalised cultural norms and patriarchal definitions of masculinity within the African family unit, which views men as the head of the family and therefore the main

[3]FAO/ECA (2018)
[4]World Health Organisation (2020)
[5]UN Women (2020)

breadwinner. It means that the cumulative negative effects of the crisis, compounded by an increased female dependence on a male provider, is particularly more acute for young, married and unemployed women in Africa.

Globally, the annual economic loss of female dependence on a male provider is estimated in the region of $1.5 billion.[6] From all indication, Africa, perhaps, bears a larger percentage of this annual economic loss. Dependence on a male provider thwarts women's access and equal participation in both education and employment and consequently their ability to contribute to household income, make healthy nutritional choices for their children and free themselves from domestic violence. Moreover, young women with little education and a family tend to work in the hardest-hit sectors including retail, hospitality and the informal sector without employment rights and protection. The International Labour Organisation (ILO) estimates that the first month of the crisis resulted in a drop of 60 percent fall in the income of informal sector workers globally. This translates into a drop of 81 percent in Africa where between 70 percent and 90 percent of mostly youths and women are employed.[7]

Because of the crisis, the African Union (AU) estimates that nearly 20 million jobs, in both formal and the informal sectors, may no longer exist.[8] In addition to job losses, coupled with hunger and food insecurity, the COVID-19 pandemic has also had an unprecedented effect on educational systems across the world, but with far-reaching social and economic consequences for many young Africans. Although comparably Africa has recorded low rates of COVID-19-related fatality, young Africans unfortunately are far more at risk of being 'left behind' in education and employment opportunities as a result of the disruption from the crisis. Thus, compared to the rest of the world, Africa has the lowest capacity and opportunity to provide its young populations with income protection benefit and continuous learning through transition to online distance learning (ODL) which has supported many workers and learners during the crisis.

Disparities in access to education during the pandemic are more acute in low-income African countries where 89 percent of young learners do not have access to household computers and 82 percent lack internet access.[9] Lack of inclusive digital education means than about 56 million young learners kept out of the classroom by the crisis live in SSA. This is in locations not served by mobile networks and without ICT infrastructure. For these young learners, whose teachers equally lack ICT and digital skills and access, transitioning to online learning has been impossible, leading to further marginalisation. As the resulting economic turmoil continues, this marginalised young populations and the families that they support will have no means of survival even after the pandemic.

Even before the COVID-19 pandemic, the demographic trends show that young Africans are twice more likely than their global counterparts to suffer marginalisation in access to general education and digital infrastructure. Consequently, they are likely to have poor digital skills. Thus, in comparison to their global counterparts, the marginalisation of young Africans in education and digital skills access as a result of the pandemic may have come at an even far greater cost than the pandemic. Marginalisation in access to education impairs people's ability

---

[6]UN Women (2018)
[7]International Labour Organisation (2020)
[8]African Union (2020)
[9]United Nations Educational Scientific and Cultural Organisation (2020)

to make any intellectual and meaningful contribution to relevant areas of their personal lives, which ultimately affects their ability to contribute to national development. From all indication, particularly judging by the economic effects of the COVID-19 pandemic on young Africans compared to their global counterparts, it seems Africa, more than any other region, is struggling to cope with the social and economic challenges associated with global demographic transition.

4.1 AFRICA'S DEMOGRAPHIC TRANSITION

At the intersection of global demographic transition is Africa's youth population surge, which is estimated to rise to 450 million by 2050, representing more than 40% of the region's projected 2.6 billion population in that year. With a median age of 19.5 years, compared to the global median age of about 26.9 years old, young people currently make up more than 65% of Africa's 1.2 billion population.[10] The latest forecast in *The Lancet* shows that Africa's population is set to increase three fold to about 3.07 billion by 2100.

In fact, by 2100 the population of Africa will outsize Asia (currently the largest) as the latter recedes in population size. Nigeria, predicted to buck these projections with a population size of 791 million, will be ahead of China and the United States as both economic superpowers decline progressively in population size to 732 million and 336 million, respectively.[11] If *The Lancet*'s projections are anything to go by, then, as shown in Figure 4.1, it will probably take Nigeria another 80 years to join the G8 league based on GDP per capita.

In any case, these demographic shifts have helped to secure Africa's status as the youngest continent in the foreseeable future until 2100, when the global population is projected to decrease to 8.8 billion from a peak of 9.7 billion in 2064 because of declining global fertility rates. Rising population, combined with large cohort of working age population, has implications for meeting the SDG targets linked to other socioeconomic indicators of quality education, health and GDP per capita income. Against the backdrop of these demographic trends is the connection between demography and socioeconomic development, which is underpinned by the concept of demographic dividend. Demographic dividend is the economic surplus arising from a relative increase of the working-age population compared to the dependents.[12]

Historically, the idea of demographic dividend was mooted, and perhaps formulated, following the analysis of economic rise of Asian economies. To better understand the underlying factors that led to the rapid rise of Asian economies from the 1960s onwards, economists, demographers and development experts considered the effects of the shifting age structures in Asian societies. They found that the rising number of active adults in the workforce population relative to their dependents affected the significant economic growth observed in East Asia, at least.[13] Paradoxically, the unpredictable outcome of having large cohorts of young populations underlies the dual nature of demographic dividend, which presents both a challenge and opportunity.

---

[10]Population Reference Bureau (2017)
[11]Vollset et al. (2020)
[12]Turbat (2017)
[13]World Bank (2015)

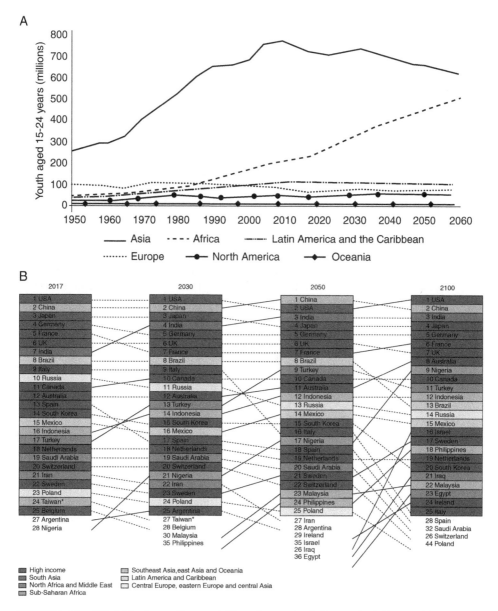

FIGURE 4.1 (A) Africa's youth population rise against the rest of the world. (B) Ranking of the top 25 countries by total GDP in 2017 and the reference scenario in 2030, 2050 and 2100

Source: (A) World Economic Forum (WEF), January 2020. (B) *The Lancet*, July 2020.

This paradox also explains why there is both an optimistic and pessimistic views of the concept of demographic dividend. On the one hand, the optimistic view perceives large populations as the gateway to the promise of accelerated economic growth and geopolitical strength through the presence of larger markets and more consumers. On the other hand, the pessimistic view perceives that social and economic turmoil looms large in a situation in which governments are unable to fulfil the aspirations and expectations of their large workforce populations.[14] From an optimistic viewpoint, to achieve demographic dividend, African governments must aggressively invest in the rapid expansion of their public services in education and health while simultaneously creating and sustaining the conditions for employment creation on a massive scale.

However, according to the AfDB and the IMF, reaping demographic dividend in Africa requires the creation of about 18 million new jobs year on year for the next 25 years. This will equate to about creating 450 million new jobs until 2040. Based on current socioeconomic indicators and forecasts, it seems Africa's formal public and private sectors formal will have a mammoth task accomplishing that target, if at all possible. Therefore, given the inability of the formal sector to create the much-needed jobs, the only way out of the current crisis of high and rising youth unemployment is to create the conditions under which self-employment can thrive, thereby prevent a demographic time bomb.

Within these insights, there is a real chance that the perceived dividends of Africa's demographic transition may be diminished if there is no serious investment in young people's future. Investment in human capital and entrepreneurial skills will be essential to productivity, entrepreneurship development and job creation, which will consequently translate into demographic dividend. As the main supplier of the continent's workforce, young people will offer vital opportunities for incremental growth in Africa's labour force and productivity, which in turn provides scope for savings, investments and sustainable economic growth.[15] The converse situation to demographic dividend is youth bulge phenomenon, which is characterised by high youth unemployment, widespread violent protest, political instability and ultimately conflict.

If a young person is unemployed, vulnerable and poor, the opportunity cost of joining an armed or a radical group is very low. Thus, it is important that Africa's young populations are not marginalised. They must be supported to be productive and remain in gainful employment with decent wages through access to continuous education and training. Unfortunately, for many development stakeholders involved in policymaking, programme design and implementation, Africa's youth population rise presents a very complex demographic challenge. Without direct access to quality education and training opportunities to either reskill or upskill themselves, young people's access to livelihood opportunity will be thwarted, thereby leading to further marginalisation, and consequently increased demographic challenges.

4.2 DEMOGRAPHIC CHALLENGES

Apart from skills mismatch with labour market needs, risk of exploitation and job loss than older workers, living conditions are notoriously daunting for many young Africans. Majority, especially young women, have heavy family burdens, less disposable income

---

[14]May & Turbat (2017)
[15]Filmer & Fox (2014)

and less access to life-changing opportunities than their global counterparts.[16] In addition to the wider socioeconomic implications that arise from these adverse conditions, other factors including lack of work experience, reduced wages due to the forces of supply and demand and threats imposed by the increasing automation and digitalisation of the workplace are among a string of structural barriers that young Africans face in today's challenging labour market.

The increased use of disruptive 4.0 technologies by organisations including Artificial Intelligence (AI) and big data means that machines are now widely predicted to do the jobs originally designed for humans. As organisations embrace and resort to using these new technologies to achieve efficiency, competitive advantage, expand existing and penetrate new markets, it becomes much harder for young Africans without the relevant skills to gain entry or even survive in today's labour market. To compound matters, the number of young Africans classified as Not in Education, Employment or Training (NEET) is on the rise.

The latest ILO records show that there is an average increase of 0.7 percent from 21.7 percent in 2015 to 22.4 percent in 2020 of Africans aged 15–24 years old who are not in education, employment, or training. Currently, one-fifth of the global youth population, that is, 267 million young people, have a NEET status with the figure projected to reach 273 million by 2021 as a result of COVID-19 pandemic.[17] The upward trend in young people's NEET status has several ramifications for their own socioeconomic well-being and their societies. It means that they are neither productive and gaining the necessary experience from work nor receiving income from employment in the labour market or improving their education and skills to help contribute to personal and societal growth.

As such, the rising number of young Africans excluded from education, employment and training will adversely affect any possibility of meeting the global SDG target of reducing the NEET rate among youths by 2020. Many poor African countries that have large cohorts and growing youth population neither have the capacity to provide the relevant education and training for their young population to earn a decent income, nor are their labour markets able to absorb the growing number of young people ready and willing to enter the workforce. With an acute number of young Africans in NEET category, lack of proper investment in quality education and their training has been linked to bad planning, misgovernance and corruption.

Large cohorts of young people with a NEET status has a knock-on effect on other social ladders that negatively affect their economic survival and life chances. In Africa, as high as 19 percent of the young female population have a NEET status, which makes them particularly more vulnerable to exploitation including domestic abuse and violence. For instance, because of the prevailing cultural norms in some African countries, more employed young women than men are trapped in poverty due to low income and income instability. Lack of education, low income and income instability are some of the socioeconomic factors that can prevent female adolescents and even adults from recognising their rights, including exercising their reproductive rights.

---

[16]Anosike (2017)
[17]International Labour Organisation (2020)

As a result, their experience as youths could be blighted by unwanted pregnancy, early or forced marriage and consequently premature parenthood. With no education and the prospect of decent work, their only chance of income and survival is either through their male partners or vulnerable employment in the informal sector where they are condemned to a lifetime of in-work poverty. In-work poverty (discussed fully in Chapter 7) particularly among young people is triggered by low growth in earnings and the rapid rise of informal employment. In-work poverty is a serious and very complex growing phenomenon globally.

This complexity is heightened by other socioeconomic concerns, such as rising inequality, which is made worse by other global challenges in relation to climate change which has implications for food security. But if governments in Africa view their large youth population as an opportunity, rather than a liability, and put in place the appropriate policy measures and interventions including creating direct opportunities and investment in education, training and employment as a way to engage more meaningfully with young people, then it is possible that young people's productivity can lead to demographic dividend. Access to quality education and work-based skills can provide young people with a lifeline for survival in the labour market.

Harnessed properly, the economic prospects of Africa's demographic transition can be transformed into dividend with enormous regional benefits in form of economic growth, social cohesion, political stability and sustainable development.[18] But these benefits can only be realised if the marginalisation of young Africans in all kinds of sectors, especially in employment and political leadership is addressed.

4.3 YOUTH MARGINALISATION, WHY IT MATTERS?

Policies and actions targeted at reversing the vulnerable conditions of many young Africans have taken upward and downward tracks. But none has been more concerning than how to deal with the issue of high unemployment amid rising poverty among young Africans. Generally speaking, youth population rise either brings enormous economic benefit in form of demographic dividend or causes social, economic and political consequences depending on government's response to young people's livelihood priorities and needs. Besides, the age structure of any society and the relative size of its youth cohort are crucial determinants in the size and growth of the labour force. As a result, large cohorts of the youth population tend to put pressure on the economy in terms of job creation.

Apart from job creation, a rapid growth in the size of the youth population also puts pressure on public institutions, thereby reducing the capacity of countries to provide basic public services, such as education and healthcare. For this reason, governments are predictably nervous and view an unprecedent rise in the youth population as a very difficult challenge. From an employment viewpoint, governments must provide young people with education, training and decent employment, which are critical to the peace and stability of a country. Because of this, serious questions must be asked about how African governments are dealing with the demographic challenge of rising youth unemployment and poverty amid the political conflicts in the region.

---

[18]United Nations Department of Economic and Social Affairs (2018)

About 90 percent of the global youth population, that is, one in every ten young person, live in developing countries, particularly in Africa where barriers to their development and fulfilment of their potential are the highest due to structural inequality and poverty.[19] Poverty is the main reason why many young Africans are denied access to basic education, livelihood opportunities and critical healthcare needs. Without access to education and healthcare, young people's ability to influence political decisions that affect their well-being and that of their commnunities is diminished. This situation is particularly worse for young girls in Africa who bear the social and economic scars of increased marginalisation in education, conflict and violence.

As explained in Chapter 2, youth poverty, coupled with a lack of access to education and training, can have a profoundly negative effect on the economic, social and the political lives of a country. Lack of access to education and training among young people leads to youth unemployment and unproductivity and creates the incentive for disillusionment and consequently disaffection. In any society, youth disaffection is a recipe for social unrest and political conflict. When faced with unemployment and joblessness, young people have been found to be far more vulnerable and willing to engage in social unrest, political violence, conflict and even wars.[20] Yet, surprisingly, the priorities and aspirations of young Africans have been frequently ignored by the political class. The problem is that because young people are excluded from Africa's political leadership structure, their priorities and needs are rarely ever the focus of policy priority and action. Thus, with a bleak economic future, coupled with marginalisation in political leadership, many young Africans have become increasingly disillusioned and disaffected.

4.4 YOUTH MARGINALISATION IN POLITICAL LEADERSHIP

Among a myriad of challenges facing many young Africans, their exclusion from the political process is the most perverse. Inclusive political process is needed to achieve demographic dividend. It constitutes and provides the pathway for inclusive growth and sustainable development. Although Africa has made significant political progress and reforms that paved the way for the end of apartheid in South Africa, the demise of authoritarianism, the introduction of constitutional democracy and rule-based political governance including term limits for incumbent presidents or heads of state. However, serious challenges still threaten the region's political stability and future.

While some African countries have built on these political gains, many have not yet institutionalised the principles and norms of effective democratic and inclusive political process. Notably, abuse of executive powers and constitutional coups remain a major threat to political stability and inclusion in the region. Incumbent presidents or heads of state are known to influence changes to their country's constitution to eliminate term and age limits, thereby unconstitutionally prolonging

---

[19]United Nations Population Fund (2014)
[20]Udal (2006)

their mandate in office.[21] To appreciate the extent of the threats and challenges, it is important to look at the composition of Africa's political leaders since the 1960s when majority of African countries became independent states. Although about 60 percent of Africa's more than a billion population is under the age of 25 years, the median age of political leaders in Africa is 62 years.

This is significantly older than the median age for political leaders in the OECD countries where the median age is about 43.2 years. This sharp contrast shows that Africa has not yet made sufficient progress in terms of empowering its younger population to take up political leadership. In contrast to other parts of the world, Africa's political elites are still dominated by revolutionists and pro-nationalist 'old guards' (or their protégées) who rose to power through coups d'état under the nationalist movements of the 1960s. Since then, coups d'état have persisted, occurring either under a military ruler or under a democratically elected government. In August 2020, a group of Malian soldiers overthrew the democratically elected government of Ibrahim Boubacar Keïta.

Before the Mali coup, in all 48 independent African countries across eastern, northern, western and southern Africa, there have been 80 successful coups d'état and 108 failed coup attempts over a 46-year-period between 1956 and 2001.[22] Military-led interventions are known to cause political instability, which adversely affects economic stability and progress. However, with increasing political awareness and decisive action by the African Charter on Democracy, Elections and Governance (ACDEG) under the aegis of the AU, coupled with interventions by powerful regional blocs, such as the Economic Community of West African States (ECOWAS), African political leaders with authoritarian motives are losing their grip on power. In what perhaps may be regarded as the most significant intervention yet by any regional bloc, the ECOWAS recently forced the former Gambian President, Yahya Jammeh, into exile after he failed to accept the outcome of a 2017 election by relinquishing power. As a result, military coups are becoming increasingly unattractive and less popular in Africa.

However, with changes to the constitution to eliminate term limits in countries such as Burundi, Chad, Cameroon, Egypt, Rwanda and Togo, it seems the growing unpopularity of military coups has given rise to a new type of constitutional coups, which allows sitting heads of state to prolong their stay in office. Thereby, corrupting and consequently eroding public trust in the political process. There are strong connections between Africa's entrenched political leadership structure, economic development and security challenges whereby several heads of state exploit weaknesses in the legislature or the judiciary to prolong their terms of office through constitutional coups.[23]

Entrenched political power inevitably gives rise to political intransigence and profligacy, which go hand in glove with authoritarianism and political instability. Authoritarianism and political instability breed mistrust between the ruling political class and the citizens, particularly in Africa where young people are mostly driven by liberalism, globalism and tolerance, coupled with the pressures of technological innovation, consumerism and the frustration over unfulfilled promises by those in power.[24] Arguably, in many cases, 'the younger generation of Africans in fact appears

---

[21] Mbaku (2020)
[22] McGowan (2003)
[23] Felter (2020)
[24] Kikuwa (2015)

to be more agile, knowledgeable, better equipped and prepared to address the fast-moving issues of today, such as, gender equality, climate-related challenges and social justice, than the political establishment'.[25]

Perhaps, because Africa's current political ruling class has largely failed to embrace the fresh impetus, vision, vibrancy, and innovativeness needed to bring about transformational change in the twenty-first century, their political inertia cast a shadow over the desire and campaign by young people for political change. We see this desire in Uganda with the recent political activism of a 38-year-old popular musician, Robert Kyagulanyi Ssentamu, better known as Bob Wine. Against reported widespread political violence and human rights violations in the lead up to the country's January 2021 polls, Bob Wine challenged the incumbent President Yoweri Museveni, who has been in power since 1986. A Ugandan court's ruling in 2018 upholding the constitutional amendment to remove the presidential age limit paved the way for the re-elected 76-year-old Museveni to extend his 34-year-old rule over the country.

Notwithstanding, the increased public awareness and calls for serious political reforms are now galvanizing the growing appetite among young people, including women, to participate in the political process. A growing participation of women and young Africans in political leadership has meant that some aspects of political leadership in Africa, whereby 14 percent of parliamentarians are under the age of 40 years, have at least begun to reflect global trends.[26] Despite these developments, there is something odd about the political situation in a region which the median age is about 19.5 years and the median age of the longest serving political leaders is more than 75 years. On average, only between 20 percent and 25 percent of Africans would have been born when their current leaders came to power. The issue is not the age of these political leaders *per se*, but with the age and length of time they have held on to political power compared to other political leaders in their league in other parts of the world.

As shown in Table 4.1, in just 60 years from independence, the tenures of about 17 sitting political leaders in Africa span from 20 years to 42 years and cumulatively between them amounts to a grip on political power for a staggering 556 years. The consequence of course is that there is a significant age gap between those who decide policies and those who must deal with the consequences of such policy decisions. As African governments continue to flounder in their efforts to pursue and implement serious political reforms, for young people with political aspirations and leadership ambition, this political situation will come as an awkward reality.

According to Mo Ibrahim 2019 good governance index, education outcomes in terms of quality and whether it is meeting the needs of the economy are worsening faster with greater consequences for about 53 percent of young Africans. This is more than half of Africa's youth population, which equates to nearly 120 million people. This percentage is staggering for a region that sees young people's productivity as vital to achieving the 2030 agenda on economic growth and sustainable development. Given this scenario, young people will have very little influence over the social and the economic consequences of political decisions that were made without them. Thus, with their hopes and leadership aspirations thwarted, many young Africans are understandably disaffected with the political situation in their countries.

---

[25] Dews (2019)
[26] Signe (2019)

TABLE 4.1 Sub-Saharan Africa's longest serving leaders excluding monarchs (1960-2020)

Leaders	Country	Time in office	Total Years in Office
El Hadj Omar Bongo Ondimba	Gabon	1967-2009	42 years[a]
Teodoro Obiang Nguema Mbasogo	Equatorial Guinea	1979-date	41 years[b]
Jose Eduardo dos Santos	Angola	1979-2017	38 years
Gnassingbé Étienne Eyadéma	Togo	1967-2005	38 years
Paul Barthelemy Biya'a bi Mvondo	Cameroon	1982-date	38 years
Robert Gabriel Mugabe	Zimbabwe	1980-2017	37 years[c]
Denis Sassou Nguesso	Republic of Congo	1979-1992 and 1997-date	36 years
Yoweri Kaguta Museveni	Uganda	1986-date	34 years
Felix Houphouet-Boigny	Ivory Coast	1960-1993	33 years
Joseph Mobutu Sese Seko	Zaire (now Democratic Republic of the Congo)	1965-1997	32 years
Hastings Kamuzu Banda	Malawi	1964-1994	30 years
Omar Hassan Ahmad al-Bashir	Sudan	1989-2019	30 years
Idriss Deby Itno	Chad	1990-date	30 years
Mathieu Kerekou	Benin	1972-1991 and 1996-2006	29 years
Isaias Afwerki	Eritrea	1993-date	27 years
Ismail Omar Guelleh	Djibouti	1999-date	21 years
Abdelaziz Bouteflika	Algeria	1999-2019	20 years

[a]At the time of his death, Omar Bongo was the longest serving head of state in Africa and the longest serving head of government globally.

[b]Currently, Africa's longest serving head of state and cumulatively the longest serving head of government in the world.

[c]Served as Prime Minister (1980-1987) and then elected President (1987-2017).

4.5 AUTHORITARIANISM AND YOUTH DISAFFECTION

Authoritarianism is a common feature of Africa's ruling political class. It breeds disaffection, which relates to a psychological state of dissatisfaction among the governed that manifests itself through protest and insurrection usually directed at those in authority. As the root and singular cause of uncertainty and disorientation among young Africans, disaffection linked with lack of inclusion in political leadership comes with serious consequences including mass uprising, political violence and even terrorist conflict, which have huge implications for economic stability and demographic dividend. Unemployed instances and poor African youths, disaffected with their governments, are known to have taken matters into their own hands, unfortunately with fatal and serious political consequences for individuals and the government. For instance, the self-immolation by a 27-year-old unemployed Tunisian street vendor, Mohamed Bouazizi, in response over the seizure of his goods by the Tunisian authorities became the catalyst for the Tunisian Revolution and subsequently the series of anti-government and pro-democracy uprisings known as the "Arab Spring", which swept through largely Middle-eastern and North African countries including Bahrain, Libya, Morocco, Egypt, and Syria in spring 2010-2011.[27] Also troubling is the political insurgency led by the Boko Haram Islamist group in northern Nigeria, which has claimed several thousands of lives.

With almost 55 percent of young people unemployed, and more than 38 percent underemployed, survival for a young person in northern Nigeria is particularly daunting. Most young people are vulnerable to the radical Islamist group – Boko Haram. Equally, in Ethiopia, survival is much harder for unemployed young people and those in vulnerable employment that makes up 22 million young Ethiopians living below the national poverty line.[28] Ethiopia's ethnic-fuelled political conflicts in the Tigray region, which has forced millions from their homes, were triggered by disaffection among mostly unemployed young people who are sympathisers of the Oromo movement.[29]

Apart from Tunisia, Nigeria and Ethiopia, 90 percent of all unemployed Kenyan youths (18.5 percent compared to national unemployment rate of 9.31 percent) involved in political conflict, especially during election cycles, cited frustration and disaffection with the political class as the major incentive for their involvement. In Africa, many young people involved in political conflicts often end up either dead, badly disfigured or as internally displaced persons or migrants in refugee camps. The psychological effects of disaffection are far greater and complex for young people living in poor shelters and humanitarian settings as migrants. They face a higher risk of discrimination and exploitation in the labour market. As a result of disaffection with authorities and the status quo, many young Africans are forced to emigrate to countries outside Africa in search of better economic opportunities.

4.6 EMIGRATION BY AFRICAN YOUTHS

Contrary to widely held notion that huge swathes of young Africans are leaving the continent in mass migration, the reality is suprisingly different. Globally, about 272 million people, equivalent to 3.5 percent of the world's population, come under the international migrants' population. India (17.5 million), China (11.8 million) and Mexico (7-8million), are home to the largest contingent of international migrant populations.[30] Of this migrant population, only 2.5 percent Africans (about 6.8 million people) are international migrants compared with a global average of 3.4 percent. Of those African international migrants, only less than half, about 2.5 - 3

---

[27]Saleh (2010)
[28]United Nations (2018)
[29]Jalata (2017)
[30]International Organisation for Migration (2020)

million people, actually leave Africa.[31] This analysis is revealing and equivalent to IMF's 2016 survey, which concluded that the rate of international migration in SSA was low relative to other regional trends.

In other words, 'the stock of African migrants to total international migrant population was found to be about 2 percent, which was low compared with the rest of the developing world, where 3 percent of the population live in a foreign country'.[32] These findings show that, if anything, Africa is not a 'continent of exodus' as widely portrayed in the popular media and amplified by sections of the development community. Africans that come under the international migrant population originate from only nine countries across East Africa (27.1 percent), North Africa (25.8 percent) and West Africa (24.1 percent), with Egypt (9.4 percent of the population) leading the largest stock of international African migrants outside Africa.[33]

Thus, despite the scaremongering by mainly Western populist politicians with ulterior motives – which has led to anti-immigrant sentiments in rich Western societies – the truth is that much of the global population, some 96.5 percent, actually reside in countries in which they were born. Migration from Africa is mostly an intra-regional phenomenon with Ivory Coast, South Africa and Nigeria, the top three recipient countries of international African migrants. Notwithstanding, the humiliating images of exhausted young Africans in unseaworthy conditions in the Mediterranean Sea, or those sardined in cargo trucks across Europe often generate negative headlines about African migrants.

The harsh experiences they are often forced to endure at the mercy of human traffickers reinforce the negative public perceptions in destination countries which view and mischaracterise African international migrants as 'desperate invaders'.[34] This negative perception feeds into anti-immigrant riots, racial attacks, labour exploitation and labour market discrimination, which are social vices disproportionately experienced more by African international migrants than other migrant populations. Attracted by the promise of a better life elsewhere, coupled with the illusion and frustration of failing to realise that promise, young African migrants encounter harsher realities as victims of forced migration to other parts of the world.

The arduous, often dangerously dehumanising journey, facilitated by well-organised criminal gangs, sometimes in complicit with corrupt government officials, is only a tip of the iceberg in a very complex global web of clandestine migratory trade in illegal migration and human trafficking. Emigration route outside Africa stretches from several countries of origin and transits along the Sahel including conflict-torn and economically fragile Niger and Libya to central Mediterranean route connecting Italy, Spain and Malta in Europe. The weak governance institutions in these countries are helping to facilitate this highly lucrative but illegal trade in forced human migration. The exact number of young Africans affected by this phenomenon is hard to establish. This is because many who are pushed by political and economic factors beyond their control to undertake such perilous journeys are either traded, raped, abandoned or even tortured to death in the dessert.[35]

---

[31]The Economist (2020)
[32]Gonzalez-Garcia et al. (2016)
[33]MO Ibrahim Foundation (2019)
[34]Adedeji (2019)
[35]Kah (2019)

However, between 2010 and 2017, about 1 million desperate young African migrants, including women and children, may have arrived in Europe as asylum seekers through various entry ports. The main concern is not so much the destination of many of these young migrant Africans, but the underlying drivers for their actions. The main drivers of emigration and the pathways migrants choose in order to achieve their ambition vary from country to country and from individual to individual. Also, because international migration is closely related to short-term acute events, such as severe instability, economic crisis or political conflict, as well as longer-term trends including demographic changes and geographic factors, such as climatic shocks, it is difficult to predict with accuracy the main drivers of emigration.

However, disaffection and desperation because of joblessness, poverty and conflict have been linked with high rate of emigration among young Africans. A survey undertaken in 2018 by the Pew Research Centre revealed that 4 in 10 young Africans in each six most African migrants' Countries of Origin (COO) said that they would like to migrate to another country if the means and the opportunity presented themselves. In particular, roughly three-quarters of those surveyed in Ghana (75 percent) and Nigeria (74 percent), more than half in Kenya (53 percent) and South Africa (51 percent), and nearly half in Senegal (46 percent) said they would like to move and resettle in another country, particularly Europe and the United States.[36]

These findings are similar to the outcome of a different survey a year earlier undertaken by Afrobarometer – a non-partisan pan-African research institution, and the Nigeria's arm of the US-based MacArthur Foundation. Afrobarometer found that one-third of Nigerians and Ghanaians have thought about emigrating. Around 11 percent of those surveyed said that they have thought about it considerably, while 12 percent acknowledged that they were taking concrete steps, such as procuring a visa with the intention of emigrating. A substantial (31.5 percent) number of young populations, that is, one-third or eight in ten potential emigrants aged 35 years or younger, including 45 percent of those aged 25 years or younger, cited economic hardship as the main reason for planning to emigrate.

Young Africans who have considerably thought about moving abroad are almost twice as many as those older than 35 years old. In other words, about 44 percent of young Senegalese, 42 percent of young Ghanaians and 38 percent of young Nigerians, respectively, are currently either contemplating or on their way to resettling outside Africa. Majority are from the urban areas (52 percent), whereas 45 percent and 35 percent have secondary school and post-secondary school certificates.[37] Although many of these young people may probably never realise their ambitions, their intentions, however, underscore the magnitude of the emigration challenge facing the region. It is such that many young Africans, as high as 10 percent in Democratic Republic of the Congo, 8 percent in Liberia and Sierra Leone and 6 percent in Ghana (about 1.7 million Ghanaians), had in 2017 actively sought to settle in the United States under the diversity lottery visa, which admits only 50,000 qualifying applicants worldwide.[38]

---

[36]Connor et al. (2018)
[37]Afrobarometer (2017)
[38]Connor (2018)

4.7 EMIGRATION TRENDS, PATTERNS AND SPILLOVERS

Put off by lack of resources and attracted by the prospect of financial independence and promise of a better life, droves of young Africans are migrating from their rural communities to densely and overpopulated urban cities in Africa, thereby putting increased pressure on limited resources, physical infrastructures and the employment sector in Africa's megacities. As shown in the previous chapter, rural–urban migration among a predominantly unemployed young people leads to overcrowded accommodation and increased presence of ghettos in big cities. As a result, and coupled with poor human settlements, there is increased risk of poor sanitation, diseases and violent crimes in Africa's biggest cities.

Emigration by young Africans generally follows three distinct patterns. The most common is rural–urban migration, then intra-regional migration, that is, within Africa and emigration outside Africa, mainly to Europe and North America. Ivory Coast, South Africa and Nigeria were the top three countries with the largest stock of intra-African migrants population. These countries have relatively large and diversified economies, and between them hosted about 2.3 million, 2 million and 0.9 million African migrants as of 2013. This pattern followed the main intra-regional migration corridors, with the largest stretching from Burkina Faso, Guinea Bissau and Mali to Ivory Coast, followed by the corridors from Zimbabwe, Mozambique, Botswana and Lesotho to South Africa and from Benin, Ghana and Niger into Nigeria.[39]

Each emigration pattern presents Africa and the migrants' destination countries with positive and negative spillovers. In addition to the availability of cheap labour in destination countries, emigration restricts the efficiency of public institutions including schools, transportation and hospitals. There is also the issue of brain drain, which suppresses productivity and socioeconomic development in African countries of migrants' origin, while benefitting their destination countries. Although the majority of emigration among young people occurs within Africa, it has implications for some of Africa's megacities in terms of rapid urbanisation, pressure on public services, poor housing and sanitation.

On the flip side, besides draining Africa of its educated and talented young population, emigration within and outside Africa brings tangible benefits. It is thought to enhance knowledge transfer and cultural exchange, especially in music and arts, as well as increases education and skills acquisition across the continent.[40] Also, against the excessive and extortionist transfer fees charged by money transfer agents, migrants outside Africa often repatriate a sizeable percentage of their earnings through remittances back home. As discussed in Chapter 1, migrants' remittances in most African countries, as a share of external income, are several times more than development aid from donor countries and foreign investments. In most cases, migrants' remittances are much better spent than foreign aid.

This is because remittances tend to go directly to migrants' families and friends who use them to supplement household income, support business and improve their

---

[39]Abebe (2010)
[40]Smith (2019)

housing. Also, Africans who are exposed to global best practices and who have a diasporic orientation tend to have and exhibit increased sense of civic duty; therefore, they are much more willing to share and exchange knowledge of such practices. Through their experiences, for instance, they influence business and innovation in their countries of origin,[41] promote and influence the democratic process and tolerance through support for political opposition.[42] Although these experiences provide the region with social and economic benefits, they however raise a spectre of a 'brain gain'.

Despite the spillovers, the combined human capital and economic costs of emigration and brain drain to Africa remain significantly huge by comparison. The reasons for the unusually high rate of youth emigration and brain drain go further than mere economic hardship and disaffection with the political class. They stem from long-standing social, economic and political marginalisation, which can only be resolved through young people's increased participation in political leadership. Young people must be empowered and encouraged with access to mainstream political platforms to help shape policies that affect their future. It is only through active political participation can they develop a strong sense of belonging, and ultimately see themselves as the 'change agents' – thereby curtailing the incidence of brain drain and its debilitating effect on the region.

4.8 COST OF BRAIN DRAIN

Brain drain is the net negative socioeconomic effect of emigration of highly trained and qualified young Africans to other parts of the world. This human capital flight phenomenon is more prevalent and not new to SSA. It began as far back as the 1960s when majority of Africans were awarded scholarships to study abroad, mostly in former colonies as part of the nationalist campaign to train high calibre Africans that would help to deliver the promises of a free, independent and prosperous Africa. It followed an unproven logic that the wider global migration movement was temporary, at least in intention.

However, it was not until the 1980s when the post-independent euphoria and promise of a better life gave way to disillusionment, amid political instability and conflicts, that most African students abroad abandoned the idea of returning home.[43] Also, frightened and discouraged by the political, social and economic upheavals back home, and propelled by the forces of globalisation, which forced open the global job market – thus, resulting in greater international mobility, most African students abandoned their nationalist sentiments and enrolled into courses that allowed them to compete in various professions in health, finance and technology in countries abroad in which they have studied.

This phenomenon has continued well into the twentieth and twenty-first centuries, thereby prompting many former colonies that make up the OECD countries to impose

---

[41]Chand (2016)
[42]Beyene (2014)
[43]Ngwé (2019)

stricter immigration controls that are disproportionately biased against many African countries. By 2016, an IMF migration report had estimated that 'migrants from SSA in OECD countries could reach about 34 million by 2050'. It also concluded that 'the migration of young and educated workers from SSA takes a large toll on a region whose human capital is already scarce'. By its very complexion, brain drain impedes the prospect of realising the demographic dividend, thereby limiting the chances of achieving inclusive growth in Africa. It also causes considerable social and economic damage in terms of human capital flight and loss of work-force productivity.

As such, brain drain poses a serious threat to Africa's potential as a future economic force and global competitiveness. Because brain drain grows out of other social, economic and political problems that lead to forced migration, it is hidden away and rarely ever the focus of public policy priority in Africa. More than any other race, talented Africans who are immigrants in all kinds of enviable professions including academia, medicine, arts, science and engineering in OECD countries are immeasurable. It will require many more years of reversal, if at all possible, to regain the loss of these tangible assets and the attendant human capital cost which Africa has suffered as a consequence of the mass emigration abroad of its mostly young and talented citizens.

For instance, an estimated 400,000 Africans currently study at various universities outside Africa. This is equivalent to about a tenth of all foreign students globally, about as many as India today, and about the same number of Chinese students that studied abroad in 2005.[44] Indeed, majority of Chinese, and to some extent Indian students, tend to return home after their study abroad. Unlike African students, majority prefer to either seek other means of settling in countries in which they have studied or migrating to countries other than in Africa. This phenomenon comes at a huge cost to the region. Also, analysis of publicly available data shows that the human capital cost of qualified medical practitioners alone emigrating from Africa including Ethiopia, Kenya, Malawi, South Africa, Uganda, Tanzania, Zambia and Zimbabwe to Europe and North America was $2.17 billion as of 2011.

On the contrary, the financial savings and benefits including from not having trained the recruited these qualified and trained medical practitioners from Africa to the destination countries, such as Australia, Canada, the United Kingdom, and the United States, were estimated at $2.7 billion in the same year.[45]

Based on this, if one were to compute a roughly conservative cumulative human capital loss over a nine-year period from 2011 to 2020, then the loss in financial asset to these African countries will probably more than quadruple to more than $19.5 billion.

Equally, the same destination countries in Europe and North America may have probably gained roughly similar, if not more, in financial savings and benefit over the same period. If the total contributions including productivity, taxation and consumption of goods and services by each qualified medical practitioner were to be computed over the same period, then the cumulative financial and non-financial gain to these destination countries would be far more significant. Whether these estimated losses and gains are accurate or not is beside the point. On average, about

---

[44]The Economist (2020)
[45]Mwang'ombe (2017)

$30,000 if not more is believed to be lost for each medical school graduate that emigrates from SSA to either Europe or North America.[46]

Even if one were to disregard these financial losses, the socioeconomic loss to Africa in human capital terms is still immeasurable. Because those who are forced to emigrate are usually young people, some with children of school age, the health, education and the psychological outcomes for those children who stay or are left behind due to parental emigration may never be accurately measured or yet even known. Parental migration leads to fragility or disintegration of the family unit, which is a crucial stabilising force in the formative stages of a child's development.[47] Thus, regardless of the stability of the care arrangements with trusted family relatives, unstable family units due to parental emigration often result in overall poorer well-being and out-comes for the children, which hamper their ability to thrive and make meaningful contribution to the society as adults.[48]

4.9 ROADMAP FOR DEMOGRAPHIC DIVIDEND

It is not unusual to find a plethora of competing programmes targeting young people in Africa. However, the main concern relates to why such programmes have not yet addressed the problem of young people's marginalisation in education, employment and healthcare. Apart from lack of joined up thinking and collaboration among the relevant stakeholders, there is a lack of cooperative effort and better use of resources and synergies among competing stakeholders, including governments, policymakers, development partners, educators, and even the private sector and their representa-tives. Consequently, the benefits of such programmes have not been widely felt as envisaged. If anything, their impact on young people has been marginal and uneven.

Also, because such programmes have not been co-created with young people and youth representative organisations, they are rarely aligned with young people's immediate needs and priorities. Coupled with this is the lack of stakeholder collab-oration in policy formulation, programme design and implementation, which presents a serious barrier to the prospect of achieving demographic dividend. Notwithstanding these challenges, there are strong prospects for achieving a demographic dividend. To achieve demographic dividend, the diverse often disparate socioeconomic pro-grammes that exist to support young Africans will need to be harmonised and inte-grated into a more coherent policy framework across the region. What is required is strong commitment to investing in and engaging with young people in a much more meaningful way than has ever been done.

As such, rather than the lopsided approach to engaging with young people, there is a need for a more inclusive approach that seeks to put young people at the heart of programme design and leadership based on collaboration, knowledge exchange and partnership. An inclusive approach that integrates young people's ideas, creativity and leadership with planning, policymaking and implementation is more likely to instil in

---

[46]*Op. Cit.*
[47]Caarls et al. (2018)
[48]Mazzucato et al. (2015)

young people a greater sense of belonging and responsibility, thereby leading to better and beneficial outcomes for all stakeholders. Thus, from a policy standpoint, the AU has set out four distinct but related strategies to encourage an inclusive approach to engaging Africa's youths.

Guided by *Agenda 2063* – Africa's transformation blueprint, and the United Nation's SDGs, the AU's flagship '1 Million by 2021 Initiative' provides a powerful platform for engaging more meaningfully with young people in four strategic areas of interventions, namely, 'Employment', 'Entrepreneurship', 'Education' and 'Engagement' (4Es). Launched in April 2019, the scheme seeks to promote African solutions and innovations, co-created with and driven by young people through building and strengthening the institutions and structures for effective stakeholder engagement. At the heart of this new 'pan-African' vision is an attempt to foster more effective collaboration with youths in accelerating the process of inclusive growth in Africa. By building on the African Youth Charter (AYC) established in July 2006, the aim of the 1 Million by 2021 Initiative is to offer a powerful continental platform to provide young people with direct opportunities to realise their dreams and thereby contribute to Africa's transformation agenda.

Embraced by the 55 member countries and organs of the AU, if correctly and fully implemented with all stakeholders on board, there is no doubt that the outcomes from these four intervention areas will ultimately translate into a demographic dividend. Therefore, in seeking to champion youth-led initiatives, African governments and their development partners must look to this new approach by working more collaboratively with young people including with organisations and groups that represent their interest.

There are several ways in which to engage young Africans guided by these four strategies, thereby helping to achieve demographic dividend. The focal point must be on participation and engagement by treating young people as cocreators and as the agency of development and implementation of novel solutions to Africa's social, political and economic challenges. As outlined in Table 4.2, the overriding aim must be to support millions of young Africans with direct interventions in those 4Es priority areas through partnerships. However, to ensure that the 4Es pathways live up to young people's expectation, it is important that their ideas are always nurtured and supported through an approach that recognises the importance of their input in driving the partnership.

Although some may view these four key priority themes as common, and even overused, it would be misjudged to dismiss too quickly the contrary evidence that shows young people view them as a profoundly significant way to work with others to achieve their personal and professional aspirations in the twenty-first century. To test the importance and efficacy of the 4Es, 400 young people from different walks of life across Africa, including those in education and employment, were invited and split into small focus groups over 2 days tasked with developing scalable ideas within the 4Es framework.

Prospectively, participants were tasked with weighing the ideas proposed as solutions to the 4Es pathways against the gains, drawbacks and regional experiences of other well-known continent-wide youth development programmes in their own countries. Emerging from the focus group was a firm belief and consensus that the 4Es pathways captured what young people value today to achieve personal growth, economic well-being and consequently ensure the political stability of their communities. By bringing young people

TABLE 4.2 One million by 2021 initiative

Thematic areas	Solutions pathways
Education	• **Scholarships:** Provide scholarship opportunities to young people especially young women at all levels of education (i.e. secondary, post-secondary, TVET) • **Alternative pathways:** Provide alternative education pathways including remote learning resources and tools for skills development and to help young people to access training through alternative delivery options • **Models for teacher development:** Establish a Teachers Without Borders programme to address quality of delivery and availability. Deploy teachers across the continent under this new model
Entrepreneurship	• **Growth capital:** Mobilise and catalyse capital to allow youth-led companies to grow, achieve economies of scale and move into underserved markets • **Nurture start-ups:** Provide scale-up opportunities including physical and virtual mentorship initiatives for young entrepreneurs; entrepreneurial and business development education delivered within a network of in-person and virtual and incubation spaces, formalise businesses and create access to online knowledge hubs for young entrepreneurs
Employment	• **Internship and apprenticeships:** Provide new professional internships and new apprenticeship programmes to ensure young people are able to contextualise learning to the world of work • **Job centres:** Establish physical and virtual job preparedness and matching services to connect at young people to available job opportunities • **Digital skills:** Develop a digital skills programme to prepare young people for new skills that enable them to be globally competitive and access roles outside their traditional geographical areas
Engagement	• **Leadership programmes:** Identify virtual and physical leaders to coach, nurture and continuously mentor emerging leaders • **Exchange programmes:** Facilitate the promotion of physical and virtual exchange of young Africans and with the rest of the world leveraging extra-curricular opportunities including in sports and the creative sectors • **Forums:** Establish a framework for youth consultation including an annual consultative forum and regional consultations to reach young people • **Youth engagement:** Develop a youth engagement mechanism to engage with at least 1 million unique young Africans

Source: AUC '1 Million by 2021 Initiative' Communications Toolkit, April 2019.

together in a co-creation approach to test the relevance and efficacy of the 4Es, the aim was to demonstrate that their ideas were valued and respected.

From their views, it emerged, for instance, that education must be equitable, accessible, affordable and above all relevant to the changing and new realities of the workplace in a globalised knowledge economy. Thus, by integrating young people's education with work-based schemes, such as internships and apprenticeships, digital skills, financial support youth-led start-ups, there is no doubt that young Africans will begin to enjoy and value the potential positive impact their educational experience will have on their future career. Of course, for stakeholders seeking to embrace this new approach, the main question is how to effectively use the 4Es platform to alter life chances for young Africans, thereby make Africa work better for young people, and consequently for the region.

4.10 MAKING AFRICA WORK FOR YOUNG PEOPLE

To help forge a new path with young Africans in a much more inclusive and meaningful manner, what is needed is a strategic alignment among all development stakeholders, coupled with structural transformation. Strategic alignment is vital to help pave the way for better contextualisation, harmonisation and streamlining of ideas and efforts devoted to improving social and economic conditions for young people. It will also help to promote a better understanding and proactive response to young people's needs in a much more concrete way than ever before, thereby helping to achieve greater synergy and impact. Achieve this entails a new way of thinking, as well as a new approach to policy formulation, programme design and implementation.

It is therefore crucial that planning, policy, resourcing and support for youth-driven programmes enjoy the flexibility, collaboration and the support of all stakeholders with young people at the heart of leadership and implementation. Within this, the broader goal and emphasis must be on enabling the conditions that encourage human capital development and youth entrepreneurship. As shown in Chapter 6, from education, training and employability skills perspectives, this can be achieved through investment in programmes that support learning-by-doing strategies and human capital development. High human capital is pivotal to the economic prosperity and stability enjoyed by many emerging and industrialised economies of the global North. Thus, investment in human capital is key to supporting young people to enable them to make a seamless school-to-work transition and raise their productivity. This will have a multiplier effect on other social and economic ladders for the benefit of the wider society.

As such, investment in human capital must be prioritised if Africa is to enjoy demographic dividend, and through that build the social and economic planks for sustainable development. As discussed in the next chapter, high levels of educational attainment and training coupled with experience and practical skills are essential to young people's employability skills, productivity and will lead to overall societal well-being. Productivity has been linked to high income, economic growth and sustainable development, which in turn raises national competitiveness.[49] Besides, increased human capital investment, particularly in health and education sectors, is likely to increase Africa's GDP per capita. Conclusive evidence supports the notion that increased aggregate labour productivity is correlated with a predominantly young demographic workforce.[50]

Also, labour productivity is found to be a key driver of economic growth and changes in living standards, as well as of international competitiveness, measured primarily by GDP per capita.[51] Through education, training and skills acquisition,

---

[49]Hunt (2000)
[50]Feyrer (2007)
[51]OECD (2013)

human capital helps to improve individual's productivity, which in turn boosts income and leads to better health outcomes. Better income and good health both have a net positive effect on living standards, which leads to wider societal growth.

Thus, education, training and skills are the components of human capital that influence young people's ability to support themselves and contribute to economic growth. Since education and training are not learning *per se*, practice and experience acquired through 'learning-by-doing' becomes a more effective and meaningful strategy needed to make education and training pay off for young people, thereby helping to transform their lives. Learning-by-doing or work-based learning enables learning to occur at the same time as developing specific work-based problem-solving skills and techniques needed to survive in a knowledge-based economy.[52] Thus, based on empirical observations as summarised in Table 4.3, if Africa is to work better for young people, then all stakeholders must embrace the 4Es as basis of action by prioritising the following:

- Increase opportunities for education and training through widening participation and access to scholarships, particularly in STEM subjects for young women. Ensure there is equitable access that addresses the educational and training needs of female and rural populations. Improve education quality and ensure education provision and outcomes are relevant to labour market needs. To achieve this, there is a need to create the incentives for academic-industry collaboration. Investment in non-traditional methods of teaching and learning (e.g. 'open spaces for informal learning, mentoring and creativity') for increased access and affordability of education and training. Support strategies and programmes that seek to introduce and adopt a learner-centred approach to education provision, de-emphasise rote learning and institutionalise entrepreneurship education programmes across the education value chain.
- Promote and support confidence-building educational programmes targeting nascent or student entrepreneurs, as well as the disabled and young women entrepreneurs.
- Encourage intra-Africa academic mobility by investing in the development and implementation of a Credit Transfer System.
- Programmes that help young people to acquire a combination of soft, digital and vocational skills, as well as investment in upskilling and reskilling are vital to improve productivity and secure sustainable livelihoods in a knowledge economy. In collaboration with youth representative organisations, work with educators and the private sector to devise frameworks for increasing and diversifying the uptake of internships and apprenticeship programmes across Africa. Although internships and apprenticeships deliver great benefits to both the employer and the trainee, they differ in duration, design and outcomes. Apprenticeship usually lasts between 12 months and 48 months depending on the provider and the nature of the programme, ultimately leading to a recognised formal qualification and pay. Whereas for employers that offer internship schemes or work placements, the main goal is to provide work-based training without pay, which usually lasts between 4 months and 12 months. Also, the development and accelerated use of

---

[52]Anzai & Simon (1979)

TABLE 4.3 Ecosystem-based framework for youth empowerment in Africa

Programmes	Barriers	Actions and recommendations
Education and Skills Development	Access	• Increase education access through widening access to scholarships. STEM subjects, female and rural population may be prioritised
	Quality	• Improve education quality through development and review of curricula and pedagogies in collaboration with employers of labour
	Relevance	• Provide incentives for education providers and private sector to make secondary and higher education relevant to labour market needs/challenges
	Human capacity and delivery modes	• Invest in alternative education models that embrace non-traditional teaching pathways, e.g. teachers without borders, encourage open spaces, mentoring and experiential learning tracks
	Linkage with private sector and lack of academic mobility	• Support educational strategies that institutionalise entrepreneurship education, deemphasise rote learning and elevate learner-centred approach to education provision
		• Invest in a continental credit transfer programme, e.g. Credit Accumulation and Transfer Scheme (CATS/ECTS) to encourage intra-Africa academic mobility
Youth Entrepreneurship	Financing/capitalisation	• Provide incentives to scale-up and nurture youth-owned businesses through start-up grants, continued financing for incubation of start-ups and facilitate links to investors
	Networks and mentorships	• Support alternative mechanisms for financing youth start-ups (e.g. crowdfunding) and sustainability, e.g. mentoring and networking throughout the incubation lifecycle
	Business knowledge/skills gap	
	Infrastructure	
	Corruption, regulation and gender bias	

		• Support educational schemes that adequately prepare youths for successful career in entrepreneurship through investments in campus innovation/entrepreneurship hubs
		• Jointly with the private sector, recognise and support policy and youth efforts that encourage rural enterprise (e.g. in agribusiness sector) and transition from informal to formal enterprise
		• Encourage and recognise efforts to build reliable and stable infrastructure including power and renewable energy, market access, communication and transport systems needed to catalyse and sustain youth entrepreneurship
		• In partnership with governments, encourage policies that foster conducive ecosystem for youth entrepreneurship through ease of business registration, standardised tax system and minimal 'red tape' for youth start-ups
		• Support confidence-building programmes targeting women entrepreneurs' through networking and mentorship
Employment & Career Development	Skills mismatch	• Establish joint formats for education provision with the private sector through employer-informed curricula, apprenticeships, internships and knowledge transfer partnerships
	Employability skills	• Establish frameworks with education providers and private sector for career centres and commercialisation of knowledge/research, e.g. technology transfer offices
	Lack of pathways for knowledge and research commercialisation	• Support programmes that create mechanisms for youths in low employment to upskill, reskill and acquire leadership and soft skills for carer progression
	Underemployment	

(Continued)

TABLE 4.3 Ecosystem-based framework for youth empowerment in Africa (Continued)

Programmes	Barriers	Actions and recommendations
		• Support and promote digital literacy and inclusion of digital skills in youth training and education • Invest and promote initiatives that educate youths for a career in self-employment through vocational education, e.g. TVET
Youth Engagement	Coordinated youth forum at continental level Impact monitoring and evaluation	• Institutionalise ACJs as the continental platform for peer-to-peer youth engagement and with key stakeholders including African diaspora with shared interest in youth-oriented enterprise • Invest in a framework that tracks progress in youth-led initiatives – the mechanisms to effectuate this will vary from region to region and from country to country

credit-bearing apprenticeship programmes as part of higher education offering may help to increase uptake among young people.

- Establish policy formats and guidelines for public–private partnership in higher education provision through employer-informed curricula structure and knowledge transfer partnership. This will enhance young people's employability skills.
- Facilitate the commercialisation of knowledge, research and other intellectual assets through investment in business incubators, campus innovation hubs, entrepreneurship centres and technology transfer offices to support students' start-ups. With a few exceptions, these facilities are either partially present, or completely lacking in Africa's higher education sector.
- Work with the private sector to provide and create seamless opportunities to scale up youth-led start-ups through business accelerator programmes, start-up grants as well as increase access to investors and markets.
- Within these, the scaling of youth start-ups in the rural agro-business sector, start-ups that seek to transition from an informal to a formal enterprise should be prioritised. In addition, or alternatively, develop appropriate structures and support mechanisms to ensure that the informal sector is fit for purpose in a way that encourages operators to fulfil their civic duties through contribution to an efficient and effective taxation system.
- In partnership with government and other support agencies, encourage policies and support programmes that foster a conducive youth start-ups ecosystem through infrastructural development and regulatory mechanisms that incentivise and encourage the formation and sustainability of youth-led ventures, reduction in 'red tape' and ease of business registration.
- Introducing capacity-building strategies and models to enable higher education sector to drive Africa's entrepreneurship and innovation ecosystem will be vital to success in supporting student-led start-ups. Alongside these interventions must be an emphasis on educating and training young Africans to be fully prepared to embrace the opportunities offered by the knowledge economy

4.11 EDUCATING YOUTHS FOR THE KNOWLEDGE ECONOMY

The knowledge economy requires both employability skills that can be acquired through work-based learning and transferable from one work context to another. Work-based learning relates to all forms of education, training and learning, both at the beginning and continuous, that occurs in a real work environment and not just in a classroom setting. Work-based learning has a direct beneficial relationship for the learner and the employer. The latter benefits from the learner's productivity and creativity, and the learner in turn benefits from work-based related training and skills acquisition, increased prospect of a job offer and a smooth school-to-work transition.

Also, there is a growing shift in thinking across the world towards combining classroom-based education with work-based learning. This entails not just embracing university or college credentials and certification, but also ensuring there is a fit between the skills possessed by an individual and the skills required to do a job effectively. Given the fast-changing labour market needs of the knowledge economy, it is more than likely that work-based skills – and not merely university or college degrees and certificates, which hitherto served as the 'professional passports' that paved the way for the rest of our working lives – will increasingly define and shape the future of work. In recent years, many well-known global companies including Google, Facebook and International Business Machines Corporation (IBM) are demanding more than an education certificate. They are fast embracing the employability needs of the knowledge economy by recruiting candidates with work-based skills and through increased investment in continuous learning for their workforce.[53]

Work-based learning can provide young Africans with the skills they need to obtain, keep and succeed in employment in a knowledge economy. Work-based learning can be particularly effective when integrated into an education and training systems that combine classroom and workplace learning. In different parts of the world including in many OECD countries, such as the United Kingdom and Germany, work-based learning occurs in form of formal, structured and certified apprenticeship programmes. These programmes offer young people the security and stability of 'on-the-job' and 'off-the-job' training in a technical and vocational education and training (TVET) settings, supported by the government, the employer and the learner. This tripartite arrangement ensures that there is a synergy between the demand in the labour market and the skills acquired by the learner.

However, in Africa, the situation is somewhat different. Many young people rarely benefit from the security and stability of work-based training programmes. Most work-based learners tend to benefit from their employers in an informal way, often in an unstructured setting without formal contracts. In such settings, learning is episodic and often mixed with other unskilled tasks, such as domestic chores. Because of the poor quality of learning and training provision, the skills acquired can quickly become depleted and outdated. This adverse situation, coupled with limited work-based training providers, also means that there is no clear direct relationship between work-based learning programmes, the skills of the learner, the needs of the employer and the economic priorities of the government as determined by labour market needs.

Consequently, it is unclear how to reward the knowledge, creativity and productivity of work-based learners or even assess the relevance of their skills against labour market needs. In addition, the difficulty in career progression or smooth school-to-work transition for work-based learners feeds into the public misperceptions and negative attitudes towards work-based learning programmes, such as TVET.[54] As a result, young people with only work-based learning have a hard time justifying the relevance of their skills to an employer and the wider society. Thus, they tend to face a greater risk of job loss in the labour market than those with university education.

In conclusion, implementing these policy priorities is by no means an easy process. But by always valuing and nurturing young people's ideas through creating the social, economic and the political conditions that foster trust and cooperation, success can be achieved. This entails that all stakeholders including governments, policy makers and development partners must begin to recognise that young Africans are the architects of

---

[53]Kumar & George (2020)
[54]Amedorme & Fiagbe (2013)

their own future. They have desires and aspirations far greater in scope than obtaining mere certificates education and training. They desire to acquire quality education and training that provide them with access to sustainable livelihoods to enable them make a meaningful contribution to their communities as well as shape their future through political representation and leadership. Hence, the emphasis must shift towards ensuring that education and training deliver to young people the employability skills and livelihood options they need to survive in a fast-globalising world.

BIBLIOGRAPHY

Abebe, S. (2010). *Migration patterns, trends and policy issues in Africa.* African Development Bank Working Paper Series No. 119. Abidjan: African Development Bank Group.

Adedeji, A. (2019). Accessing sub-Saharan African migrant group for public health interventions, promotion, and research: the 5-wave-approach. *Comparative Migration Studies,* 7(1).

African Union. (2020). *Impact of the coronavirus (COVID-19) on the African economy.* Retrieved from https://au.int/sites/default/files/documents/38326-doc-covid-19_impact_on_african_economy.pdf. Accessed on 8 July 2020.

Afrobarometer. (2017). *One-third of Nigerians – most of them young and educated – have considered emigrating, study shows.* Afrobarometer. Retrieved from http://afrobarometer.org/sites/default/files/press-release/Nigeria/nig_r7_pr2_youth_large_majority_of_potential_nigerian_emigrants_18122017_1.pdf. Accessed on 21 July 2020.

Amedorme, S. K., & Fiagbe, Y. A. (2013). Challenges facing technical and vocational education in Ghana. *International Journal of Scientific and Technology Research,* 2(6), 253–255.

Anosike, P. (2017). *Transforming Africa's socio-economic landscape through entrepreneurialism, Africa Policy Review Journal,* 2017/18 Special Report, London: Kempstone Media Retrieved from http://africapolicyreview.com/special-reports/

Anzai, Y., & Simon, H. A. (1979). The theory of learning by doing. *Psychological Review,* 86(2), 124–140.

Beyene, H. G. (2014). Are African diasporas development partners, peace-makers or spoilers? The case of Ethiopia, Kenya and Nigeria. *Diaspora Studies,* 8(2), 145–161.

Caarls, K., Haagsman, K., Kraus, E., & Mazzucato, V. (2018). African transnational families: Cross-country and gendered comparisons. *Population, Space and Place,* 24(7), 1–16.

Chand, M. (2016). Leveraging the diaspora for Africa's economic development. *Journal of African Business,* 17(3), 273–290.

Connor, P., Lopez, M., & Bell, J. (March 2018). *At least a million sub-Saharan Africans moved to Europe since 2010.* Pew Research Centre - Global Attitudes & Trends. Retrieved from https://www.pewresearch.org/global/2018/03/22/at-least-a-million-sub-saharan-africans-moved-to-europe-since-2010/. Accessed on 21 July 2020.

Connor, P. (August 2018). *Applications for U.S. diversity visa lottery remained near record in 2017.* Pew Research Centre. Retrieved from https://www.pewresearch.org/fact-tank/2018/08/23/applications-for-u-s-visa-lottery-more-than-doubled-since-2007/. Accessed on 21 July 2020.

Dews, F. (2019). *Charts of the week: Africa's changing demographics.* Brookings. Retrieved from https://www.brookings.edu/blog/brookings-now/2019/01/18/charts-of-the-week-africas-changing-demographics/. Accessed on 13 July 2020.

Felter, C. (2020). *Africa's leaders for life.* Council on Foreign Relations. Retrieved from https://www.cfr.org/backgrounder/africas-leaders-life. Accessed on 13 July 2020.

Feyrer, J. (2007). Demographics and productivity. *Review of Economics and Statistics,* 89(1), 100–109.

Filmer, D., & Fox, L. (2014). *Youth employment in Sub-Saharan Africa, Africa development series.* Washington, DC: World Bank.

Food and Agriculture Organisation and Economic Commission for Africa. (2018). *Africa: Regional overview of food security and nutrition. Addressing the threat from climate variability and extremes for food security and nutrition,* Retrieved from http://www.fao.org/3/CA2710EN/ca2710en.pdf. Accessed on 8 July 2020.

Gonzalez-Garcia, J., Hitaj, E., Mlachila, M., Viseth, A., & Yenice, M. (2016). *Sub-Saharan African migration: Patterns and spillovers. International monetary fund spillover taskforce,* Washington DC: IMF Publications.

Hunt, S. D. (2000). *A general theory of competition – resources, competences, productivity, economic growth.* Thousand Oaks, CA: SAGE.

International Labour Organisation. (2020). *COVID-19: Stimulating the economy and employment.* Retrieved from https://www.ilo.org/global/about-the-ilo/newsroom/news/WCMS_743036/lang–en/index.htm. Accessed on 8 July 2020.

International Labour Organisation. (2020). *Youth and COVID-19 impacts on jobs, education, rights and mental well-being.* Retrieved from https://www.ilo.org/wcmsp5/groups/public/—ed_emp/documents/publication/wcms_753026.pdf. Accessed on 9 September 2020.

International Labour Organisation. (2020). *Global employment trends for youth 2020 – technology and the future of jobs.* Geneva: International Labour Office.

International Organisation for Migration. (2020). *World migration report 2020.* Retrieved from https://publications.iom.int/system/files/pdf/wmr_2020.pdf. Accessed on 22 July 2020.

Jalata, A. (2017). The Oromo movement: The effects of state terrorism and globalisation in Oromia and Ethiopia. *Social Justice,* 44(4), 83–106.

Kah, H. (2019). 'Blood money', migrants' enslavement and insecurity in Africa's Sahel and Libya. *Africa Development,* 44(1), 25–44.

Kikuwa, D. (2015). *Africa is young. Why are its leaders so old?* Cable News Network. Retrieved from https://edition.cnn.com/2015/10/15/africa/africas-old-mens-club-op-ed-david-e-kiwuwa/index.html. Accessed on 13 July 2020.

Kumar, R., & George, S. (2020). *Why skills – not degrees – will shape the future of work.* World Economic Forum. Retrieved from https://www.weforum.org/agenda/2020/09/reckoning-for-skills/. Accessed on 29 September 2020.

May, J., & Turbat, V. (2017). The demographic dividend in sub-Saharan Africa: Two issues that need more attention. *Journal of Demographic Economics,* 83, 77–84.

Mazzucato, V., Cebotari, V., Veale, A., White, A., Grassi, M., & Vivet, J. (2015). International parental migration and the psychological well-being of children in Ghana, Nigeria and Angola. *Social Science and Medicine,* 132, 215–224.

Mbaku, J. M. (2020). *Threats to democracy in Africa: The rise of the constitutional coup, brookings, Africa in focus.* Retrieved from https://www.brookings.edu/blog/africa-in-focus/2020/10/30/threats-to-democracy-in-africa-the-rise-of-the-constitutional-coup/?utm_campaign=Brookings%20Brief&utm_medium=email&utm_content=99323007&utm_source=hs_email. Accessed on 30 October 2020.

McGowan, P. J. (2003). African military coups d'état, 1956-2001: Frequency, trends and distribution. *Journal of Modern African Studies,* 41(3), 339–370.

Mo Ibrahim Foundation. (2019). *Africa's youth: Jobs or migration? Demography, economic prospects and mobility.* 2019 Ibrahim Forum Report. Retrieved from https://mo.ibrahim.foundation/sites/default/files/2020-01/2019_Forum_Report_2.pdf. Accessed on 22 July 2020.

Mwang'ombe, N. (2017). The African health workforce brain drain. The socioeconomic and geopolitical realities. *Scifed Journal of Surgery,* 1(1), 1–3.

Ngwé, L. (2019). *African brain drain: Is there an alternative?* The UNESCO Courier. ISSN 2220-2269. Retrieved from https://en.unesco.org/courier/january-march-2018/african-brain-drain-there-alternative. Accessed on 29 September 2020.

Organisation for Economic Cooperation and Development. (2013). *GDP per capita and productivity growth.* Retrieved from https://www.oecd-ilibrary.org/employment/data/oecd-productivity-statistics/gdp-per-capita-and-productivity-growth_data-00685-en. Accessed on 5 August 2020.

Population Reference Bureau. (2017). *PRB projects 2050 world population at 9.8 billion*. Retrieved from https://www.prnewswire.com/news-releases/prb-projects-2050-world-population-at-98-billion-300504448.html. Accessed on 20 December 2019.

Saleh, H. (2010). High unemployment sparks Tunisian riots. *Financial Times*. Retrieved from https://www.ft.com/content/0249621c-0d1f-11e0-82ff-00144feabdc0. Accessed on 18 June 2020.

Signe, L. (2019). *Africa youth leadership: Building local leaders to solve global challenges*. Brookings. Retrieved from https://www.brookings.edu/blog/africa-in-focus/2019/03/27/africa-youth-leadership-building-local-leaders-to-solve-global-challenges/. Accessed on 13 July 2020.

Smith, S. (2019). *The scramble for Europe – Young Africa on its way to the old continent*. Cambridge: Polity Press.

The Economist. (2020). *Migration is helping Africa in many ways*. Retrieved from https://www.economist.com/special-report/2020/03/26/migration-is-helping-africa-in-many-ways. Accessed on 17 July 2020.

Turbat, V. (2017). The demographic dividend: A potential surplus generated by a demographic transition. In: H. Groth & J. May (Eds.), *Africa's population: In search of demographic dividend*, (pp. 181–195). Cham, Switzerland: Springer International Publishing.

Udal, H. (2006). A clash of generations? Youth bulges and political violence. *International Studies Quarterly*, 50(3), 607–629.

United Nations. (2018). *Ethiopia's progress towards eradicating poverty*. Retrieved from https://www.un.org/development/desa/dspd/wp-content/uploads/sites/22/2018/04/Ethiopia's-Progress-Towards-Eradicating-Poverty.pdf. Accessed on 15 July 2020.

United Nations Department of Economic and Social Affairs. (2018). *World youth report – youth and the 2030 agenda for sustainable development*. New York, NY: United Nations Publication.

United Nations Department of Economic and Social Affairs. (2020). *Protecting and mobilising the youths in COVID-19 responses*. Retrieved from https://www.un.org/development/desa/youth/news/2020/05/covid-19/. Accessed on 8 July 2020.

United Nations Educational Scientific and Cultural Organisation. (2020). *Startling digital divides in distance learning emerge*. Retrieved from https://en.unesco.org/news/startling-digital-divides-distance-learning-emerge. Accessed on 8 July 2020.

United Nations Population Fund. (2014). *The power of 1.8 billion adolescents, youth and the transformation of the future*. Retrieved from https://www.unfpa.org/sites/default/files/pub-pdf/EN-SWOP14-Report_FINAL-web.pdf. Accessed on 13 June 2020.

United Nations Women. (2018). *Facts and figures: Economic empowerment – benefits of economic empowerment*. Retrieved from https://www.unwomen.org/en/what-we-do/economic-empowerment/facts-and-figures. Accessed on 8 July 2020.

United Nations Women. (2020). *Violence against women and girls: The shadow pandemic*. Retrieved from https://www.unwomen.org/-/media/headquarters/attachments/sections/library/publications/2020/issue-brief-covid-19-and-ending-violence-against-women-and-girls-en.pdf?la=en&vs=5006. Accessed on 8 July 2020.

Vollset, S., Goren, E., Yuan, C. W., Cao, J., Smith, A. E., Hsiao, T. ... Murray, C. J. L. (2020). Fertility, mortality, migration and population scenarios for 195 countries and territories from 2017 to 2100: A forecasting analysis for the Global Burden of Diseases Study. *The Lancet*, 396, 1285–1306. Online First. Retrieved from https://www.thelancet.com/pdfs/journals/lancet/PIIS0140-6736(20)30677-2.pdf. Accessed on 15 July 2020.

World Bank. (2015). *Demographic transition: dividend or disaster? Africa Development Forum*. Washington, DC: The World Bank Group.

World Health Organisation. (2020). *COVID-19 could deepen food insecurity, malnutrition in Africa*. Retrieved from https://www.afro.who.int/news/covid-19-could-deepen-food-insecurity-malnutrition-africa. Accessed on 8 July 2020.

YOUTH EMPLOYABILITY

5

Globalisation and technological advancements, coupled with the economic fallout of the COVID-19 pandemic, have dramatically altered the way in which work is organised and done in organisations. As a result, how organisations behave, where work is done, whether remotely or onsite, who can do it and under what conditions have been affected in varied and significant ways. These changes have implications for job security, the quality and stability of jobs, the kind of education and training as well as the types of skills needed to work effectively in an increasingly interconnected workplace. Also, the changes have not only dislocated traditional employment patterns and created new job opportunities, but they have challenged the modernist job-for-life argument of the Third Industrial Revolution, thereby paved the way for the emergence of the knowledge economy.[1]

Notably, with the disappearance of job-for-life comes an increased risk of excluding certain workforce population groups, while simultaneously expanding employment opportunities for others who may be more responsive to labour market needs of the knowledge economy. Importantly, without the relevant skills and the ability to adapt to these changes, individuals are faced with either long-term unemployment or the prospect of a low pay in an unstable work. Thus, to make employment more inclusive and boost labour market productivity, there is a need to increase workforce employability through flexible vocational education and innovative work-based training systems that foster transferable skills and the adoption of new technologies.[2]

Africa's demographic position as the continent with the youngest population offers the opportunity and unrivaled advantage to increase the employability skills and productivity of its workforce population, champion innovation and thereby enable the region to enjoy the socioeconomic benefits that come with a young and highly skilled workforce. A young and highly skilled workforce can provide a unique opportunity to enjoy a greater share of the benefits of the knowledge economy. This is achievable through the provision of quality education and acquisition of work-based skills, labour productivity, savings and investments, all of which can lead to shared economic prosperity. Unfortunately, apart from having the least skilled workforce globally, Africa faces the dire situation of a mismatch between the skills attainment of its highly educated and trained youths and the skills needed to access and succeed in employment in a globalised knowledge economy.

[1]McQuaid and Lindsay (2005, p. 203)
[2]OECD (2016)

Also, with the region off-track in meeting its education and skills revolution aspiration under AU's Agenda 2063, and with majority of its young population struggling to obtain employment with decent income, there is a real danger that a significant percentage of Africa's working age and youth population may be unproductive and consequently condemned to a lifetime of unemployment and poverty. Because of this, it is vital to empower the growing youth population in Africa with the correct employability skills to thrive and access livelihood opportunities in today's highly competitive and globalised knowledge economy.

5.1 EMPLOYABILITY SKILLS AND LIVELIHOOD

Seen as 'the ability to obtain and maintain a paid job – salaried or unsalaried, employability is associated with identifying the problems and priorities of persons and institutions involved in the access to work and employment'.[3] It is an agenda that activates and justifies employment expenditures based on promoting education and training opportunities as well as targeted incentives that are aimed at 'putting the unemployed back into work'. More than just a fixed socioeconomic agenda, the composition and applicability of employability varies widely according to a set of social and economic norms, as well as the socioeconomic priorities of each country and region.

With the increasing disappearance of job-for-life, triggered by the shift from manufacturing to service economy, the concept of employability has assumed a variety of meaning depending on the nature of economic development and progress within each country. From a higher education standpoint, employability has been considered as 'a set of achievements – skills, understanding and personal attributes – that make graduates more likely to gain employment and be successful in their chosen occupations, which benefits themselves, the workforce, the community and the economy'.[4] Analysis of the employability literature points towards several competing versions of the concept, namely 'dichotomic employability' and 'labour-market performance employability', 'initiative employability' and 'interactive employability'.[5]

Common among these are initiative and interactive employability, which are used by most governments to characterise and justify employability policies. Initiative employability recognises that an individual has the responsibility to acquire the human capital, that is, knowledge and productive skills, and the learning ability which are considered necessary to strengthen his or her position in the labour market. It favours the entrepreneurial model, whereby the most employable person is encouraged to use his or her skills and connections to either obtain or create employment.

Similarly, interactive employability emphasises human capital and individual responsibility, but further recognises that an individual's employability is based on personal skills, characteristics and competencies relative to the employability of others and labour market dynamics including opportunities, what employers seek and the institutional rules that govern the labour market. As a central feature of the labour market, employability plays an important role in determining the education and

[3]Gazier (2001, p. 5)
[4]Yorke (2006, p. 8)
[5]Gazier (2001)

training strategies including the skills, attitudes and competences (the *supply side*) that employers (the *demand side*) believe are necessary to ensure and preserve employees' productive capacities and performance throughout their working lives.

Emerging from these perspectives is the importance of continuous education and training through lifelong learning. Lifelong learning is more than just a second-chance education and training for adults. It provides individuals, whether young or old, with the opportunity to acquire the relevant employability skills needed to obtain and survive in a gainful employment. It encompasses the idea that individuals, regardless of age and background, should be 'motivated and actively encouraged to learn in all kinds of settings – formally, in schools, vocational, tertiary and adult education institutions; and non-formally at home, at work and in the community – throughout life'.[6] Thus, references to employability skills should not be limited to the implicit assumptions that these are skills limited to, or needed by only young people or graduates.

Thus, from a lifelong learning viewpoint, employability may be regarded as 'the capacity to be productive, to be equipped with up-to-date skills and competences and to hold rewarding jobs throughout one's working life'.[7] The International Labour Organisation describes employability as the result of several factors including education and training access, which enable workers to obtain decent work, manage change, succeed in enterprise and adapt to the changing demands of the labour market. Beyond access to education and training, there is a need to invest in the acquisition of core portable skills, such as teamwork, problem-solving, information and communications technology and language skills through continuous learning.[8]

As such, employability involves all actions taken to ensure that all those capable of working are encouraged to develop the relevant knowledge and skills to enable them to enter and remain in employment throughout their working lives.[9] From the viewpoint of knowledge economy, employability has implications for education and economic development. In particular, in relation to how learning and training are designed and provided as well as how governments respond to the employability needs of individuals and employers. For individuals, particularly young people and the less skilled, it means that they will have to learn, not just in formal and informal educational settings, but throughout their working lives under different learning conditions.

Similarly, employers will have to find more inclusive and stimulating ways of supporting workers who may have varying employability needs and circumstances. It means that to succeed in employment or self-employment, the knowledge acquired through education and training must always be relevant and the skills transferable. Thus, notions of employability have come to signal a shift towards a 'new work agenda' in which there is a strong relationship between education and the economy. This notion is rooted in the idea that work must enable people regardless of their background to achieve fulfilment and dignity in their profession by providing them with decent wages to help reduce inequality and poverty. This new work agenda recognises that all forms of education and training must at least serve the livelihood needs of learners, trainees and employers alike.

---

[6]OECD (1997a)
[7]McKenzie and Wurzburg (1997)
[8]Brewer (2013)
[9]McQuaid and Lindsay (2005, p. 199)

In other words, education and training interventions must be designed and delivered in innovative ways that ensure certain marginalised groups, particularly youths, do not face added hurdles (e.g. lack of relevant skills, discrimination) in the labour market. The goal ultimately must be to create the conditions under which opportunities for increased productivity in both employment and self-employment can thrive simultaneously, thereby spur economic prosperity and growth. In an effort to embrace this 'new work agenda', developed countries have adopted various policy norms to work with employers and job seekers to establish conditions that boost workforce productivity in a knowledge economy. In many OECD countries, education policies that focus on employability have prioritised investments in vocational education and training (VET).

The main goal is to upskill and reskill mostly young people and the long-term unemployed with an aim towards supporting them to enter and re-enter the labour market – either as fully employed or self-employed individuals. Wide public support for the shift in policy towards employability skills was prompted by a better understanding of the relationship between education and economic development. In the United Kingdom, for instance, the publication in the mid-1990s of the Dearing Report – which was an outcome of a major national enquiry into the future of higher education, led by Professor Ronald Dearing – increased public awareness of the relationship between education and the modern economy.

With several recommendations spanning funding, quality, maintenance of academic standards and expansion, the Dearing Report gave a much-needed momentum to the vital role of higher education in a globally competitive knowledge-based economy. Building on previous enquiries, such as *The Management of Higher Education in the Maintained Sector*,[10] Dearing's Report traces the long-standing relationship between higher education and economic development and asserts that 'education and training' are the human capital components that enable people in advanced societies to compete and thrive in a modern economy'.[11] Thus, in an attempt to reintegrate the long-term unemployed into the labour market, increase individual access to labour market opportunities and ultimately raise workforce productivity and people's income, the United Kingdom partnered with employers and employer representatives (e.g. Confederation of British Industry (CBI)) to determine the basis for reskilling and upskilling people through vocational training under the 'New Deal' initiative.[12] Significant investments in the New Deal programme are known to have helped to establish UK's global leadership position in the development and delivery of effective employability policies for human capital and workforce development.[13] Documented evidence has shown that the New Deal programme effectively supported many unemployed people to enter the workforce.

For instance, many young people were not only put on a staged progression route to finding and sustaining work under the New Deal for Young People (NDYP) programme, but also were offered additional support and protection through their Personal Advisers if they became unemployed.[14] But critics have argued that because United Kingdom's approach to employability skills development tended to prioritise support for those who

---

[10]Oakes (1978)
[11]Dearing (1997)
[12]Finn (1997)
[13]Lindsay et al. (2007)
[14]White (2000)

wished to enter the labour market as quickly as possible, there was always a danger that the long-term unemployed and the inactive labour force may be forced to accept low paid or ill-suited jobs,[15] thereby sacrificing the 'gainful employment with decent wage' mantra under the Sustainable Development Goals (SDGs) agenda.

The extent to which this supposedly 'quick fix' approach was a common phenomenon under the New Deal programme remains as yet unclear. However, by signalling that individual's employable skills are not merely the prerogative of labour market dynamics and that employers and governments indeed have a role to play, employability has evolved into a unifying concept through which to accelerate investment in human capital and enhance workforce productivity. The consensus seems to be that programmes like the 'New Deal' reflect greater government commitment towards human capital development (HCD) and a more inclusive approach to addressing the employability skills gaps. As such, the need to invest in employability skills by fostering conditions in Africa under which human capital can grow to support individuals and labour market productivity could not be more profound.

In debates about support for the unemployed and economically inactive people, analysts have suggested that there are differences between the 'New Deal' programme – where support tends to focus on short-term interventions that facilitate a quick return to work, and HCD – where support is more tailored towards personal development and acquisition of longer-term skills through education and training.[16] These differences clearly show that HCD, as part of a new long-term approach to building employability skills, recognises that individuals have the responsibility to take concrete actions towards obtaining and sustaining an employment, while also providing for a full range of structural measures that support people to improve their knowledge and skills, thereby increase their options and pathways to access and retention in work.[17]

Motivated by the New Deal initiative, particularly the prospect of improving people's knowledge and skills through investment in human capital and to repair their fractured economies, many developing countries including in Africa began to actively embrace the idea of VET as a 'go-to strategy' for producing highly skilled and productive workforce. Particularly, in an attempt to distinguish various education and training initiatives geared towards providing the unemployed with relevant skills to enter the labour market, labels, such as Education and Vocational Training (EVT), Technical and Vocational Skills Development (TVSD), Technical and Vocational Education (TVE) and Technical and Vocational Education and Training (TVET) were quickly adopted by these countries.

5.2 VET IN AFRICA, ORIGINS AND DEVELOPMENT

There is evidence to suggest that some form of vocational education and training (VET) has existed in Africa long before colonization. In pre-colonial Africa, the policy, systems and institutions of VET were either embedded in traditional craft and

---

[15]Dean (2003)
[16]Lindsay et al. (2007)
[17]Bernston et al. (2006)

artisanry or largely oriented towards skilled labour purely to facilitate the extractive activities of the colonialists.[18] Since then, VET has evolved alongside Africa's economic development needs, demographic shifts and labour market changes. As a long-term approach to investment in employability skills, VET intervention in Africa has undergone three important phases of development around the transition from colonialism to independence in the 1950s and 1960s.

Following independence, and with the era of Industrial Revolution receding, many African countries prioritised investment in vocational education and training to develop the local skills needed to usher in state formation and industrialisation in the region. But with many well-trained and skilled people unemployed in early post-independent era, critics began to advocate that what Africa needed was perhaps basic and general education and not vocational training. Many critics, including the World Bank, viewed vocational education as 'expensive' and 'inefficient'. However, many African leaders were adamant and felt that expanding general education might worsen the problem of unemployment among mainly educated professionals.

Notwithstanding, the World Bank and other international lending institutions, pushed ahead, rather controversially, with prioritising investment in general education through global initiatives like the 'Education for All' (EfA) and the Millennium Development Goals (MDGs) frameworks. These developments introduced and defined much of the second phase of VET development in Africa. Added to this was publication of the 'Vocational School Fallacy' by the influential education and development expert, Philip Foster. In development literature his publication marked a turning point in debates about the relevance of general education and vocational education as a way of unlocking Africa's emerging modern sector.

Drawing from his research on the effectiveness of the school system as a way to influence students' attitudes towards employment and self-employment in preindependence Ghana, Foster argued that vocational instruction in African schools was unlikely to have any determinative influence on the occupational aspirations and career destinations of students.[19] But several decades later, Foster's position was challenged as post-independent reforms in Ghana's school system were found to have had a 'substantial' positive influence on students' attitudes towards employment and self-employment.[20]

Besides dichotomising basic education and vocational training, the second phase witnessed an increased surge in public calls for more investment and structural transformation of the entire education sector. Under increased public pressure to reform the education sector, many African countries were forced to introduce new governance structures, which granted educational institutions autonomy, and the private sector more involvement in education and training provision.[21] However, a greater emphasis on VET only came into a sharper focus with the radical changes to the global economic system, coupled with technological advancements, which saw a dramatic shift from industrial manufacturing to knowledge-based services economies.

With these changes came increased demands for new ways of equipping young people and adults with vocational skills to enable them rise to the challenges of labour

[18]McGrath (2018)
[19]Foster (1965)
[20]King and Martin (2002)
[21]McGrath et al. (2019)

market demands in a globalised knowledge economy. These developments, which marked the beginning of the third phase of VET development, coincided with the launch of TVET in Africa. Many African governments view TVET potentially as a more effective strategy to provide particularly young people with practical skills needed to access and survive in employment. Since then, despite the introduction of a new vision under the SDG framework for transforming TVET, not much has changed in terms of VET-specific strategy across Africa.

The central idea of transforming TVET, mainly propagated by multilateral organisations, such as the World Bank and UNESCO, required an 'enlarged stakeholder involvement that brings the relevant actors, such as Ministries of Education, workers' associations, civil society and the private sector together in the planning, design, delivery and governance of TVET'.[22] To a great extent, enlarged stakeholder involvement reflects the current public thinking and understating across the world of how TVET should work in reality. Nevertheless, the need to transform the current TVET strategy across Africa has been overshadowed by the dichotomy over whether to prioritise investment in general education or in VET-related programmes, with many African countries deeply confused about how best to address the dilemma. The confusion, perhaps, stems from the fact that the underlying rationale and direction of the new vision of VET were in favour of the economic dynamics and needs that have their origins in a Western context rather than in Africa.

However, today TVET broadly refers to educational process that involves, in addition to general education, the study of technologies and related sciences and the acquisition of practical skills, attitudes, understanding and knowledge related to jobs in various sectors of the economy.[23] It is also involves 'aspects of education that are technical and vocational in nature, provided either in educational institutions or under their authority by public authorities, the private sector or through other forms of organised education, formal or non-formal, to ensure that all members of the community have access to the pathways of lifelong learning'.[24]

Across Africa, TVET is seen to hold the key to overcome youth unemployment, boost national productivity and realise demographic dividend in an increasingly globalised world.[25] The African Union (AUC) may have given momentum to the significance of TVET through one of its former Commissioners, Dr. Martial De-Paul Ikounga, who once declared publicly: 'TVET was Africa's response to youth unemployment and the magic instrument that will convert African youths into entrepreneurs'. By implication, TVET covers all aspects of work-based VET and skills development from employability skills to self-employment as well as for reskilling and upskilling.[26] Despite this broad understanding, it would be misguided to expect TVET to solve many of Africa's unemployment and socioeconomic challenges. Yet, by investing and relying heavily on TVET to tackle their youth unemployment crisis, many African countries appear to be oblivious to the limitations of TVET as employment creation strategy.

---

[22]Ngcwangu (2015)
[23]UNESCO (2016)
[24]UNESCO/ILO (2003)
[25]Oketch (2017)
[26]Psacharopoulos (1997)

5.3 TVET IN AFRICA

The massive investment in TVET by many African governments has not been a complete failure. A few African countries in which TVET has been integrated into the wider general education strategy and operationalised correctly as a work-based skills acquisition initiative have seen some positive, although marginal, relationship between TVET and young people's occupational choices. Analysis of the World TVET database compiled by UNESCO and the International Centre for Technical and Vocational Education and Training (UNEVOC) showed that Botswana has had the most successful experience in Africa in terms of evidencing this positive relationship. Botswana has achieved this success by aligning its TVET strategy with its national general education system.

Influenced by the national qualifications framework of New Zealand, South Africa and the United Kingdom, Botswana has an established National Vocational Qualification Framework (BNVQF) through which it regulates and evaluates the delivery of all TVET programmes across the country. In addition, the Department of Technical and Vocational Education (DTVET) is the government body responsible for the provision and coordination of the country's TVET programmes. Under its National Policy on Vocational Education and Training (NPVET), supported by the Vocational Training Act and the Tertiary Education Act (2000), Botswana has more than 290 (2020 figures) registered TVET providers overseen by the Botswana Training Authority (BOTA).

By law, to have their programmes recognised under Botswana's NVQF, all TVET providers must apply and be accredited by BOTA. This centralised governance structure is instrumental to ensuring that all students taking the compulsory practical subjects, such as, Design Technology and Commerce during their 10-year basic education at least have a flexible pathway to gain national certification as well as onward progression to further and higher education if they desire. It works on the principle that students entering a TVET programme after 10 years of basic education will normally join the Artisan Programme, while those entering after 12 years will join a Technician Programme in a Technical College leading to the award of National Craft Certificate (NCC) in 17 nationally recognised trades.[27]

To strengthen the quality and ability of TVET programmes, and to prepare and equip students with the competences to initiate, start and run their own business, the DTVET in collaboration with employers in 2001 launched the Botswana Technical Education Programme (BTEP) with entrepreneurship education embedded as an integral part of BTEP. BTEP is delivered in public technical colleges leading to Foundation, Certificate, Advanced Certificate and Diploma awards. All TVET programmes, expected skills and competencies are developed and approved with industry stakeholders and employers, thereby ensuring that the skills students have acquired are needed by employers.

Similarly, there is evidence of marginal success in other parts of Africa. In Ethiopia, for instance, evidence shows that the supply-driven nature of TVET has led to its integration into wage employment.[28] Although under the country's current TVET

---

[27]World TVET Database (2012)
[28]Garcia and Fares (2008)

scheme allocation of enrolment slots to students needs to be efficient, equitable and guided by labour market needs.[29] In addition, there has been attempts to use TVET programme to create pathways to self-employment through informal sector apprenticeships in Tanzania[30] and Malawi.[31] Also, since the 1980s, the basic educational systems in Kenya and Ghana have required students to study a combination of general and vocational or technical subjects to equip them with skills for both employment and self-employment.

However, across Africa, as a deliberate 'new work' agenda used by many governments to offer young people a differentiated progression into the labour market, the extent to which TVET has been a successful work-based education and training strategy remains an open question. In Kenya, the policy investments and adjustments towards integrating TVET into the general education system to solve the country's youth unemployment crisis were found to have been largely ineffective.[32] Today, many young Kenyans and their education sponsors including parents continue to view TVET in a negative manner. Among many Kenyans, university education remains the preferred progression route and perceived as the only 'elite' pathway to decent employment and economic success. This is also the case in Ghana where various policy attempts to integrate TVET and general education were found to have failed to 'alter the negative perceptions associated with TVET'.[33]

While the scale and scope of success in attempting to use TVET to provide people with employment may differ from one country to another, it remains unattractive to many young Africans who view it less favourably compared to higher education. Notwithstanding, the main question for African leaders should be whether TVET can provide their unemployed young people with skills for employment and self-employment in a knowledge economy? Integrating TVET with general education in an effective and sustainable manner, particularly aligning it with the needs of employers, may be the only way to ensure that TVET can be well received and be used to make a direct positive impact on young people and employers. Addressing these questions would first require some understanding of why TVET is failing in Africa.

5.4 WHY TVET IS FAILING IN AFRICA

Through a mix of policy incoherence, poor planning and implementation, particularly the lack of synergy with the labour market needs of the knowledge economy, TVET has not lived up to the career expectations of many young people and employers in Africa. The problem is that several years after adopting TVET, many African countries still view it merely as a way to supply skilled labour to employers in specific traditional sectors, such as manufacturing, agriculture and engineering. Because of this, its strategy, format and delivery patterns have yet to respond effectively to the changing

---

[29]Krishnan and Shaorshadze (2013)
[30]Nubler et al. (2009)
[31]Aggarwal et al. (2010)
[32]Mwiria (2005)
[33]Oketch (2017)

demands of the knowledge economy and career development needs of young people in the region. As discussed in the previous chapter, lack of work-based skills and low productivity among a predominantly young workforce population are the most critical challenges facing employers and labour market in Africa.

These challenges also constitute the major barrier to achieving demographic dividend. Without work-based skills, it will be difficult for young people to benefit from the livelihood opportunities that offer decent wages in a knowledge economy. From implementation standpoint, there are several interconnected reasons why TVET has not been as effective as envisaged in helping to address Africa's youth unemployment crisis despite several decades of its existence. Firstly, as a work-based training programme, TVET has not been sufficiently differentiated from general education even though there has been a policy shift towards integrating TVET into the general education system. Both have differences in curricula structure, pattern of delivery and learning outcomes.

In general education, age and educational attainment or qualification are the key success indicators rather than possession of practical skills in a particular craft or trade. It therefore means that the lack of a clear boundary between general education and TVET courses remains a source of confusion for many providers and beneficiaries. Another reason is that the provision of TVET in private and public institutions differs substantially in terms of content, learner profile, delivery method and the outcomes sought. Private TVET providers are known to have a deliberate strategy of targeting and linking their provision and outcomes with skills-level acquisition, access to initial or further training based on experience or aptitude rather than age or formal academic qualifications.[34] This is not the case with the provision of TVET in public educational settings, where age and formal academic qualifications are important features for admission and academic progression. To complicate matters, the profit motives of private providers are also at odds with the desire of public educational institutions to supply the economy with work-ready and highly skilled individuals.

Consequently, there is a mismatch between the profit-driven motives of private TVET providers and the vision and motivation of publicly funded TVET providers. The latter views their role primarily as helping to contribute towards achieving development goals. This lack of symmetry in vision, content and outcomes presents a significant barrier to effective collaboration between public and private TVET providers in Africa. It also makes it difficult to adopt a coherent approach to developing a common TVET strategy that can speak to the competing needs of various stakeholders. Thus, to ensure the effectiveness of TVET strategy without undermining the interests and motivation of all stakeholders, there is a need to strike a balance among providers with conflicting visions, mission and strategic priorities.

Thirdly, and most concerning is the fact that TVET has been declining in attractiveness among the general public, particularly young people and their academic sponsors. Given the low academic requirements for admission into TVET programmes, coupled with a low prospect of continuing into higher or professional education after graduation, many people view TVET as an inferior education and training option compared with general education. There is a general perception that

---

[34]Akoojee (2016)

TVET is an alternative for those in the society who inherently lack the intellectual ability to succeed, particularly in higher education, but who have a need to acquire specific work-based skills to survive.

This perception, rightly or wrongly, fuels negativity and mistrust between the government, TVET providers and the general population. The general perception seems to be that TVET leads to apprenticeship, which is widely stigmatised as socially and economically undignified in terms of building one's career pathway. Historically, the concept of apprenticeship has a negative connotation in Africa given its deep roots to 'slavery' and the protection of white hegemony through 'indentured labour'. As a result, many people, especially youths, prefer the general education or academic qualification track. This is because it is perceived as ultimately leading to supervisory or managerial job opportunities. Whereas TVET is widely viewed as "lower status" or another form of "low-grade" education different and independent of higher education'.[35]

Africa's current TVET strategy has neither altered nor countered the prevalence of such historically negative misperceptions. To appreciate the scale of the social and economic stigma attributed to TVET, one must look at the number of young people seeking enrolment in universities across Africa. While this has soared over the last decade, enrolment in TVET colleges has correspondingly declined. Fourthly, Africa's current TVET systems are neither up to the challenge nor set up to provide learners with digital skills required in a knowledge economy and to work collaboratively in the Fourth Industrial Revolution (4IR). One of the key issues is that TVET delivery mainly thrives on a rote format, which is incompatible with the collaborative learning and teamworking needed to learn effectively and survive in employment in a knowledge economy.

This is made worse by poorly trained personnel who are slow to embrace ICT skills and modern learning technologies, therefore unable to use innovative pedagogies for TVET delivery. The absence of well-trained personnel in ICT has implications for learning and assessment including TVET outcomes. Assessed outcomes are fragmented and rarely aligned with the core portable and transferable skills, such as teamworking, problem-solving and analytical skills essential to survival in a globalised knowledge economy. For TVET to be portable across providers, learning, assessment and outcome strategies would need to be harmonised under a common regulatory and qualification framework.

But because there is a lack of standardised format for TVET delivery including a common credit or points transfer system, different providers pursue different learning strategies and outcomes and issue their own certificates. It means that programmes, certifications, skills and competencies offered by a cohort of often competing providers within and across countries are difficult to evaluate and recognise. This is particularly the case between Anglophone and Francophone African countries where TVET programmes vary widely in scope, content and outcomes. Even more problematic are bilingual countries, such as Cameroon, Mauritania and Equatorial Guinea, where any attempt to integrate TVET with general education might prove to be more difficult given the dual language and legal systems that govern education and training provision in such countries.

---

[35]Nkomo et al. (2015)

In any case, a harmonised TVET strategy at both national and regional levels will help to better evaluate programme quality, learning outcomes and acquired skills. Without a harmonised framework, it may be difficult to align TVET with employability and labour market needs of the knowledge economy in a successful manner. Moreover, a lack of harmonised TVET strategy undermines the AU's vision of 'an integrated Africa, driven by its own people to take its rightful place in the knowledge economy'. These issues are further compounded by the fact that many African countries notoriously have weak foundations and systems of education and training due to inadequate funding and capacity challenges.

As shown in Chapter 3, the socioeconomic upheavals of the COVID-19 pandemic have sharply exposed the lingering weak digital education and training systems in sub-Saharan Africa (SSA). Within the worst hit sectors, such as manufacturing, hospitality and supply chain where young people have been gravely affected by COVID-19-related job losses. Many African countries that have invested heavily in TVET are unable to use it to support those who have lost their jobs to re-enter the labour market – even as their economies begin to recover and reopen.

In contrast, with their well-funded and harmonised education and training systems, many developed countries in Europe, particularly Germany and Sweden, have successfully used their vocational educational and training programmes to raise human capital and the productivity of those sectors affected by the pandemic through reskilling and upskilling of the workforce. Evidence shows that organisations in different sectors affected by a global economic crisis tend to re-strategise and restructure their operations by raising the human capital and productivity of their workforce as a way to respond to the crisis.[36] As such, for young and unemployed Africans, obtaining employment even after the pandemic would be much tougher without the relevant skills.

5.5 VET, EUROPEAN CONTRASTS

An effective system of VET is a vital component of employment creation and economic development in any society. In many advanced countries, such as Finland, Germany, Sweden and the United Kingdom, there have been tremendous success in using VET to plug the skills gap in the labour market and tackle youth unemployment.[37] With low unemployment rates, increased labour market productivity and sustained economic success in these countries, it is difficult to dismiss the effectiveness of VET in providing people with the relevant employability skills needed in today's world of work. In majority of these countries, vocational programmes by law must reflect labour market needs and are aligned or integrated into general education systems.

For instance, OECD records show that vocational educational and training programmes in key sectors of the Swedish economy, from construction, transportation to electricity and energy, are driven by labour market needs. In addition, VET providers

---

[36]Cascio (2014)
[37]Tabbron and Yang (1997)

must involve employers and social partners including Local Programme Councils (*lokala programrad*) in programme design and assessment before VET programmes can be funded by the Swedish National Agency for Higher Vocational Education (NAHVE). NAHVE is the government body responsible for formulating and administering TVET strategy across Sweden. To access further funding, VET providers must secure a mandatory work placements scheme with employers and demonstrate evidence of an established local partnership in a way that allows their programmes to be adjusted to local changing labour market needs. This robust system ensures there is always a strategic collaboration and linkages between different VET stakeholders at local and national levels. Also, vocational programmes offer Swedish VET students a clear progression path from upper-secondary diploma to advanced diploma, which allow them to ultimately obtain a university degree if they desire.

In addition, VET qualifications are recognised as meeting the Level 6 standards of the European Qualifications Framework (EQF). EQF guarantees the portability of VET skills while enhancing students' mobility and access to employment across Sweden and in other European countries.[38] Similarly, a long-standing and core strength of Germany's economic success has been its internationally respected and much-replicated dual VET system. Commonly known as the 'dual system' (*Ausbildung*), VET programmes have proven to be a highly sophisticated and effective way of providing young people and the unemployed with relevant employability skills to access jobs in Germany. By integrating work-based and school-based learning, the country's VET system prepares and equips students and young people with tools for successful transition to full-time employment. Developed and governed by legislation under the Vocational Training Act 1969 (amended in 2005), the dual training system is firmly embedded in Germany's education system and well-funded through a combination of public and private sector sources.

Regulated by the Federal Institute for Vocational Education and Training (BMBB) under the Federal Ministry of Education and Research (BMBF), Germany's VET system works on the principle of close alliance and strong cooperation between the federal government, the federated regions and businesses. Small and medium-sized companies work directly and collaboratively with publicly funded vocational institutions to provide young people with certified, usually by a competent national body (e.g. Chamber of Commerce and Industry or Chamber of Crafts and Trade), training and skills in nationally recognised occupations. With more than 330 occupations requiring formal training and qualification in Germany, employers and businesses consider the country's VET system as the most effective way to provide skills and procure skilled personnel.

This integrated process ensures that all VET-related training, assessment and certification are standardised across all business sectors. Equally, the standardisation ensures that all VET students or apprentices across the country receive the same level and quality of training as well as qualification regardless of industry and region. Moreover, the VET curricula are created and continuously updated jointly with employer representatives and the trade unions. That is not all, the trade unions drive changes in the system including regulations, research and innovation. Germany's VET system also enjoys a well-developed and institutionalised national network of research

---

[38]Kuczera and Jeon (2019)

centres, including the Federal Institute for VET, with a research capacity to study different aspects of the system and support continuous improvement and innovation.

The well-integrated VET system ensures that outcomes and certificates are widely respected. They provide evidence of what the individual has learned, earned and able to do in any occupation and sector, thereby instilling the confidence and trust that employers, parents/sponsors and students need. This level of efficiency and effectiveness was only made possible through a shared and mutually reinforcing sense of responsibility involving the government, industry representatives and trade unions. It guarantees the delivery of several benefits to various stakeholders across the VET value chain. Because of this, Germany's VET system is widely respected as the most dynamic and agile at two key levels relevant to today's world of work.

At a macro level, VET programmes are used to facilitate an open and flexible response to changing workforce and labour market needs, particularly plugging the skills gaps associated with industry 4.0 technologies and labour market challenges arising from shocks in the global economy. For instance, under the current COVID-19 pandemic, Germany has been able to effectively protect jobs than many of its European neighbours. Compelled by the crisis, it has been easy for the government and businesses to forge a new vision for VET through increased dialogue and collaboration between schools and businesses as a result of the strong partnership between the public and the private sectors. With emphasis on digital participation, educational mobility and digital transformation, the country has successfully promoted and accelerated the sharing of best practices among all stakeholders to shape digital and hybrid VET learning. This meant that the post-COVID-19 VET curriculum has opened up new opportunities for young people and adults by preparing them for the jobs of the future through training and continuing education in new technologies including Artificial Intelligence (AI), the Internet of Things (IoT), Blockchain and Augmented Reality. These new technologies have an impact on the real sector including occupational profiles and training regulations that affect how work is organised and done, particularly in modern-day manufacturing organisations.

At a micro level, companies and apprentices benefit through market-ready training, which improves employment chances in the labour market and drives down recruitment costs. This is because companies are guaranteed to hire the right employees, with first-class VET training, awareness and skills ready to respond to labour market needs and innovation. Also, through its VET system, Germany has systematically and massively injected well-qualified and technically competent employees into its key sectors, particularly its automated manufacturing sector, in a sustainable manner. By so doing, its economy has remained comparably resilient and strong even under the COVID-19 pandemic.

However, this is not to say that Germany's VET system is not without challenges. Demographic shifts are causing declining students' numbers, and graduates with weak core academic skills have limited opportunity to progress from upper-secondary VET to tertiary education.[39] An even more critically challenging for Germany is the job-specific nature of the skills acquired from its VET programme. Among most middle-aged German workers, and there are many of them, who obtained

---

[39]Deissinger (2004)

their employment by completing an apprenticeship or VET, there is a looming mid-career crisis.[40]

The skills of middle-aged workers, especially those in their late 40s who trained in their teens, are fast becoming obsolete in a technologically driven workplace of the twenty-first century where knowledge of AI and robotics define how work is done and organised. At middle age, work-based skills acquired from vocational training can easily become outdated as organisations innovate and adapt. This situation therefore makes it difficult for VET-only-trained individuals to stay in the labour force compared to workers with tertiary education, who have more generic knowledge and transferable skills, such as problem-solving, analytical thinking and organisational skills.[41] Despite these challenges, Germany's dual VET system remains one of the most robust but also widely seen as the transformative force behind the country's sustained economic success.

5.6 NEW TVET STRATEGY, OLD WINE IN A NEW BOTTLE

As seen in the cases of Germany and Sweden, there is no doubt that an effective VET strategy, if aligned with general education, can boost young people's access to gainful employment, thereby enable them to become more productive and contribute to economic growth. Given the globalising and consequently the constantly changing nature of work, to be effective, any new TVET strategy in Africa would at least require a deep immersion in the understanding of and the importance of achieving sustainable development goals targets.[42] Workplace changes and evolving labour market needs also means that TVET must form part of the region's wider long-term strategy for HCD, especially in the context of addressing present and future social and economic needs of the region.

To this end, education economist, Moses Oketch, sums up the critical challenge of using a new TVET strategy to address people's social and economic needs in Africa. While advocating for several market-led reforms, he argued that a revitalised TVET strategy must reflect the prevailing labour market reality in a post-independent Africa. Among others, he stressed the need to withdraw public sector institutions from providing vocational education, delinking TVET as an unemployment solution strategy, and instead position it to deliver high employability skills including reskilling and upskilling in technological advancements.[43]

Motivated by prevailing labour market needs, and recommendations from other stakeholders including UNESCO, but primarily in recognition of the barriers that have hindered effective TVET implementation for so long, the AU developed and adopted a new TVET strategy for Africa. The new strategy is anchored on 'promoting skills acquisition through competency-based training with proficiency testing for employment,

---

[40] Juskalian (2018)
[41] Op. Cit
[42] Karmel (2009)
[43] Oketch (2007)

sustainable livelihoods and responsible citizenship'.[44] Even though the new strategy provides a credible policy framework within which to encourage countries to develop national policies and operational strategies to transform their TVET programmes, its adoption, implementation and impact will inevitably vary from country to country. This variation is shaped by the wide-ranging social and economic factors peculiar to each country.

These factors include a country's context-specific socioeconomic challenges including skills needs, institutional arrangements and constitutional provisions for education, training and skills development. As well as the resource implications including capabilities to successfully execute such reforms, and public's response based on whether or not the public perceive such reforms as either beneficial or of little value. Without the critical human capacity and resource infrastructures, countries would be restricted in their ability to effectively operationalise the new TVET strategy. Besides, TVET reforms must be an occasion to tackle head-on some of the lingering and harshest criticisms of most VET programmes, which so far have been hidden away from public debate in Africa.

Compelling evidence has shown that VET provides a relatively short-term employment success for graduates and young people. It does not cater to the long-term employability needs of a specific workforce population. Because of this, VET graduates are known to have access to short-term employment, and then become jobless, before retraining to rejoin the workforce.[45] Also, VET has tended to ignore the employability needs of certain workforce population, such as those with severe social or health problems, which may require specific long-term interventions. However, it's not clear how Africa's new TVET strategy has addressed some of these legitimate concerns.

A review of Africa's new TVET strategy shows a rather narrow focus on providing countries with a list of roadmaps to (1) deliver quality TVET programme, (2) assure employability of trainees, (3) improve coherence and management of training provision, (4) promote lifelong learning and (5) enhance status and attractiveness of TVET. Without a clear and harmonised operational plan to implement and integrate these principles with labour market needs, TVET is unlikely to have any real socioeconomic benefit for the individual and the wider society. A further challenge relates to the 'paradox of economic growth' (discussed in Chapter 1), whereby many African countries implementing TVET have seen a sustained economic growth. Yet, there is mass unemployment crisis and lack of capacity for skills development and opportunities for job creation, especially among young people and school leavers ready to enter the labour force.

Perhaps, these problems explain why TVET has remained heavily unattractive to young people and critics, who often dismiss it as a 'training for future training, without the prospect to facilitate entry into productive and sustainable employment'.[46] Without appetite to pursue and introduce a substantial reform, any interest and government incentive to encourage stakeholders to embrace the so-called 'new TVET strategy' will only increasingly diminish.

[44]AUC/HRST (2007)
[45]Lindsay et al. (2007)
[46]Oketch (2007)

5.7 REFORMING TVET, WHAT AFRICA CAN DO

To be relevant in the twenty-first century and beyond, a TVET strategy needs to provide an attractive education and training experience and must be used to effectively address the problem of high youth unemployment and labour market needs of the 4IR. To achieve this, TVET programmes would need to address two key goals. Firstly, they must directly speak to the changing career needs and priorities of young people, which involves progression to higher education. Secondly, TVET must be inclusive and well aligned with the labour market needs of the knowledge economy including access to digital literacy. The reason why it has been difficult to achieve these two goals in the context of Africa can be traced to the region's persistently low and poor human development outcomes.

As such, efforts directed at using any type of education and training initiative to address the employability needs of young people and labour market needs of the knowledge economy must first and foremost recognise the wider institutional challenges affecting HCD in the region. The nature of Africa's demographic challenges makes HCD a social and economic imperative. The HCD-oriented approach proposed here therefore offers a unique opportunity through which to better understand the conditions under which a market-led approach to TVET transformation could lead to an inclusive and beneficial outcome for young people and the wider society.

As the labour market has become increasingly more complex and uncertain, a disposition towards entrepreneurialism and risk-taking will become increasingly more attractive to many unemployed and diverse young people as a means to access livelihood opportunity. For a long time, risking-taking and entrepreneurial disposition has existed and can be seen in the context of Africa's vibrant informal sector, which has outpaced the formal sector in generating employment and income for people. Many unemployed young people including university graduates are locked into informal sector employment with little to no prospect of a better future.

From labour market and socioeconomic development viewpoints, an HCD approach to a reformed TVET curriculum must therefore provide young people with entrepreneurial knowledge and skills. With many African countries struggling to provide basic amenities and infrastructures including health, security and food, it is unrealistic to expect the government or indeed the private sector in these countries to provide everyone with a decent job and income. In some, if not in most cases, graduates and young people may be employable and still struggle to find work because the labour market conditions are unfavourable. It therefore means that self-employment through an emphasis on HCD is vital.

In Africa, the prevalence of unemployment and underemployment among young people, including TVET and non-TVET graduates most of whom have stagnant wages, makes investment in human capital and entrepreneurship education a pressing necessity. Human capital is associated with individual productivity, economic growth and factors of production based on knowledge and skills acquisition and diffusion in a wide range of contexts. Rather than the current focus on using TVET to develop skills for paid employment, the emphasis should move towards VET initiatives that deliver the knowledge and skills for self-employment through entrepreneurship education. Entrepreneurship education will ensure that young people have the right mindset and attitude to embrace self-employment as an alternative career path. Graduates with the relevant mindset, the right entrepreneurial training and skills are most likely to have the commitment and ability to establish their own business than take up poorly paid job in the labour market.

What is needed, therefore, is a shift in thinking towards a more long-term stakeholder commitment and investment in programmes that promote human capital and entrepreneurship development. Such a focus will better prepare and empower young Africans to recognise and exploit emerging opportunities from (1) social and environmental entrepreneurship in the green economy, (2) evolving technologies in the disruptive sectors of the 4IR and (3) intra-Africa trade integration under the Africa Continental Free Trade Agreement (AfCFTA). Thus, the HCD approach proposed here emerges in response to the failure of TVET to meet the employment priorities and career aspirations of young people in a knowledge economy. This approach is rooted in the assumption that if young people acquire the relevant education and training in entrepreneurship through exposure to entrepreneurship education, they will be better able to participate in the labour market in a more effective manner. Education and training acquisition within this approach will emphasise the necessary behavioural aspects of entrepreneurial competencies, skills, creativity and risk-taking associated primarily with self-employment.

Also, some have proposed that collaboration between education and training providers, the government and employers must be strengthened under a harmonised structure of an alternative TVET strategy in Africa.[47] However, achieving this would require a more direct and definite role for various stakeholders. For instance, employers could help to shape the contents and pedagogies of TVET, whereas for governments, they could determine and enforce the regulatory framework to better guide TVET providers to deliver programmes and outcomes in a more harmonised structure. It also requires that TVET providers must be well-funded, agile and flexible to embrace emerging technologies in digital education, while teaching personnel must themselves be reskilled and upskilled in the design and use of new technologies in age of technological advancement. Teaching personnel must be particularly skilled in deploying the services of digitalised education and training delivery systems targeting entrepreneurship development within TVET courses.

Digitalised systems are important for an inclusive and more responsive education and training strategy in a globalised modern economy, whether in a crisis as in COVID-19, or in reaching out to marginalised communities, including the workforce population with long-term employability needs. Such substantial and targeted reforms have the potential to yield longer-term beneficial socioeconomic outcomes through solutions to the critical challenges of poor skills development and low productivity, human capital, employment creation and sustainable development. Besides, there is little ambiguity about the positive relationship between HCD, employability skills and socioeconomic outcomes.

Human capital theorists have long advocated that the dynamics of the labour market reward individuals who make investments in their skills development, which leads to increased productivity, access to better jobs and earnings.[48] Thus, the development of human capital promotes a market-led concept and approach to transformational change in which educational attainment through exposure to TVET programme, ultimately,

---

[47]Lewis (2009)
[48]Schultz (1961)

can begin to equate to skills acquisition relevant to self-employment and economic success. As components of human capital, education and training have been found to increase people's job creation potential and the likelihood of being economically self-independent as they increase their skill and capability to undertake risks, recognise and exploit opportunities and solve problems.[49]

For this reason, an emerging but significant question here for policymakers and researchers is whether the formation of human capital can be achieved through entrepreneurship education. The emphasis on entrepreneurship education rests on the assumption that it will create the 'general' human capital that enhances an individual's ability to acquire transferable knowledge, skills and experience for self-employment. Access to education and training for self-employment raises young people's employability skills, reduces their vulnerability to the negative consequences of joblessness and low productivity, and consequently leads to increased human development outcomes.

Besides, as a general education programme, entrepreneurship education can easily be modified to suit various individual learning ability, employability needs and contexts. If indeed, as different studies have shown, it makes sense perhaps to focus on using entrepreneurship education to provide young people with the knowledge, skills and training needed for self-employment, job creation and entrepreneurship.

BIBLIOGRAPHY

African Union. (2007). *Strategy to revitalize technical and vocational education and training (TVET) in Africa*. Addis Ababa: Final Draft. Bureau of the Conference of Ministers of Education of the African Union (COMEDAF II+), Retrieved from http://citeseerx.ist.psu.edu/viewdoc/download?doi=10.1.1.688.8559&rep=rep1&type=pdf. Accessed on 15 November 2020.

Aggarwal, A., Hofmann, C., & Phiri, A. (2010). *A study of informal apprenticeship in Malawi*. ILO, Skills and Employability Department, ILO Decent Work Team for South and Eastern Africa, Geneva: ILO Publications.

Akoojee, S. (2016). Private TVET in Africa: Understanding the context and managing alternative forms creatively! *Journal of Technical Education and Training*, 8(2), 38–51.

Bernston, E., Sverke, M., & Marklund, S. (2006). Predicting perceived employability: Human capital or labour market opportunities. *Economic and Industrial Democracy*, 27(2), 223–244.

Brewer, L. (2013). *Enhancing youth employability: What? Why? and how? Guide to core work skills*. International Labour Office, Skills and Employability Department – Geneva: ILO. Retrieved from https://www.oitcinterfor.org/sites/default/files/file_publicacion/wcms_2134 52.pdf. Accessed on 2 September 2020.

Cascio, W. F. (2014). Investing in HRD in uncertain time now and in the future. *Advances in Developing Human Resources*, 16(1), 108–122.

Dean, H. (2003). Reconceptualising welfare to work for people with multiple problems and needs. *Journal of Social Policy*, 32(3), 441–459.

Dearing, R. (1997). *Higher education in the learning society*. London: Her Majesty's Stationery Office.

Deissinger, T. (2004). Germany's system of vocational education and training: Challenges and modernisation issues. *International Journal of Training Research*, 2(1), 76–99.

Finn, D. (1997). Labour's new deal for the unemployed: Making it work locally. *Local Economy: The Journal of the Local Economy Policy Unit*, 12(3), 247–258.

---

[49]Groot and Van Den Brink (2000)

Foster, P. (1965a). The vocational school fallacy in development planning. In: A. Anderson & M. Bowman (Eds.), *Education and economic development*, Chicago: Aldine.

Garcia, M., & Fares, J. (2008). *Why is it important for Africa to invest in its youth? Youth in Africa labor market, directions in human development*, (pp. 3–14). Washington, DC: World Bank. Retrieved from https://openknowledge.worldbank.org/bitstream/handle/10986/6578/454880PUB0Box311OFFICIA0L0USE0ONLY1.pdf?sequence=1&isAllowed=y. Accessed on 14 November 2020.

Gazier, B. (2001). Employability: The complexity of policy notion. In: Weinert, P., Baukens, M., Bollerot, P., Pineschi-Gapenne, M., & Walwei, U. (Eds.), *Employability: From Theory to Practice*, pp. 3–23, New Brunswick, New Jersey.

Groot, W., & Van Den Brink, H. (2000). Education, training and employability. *Applied Economics*, 32, 573–581.

Juskalian, R. (2018). Rebuilding Germany's centuries-old vocational program. *MIT Technology Review*. Retrieved from https://www.technologyreview.com/2018/06/22/2609/rebuilding-germanys-centuries-old-vocational-program/. Accessed on 5 November 2020.

Karmel, T. (2009). TVET and sustainable development: A cautionary note. In: J. Fein, R. Maclean & M. G. Park (Eds.), *Work, learning and sustainable development. Technical and vocational education and training: Issues, concerns and prospects*, Vol.8. Springer. Retrieved from https://link.springer.com/chapter/10.1007%2F978-1-4020-8194-1_36. Accessed on 19 November 2020.

King, K., & Martin, C. (2002). The vocational school fallacy revisited: Education, aspiration and work in Ghana, 1959-2000. *International Journal of Educational Development*, 22(5), 5–26.

Krishnan, P., & Shaorshadze, I. (2013). *Technical and vocational education and training in Ethiopia*. Working Paper for International Growth Centre. Retrieved from https://www.theigc.org/wp-content/uploads/2014/09/Krishnan-Shaorshadze-2013-Working-Paper.pdf. Accessed on 16 November 2020.

Kuczera, M., & Jeon, S. (2019). *Vocational education and training in Sweden*, OECD Reviews of Vocational Education and Training. Paris: OECD Publishing.

Lewis, T. (2009). Towards reclaiming the high ground in the discourse on vocationalisation in developing countries. *International Journal of Educational Development*, 29(6), 558–564.

Lindsay, C., McQuaid, R., & Dutton, M. (2007). New approaches to employability in the UK: Combining 'human capital development' and 'Work First' strategies. *Journal of Social Policy*, 36(4), 539–560.

McGrath, S. (2018). *Education and development*. Abingdon: Routledge.

McGrath, S., Ramsarup, P., Zeelen, J., Wedekind, V., Allais, S., Lotz-Sisitka, H., … Russon, J. (2019). Vocational education and training for African development: A literature review. *Journal of Vocational Education and Training*, 72(4), 465–487. DOI: 10.1080/13636820.2019.1679969

McKenzie, P., & Wurzburg, G. (1997). Lifelong learning and employability. *OECD Observer*, 209, 13.

McQuaid, R., & Lindsay, C. (2005). The concept of employability. *Urban Studies*, 42(2), 197–219

Mwiria, K. (2005). Vocationalisation of secondary education: Kenyan case study. In: R. Maclean, D. N. Wilson, J. Lauglo & R. Maclean (Eds.), *Vocationalisation of secondary education revisited. UNESCO-UNEVOC book series technical and vocational education and training: Issues, concerns and prospects*, Vol 1, Dordrecht: Springer. Retrieved from https://link.springer.com/chapter/10.1007%2F1-4020-3034-7_6

Ngcwangu, S. (2015). The ideological underpinnings of World Bank TVET policy: Implications of the influence of human capital theory on South African TVET policy. *Education as Change*, 19(3), 24–45.

Nkomo, M., Warchal, A., & Tshikovhi, N. (2015). *History explains why black South African still mistrust vocational training*. The Conversation. Retrieved from https://theconversation.

com/history-explains-why-black-south-africans-still-mistrust-vocational-training-46998. Accessed on 16 November 2020.

Nubler, I., Hofmann, C., & Greiner, C. (2009). *Understanding informal apprenticeship: Findings from empirical research in Tanzania.* ILO, Skills and Employability Department. Geneva: ILO Publications.

Oakes, M. J. (1978). *The management of higher education in the maintained sector.* London: Her Majesty's Stationery Office.

OECD. (2016). *Enhancing employability.* Paris: OECD Publishing. Retrieved from https://www.oecd.org/employment/emp/Enhancing-Employability-G20-Report-2016.pdf. Accessed on 1 September 2020.

Oketch, M. O. (2007). To vocationalise or not to vocationalise? Perspectives on current trends and issues in technical and vocational education and training (TVET) in Africa. *International Journal of Educational Development, 27,* 220–234.

Oketch, M. (2017). Cross-country comparison of TVET systems, practices and policies, and employability of youths in Sub-Saharan Africa. In: F. Eicker, G. Haseloff & L. Bernd (Eds.), *Vocational education and training in Sub-Saharan Africa: Current situation and development.* Bielefeld: W. Bertelsmann Verlag. Retrieved from https://library.oapen.org/bitstream/id/2ffff4ec-22c7-4efc-9a2a-807686932d3a/640951.pdf

Organisation for Economic Cooperation and Development. (1997). *Lifelong Learning to Maintain Employability, Paper prepared for the Meeting of OECD Labour Ministers, DEELSA/ELSA (97)4REV2 (drafted by G. Wurzburg & P. McKenzie), DECO, Paris.*

Psacharopoulos, G. (1997). Vocational education and training today: Challenges and responses. *Journal of Vocational Education and Training, 49*(3), 385–394.

Schultz, T. W. (1961). Investment in human capital. *The American Economic Review, 51*(1), 1–17.

Tabbron, G., & Yang, J. (1997). The interaction between technical and vocational education and training (TVET) and economic development in advanced countries. *International Journal of Educational Development, 17*(3), 323–334.

UNESCO. (2016). *Strategy for technical vocational education and training (TVET), (2016–2021),* Paris: UNESCO, Retrieved from https://en.unesco.org/sites/default/files/tvet.pdf. Accessed on 13 November 2020.

UNESCO and ILO. (2003). *Technical and vocational education and training for twenty-first century: UNESCO and ILO Recommendations.* Retrieved from https://unesdoc.unesco.org/ark:/48223/pf0000220748. Accessed on 13 November 2020.

White, M. (2000). New deal for young people: towards an ethical employment policy. *Policy Studies, 21*(4), 281–295.

World TVET Database (2012). *Botswana. Compiled by UNESCO-UNEVOC International Centre for Technical and Vocational Education and Training.* Retrieved from https://unevoc.unesco.org/wtdb/worldtvetdatabase_bwa_en.pdf. Accessed on 18 November 2020.

Yorke, M. (2006). *Employability in higher education: What it is, what it is not. Learning and Employability Series 1.* York, England: Higher Education Academy Publications.

ENTREPRENEURSHIP EDUCATION AND HUMAN CAPITAL

6

Knowledge and skills for self-employment foster entrepreneurship development, which eases labour market constraints and ultimately contribute to economic growth. As such, entrepreneurship is vital to job creation, inclusive growth and sustainable development. But the major challenge in Africa has been the type of education and training that can be used effectively to influence youth entrepreneurship. Education and training mechanisms used to influence and support young people, especially students to become self-employed cannot be limited to classroom exercise. As such, for the impact of education and training systems to be felt beyond the classroom and to successfully drive youth entrepreneurship, education and training providers in Africa must embrace practice-oriented learning strategies.

In Africa, the main drivers of youth entrepreneurship have been the political calls for action led by governments, intergovernmental organisations, such as the African Union (AU) and the United Nations (UN). In the context of the UN's agenda for sustainable development, youth entrepreneurship is underpinned by both Goals 4 and 8. In particular, SDGs target 4.4 mainly aims to increase the number of young people (and adults) who have the relevant skills, including technical and vocational skills for entrepreneurship. Equally, SDG target 8.3 promotes development-oriented policies that support entrepreneurship, creativity and innovation, and encourages the formalisation and growth of micro, small and medium-sized enterprises (MSMEs).

Simultaneously, in regard to AU's strategic vision for inclusive growth and sustainable development under Agenda 2063,[1] Goals 1, 4 and 18 seek to prioritise a high standard of living and quality of life for youths in Africa through an emphasis on youth entrepreneurship development. Unfortunately, mere policies and targets, as useful and as relevant as they may be, are in themselves insufficient to bring about the necessary shift in mindset and attitude among young people, as well as provide the knowledge and skills needed to become successful entrepreneurs. Notwithstanding, the surge in interest in entrepreneurship education as a way to encourage young people in Africa to develop an entrepreneurship career, entrepreneurship education

---

[1] The vision of the African Union under Agenda 2063 is to see 'an integrated, prosperous and peaceful Africa, driven by its own citizens and representing a dynamic force in the international arena'.

has been inspired by educational and training initiatives intended to support students to initiate, start and run their own business.

But to better understand what drives young people to pursue an entrepreneurship career and the role (or lack thereof) of entrepreneurship education in that process, one must consider young people's levels of entrepreneurial knowledge and skills, the quality of education and training that they have been exposed to, as well as the livelihood opportunities open to them after school. Thus, investing in human capital development by boosting access to quality entrepreneurship education and training opportunities for young people is one of the most important levers for promoting youth entrepreneurship. Yet, the implications of human capital and of unlocking the entrepreneurial potential of young people in Africa through entrepreneurship education have only just emerged as an area of research in higher education and policy priority.

Since its introduction at Harvard University in the mid-1940s, the number of higher education institutions offering entrepreneurship education across the world has increased exponentially. Unfortunately, there remains very limited understanding of how entrepreneurship education learning strategies can be used effectively to foster entrepreneurial competencies, and how these competencies translate into entrepreneurial outcomes, and ultimately venture formation in diverse contexts.[2] Specifically, the extent to which entrepreneurship education influences the entrepreneurial intentionality, attitude and behaviour of young people, as well as whether it enables them to become effective entrepreneurs, remains unclear.[3]

As a result, more research is needed to fully understand the effectiveness of entrepreneurship education as a vehicle to foster and support youth entrepreneurship especially in Africa. Seen from a broader viewpoint of rigorous scientific debate that has spawned a vast literature, particularly in Asia, Europe and North America, research into how entrepreneurship education influences different entrepreneurial outcomes from an African perspective is comparably insignificant. Entrepreneurship education is any pedagogical process of training and developing individuals to acquire knowledge and skills for a new venture formation. It has also been referred to as the process of improving one's entrepreneurial attitudes and skills to start a new venture.[4] It can also be understood in two simple ways: 'either learning about entrepreneurship as a phenomenon or learning useful skills in order to become an entrepreneur'.[5] Yet, much is unknown about how to design an effective entrepreneurship education pedagogy, or how to use it to influence students and young people in Africa to become entrepreneurs.

Analysis of the entrepreneurship education literature shows that there is a heavy bias towards those research insights and contexts that have their origins mainly from developed Western societies rather than in Africa. This has prompted many scholars to argue that the available research evidence does not provide the sufficient intellectual space to precisely understand the contextual boundaries of entrepreneurship education outcomes.[6] Notably, Alain Fayolle, a distinguished Professor of Entrepreneurship,

---

[2] Garavan and O'Cinneide (1994)
[3] Pittaway and Cope (2007)
[4] Fellnhofer (2017)
[5] Rasmussen and Sorheim (2006, p. 186)
[6] Huang-Saad et al. (2020)

and a prominent voice in the field, has urged researchers 'to showcase how entrepreneurship education can be used to produce different set of entrepreneurial outcomes for different groups in a wide range of contexts'.[7]

6.1 SUMMARY OF ENTREPRENEURSHIP EDUCATION RESEARCH

Early entrepreneurship education researchers focused on the development, challenges and the way in which entrepreneurship education is taught in schools, particularly in higher education institutions. Since then, entrepreneurship education research has evolved in remarkably diverse forms. Some studies have linked entrepreneurship education to entrepreneurial culture,[8] human capital development[9] and students' entrepreneurial intentions.[10] While others have examined how entrepreneurship education influences entrepreneurial behaviour[11] and the ability of SME owner-managers to influence the social and economic outcomes that occur at organisational and regional levels through job creation.[12] Job creation occurs as a direct result of entrepreneurial creativity and innovation, which arises from how entrepreneurs are taught, learn and behave in a variety of contexts.

Also, individual creativity and innovation within firms, which is closely associated with the emerging subfield of corporate entrepreneurship (CE), has been associated with entrepreneurship education. CE describes entrepreneurial behaviour in relation to those entrepreneurship activities that occur within well-established organisations. More recently, emerging research interest explores how to use entrepreneurship education to model science-based and engineering courses in higher education, thereby influence non-business students to become entrepreneurs.[13] In addition, there are many cross-sectoral examples in innovation-driven countries – including the United States, Scandinavian countries and the United Kingdom – where enterprise education is used alongside entrepreneurship education pedagogies to educate students and small business owners.

Despite this broad spectrum of scholarly efforts, existing research stops short of unveiling how entrepreneurship education should be systematised as an instructional tool in schools, its content and how this content is to be designed and delivered, as well as how to align programmes with needs of individual learners in higher education.[14] Perhaps, these questions prompted the European Commission to publish a comprehensive study (available in 21 languages) on entrepreneurship education

---

[7]Fayolle (2018, p. 698)
[8]Davidsson (1995)
[9]Anosike (2019)
[10]Maresch et al. (2016)
[11]Nyello et al. (2015)
[12]Lindh and Thorgren (2016)
[13]Gorlewicz and Jayaram (2020)
[14]Béchard and Grégoire (2005)

intended to serve as a good practice guide for educators and policymakers across Europe.[15] Necessary though this may be, an entrepreneurship education guide for European educators and practitioners does not provide sufficient scope and diversity of evidence needed to advance knowledge and understanding of entrepreneurship education outcomes in other environmental contexts, such as, Africa.

To compound matters, research in entrepreneurship education is 'fragmented'[16] and lacks a legitimate theoretical foundation.[17] Besides being an ambiguous concept to grasp, it is difficult to clearly define its boundary with other disciplines with which it overlaps. If anything, educators and higher education practitioners have a hard task identifying the distinct contributions of entrepreneurship education to the broader domains of entrepreneurship, management and education, and precisely what areas of research and practice to focus on. These challenges have pedagogical and theoretical implications including whether the emphasis should be on how entrepreneurship education is taught in schools, how entrepreneurship education outcomes should be measured, or both.[18]

Apart from pedagogical issues, the social and economic roles of entrepreneurship education for individuals and society as well for higher education institutions are yet to be ironed out.[19] Thus, the research emphasis should be on whether higher education students, particularly in Africa, are sufficiently exposed to the right kinds of learning to provide them with the knowledge and skills to embrace the disruptive innovation happening in today's world of business through exposure to entrepreneurship education.[20] Apart from the need to expose higher education students to the right kind of learning, another major concern is that existing entrepreneurship education studies are mostly inconclusive in their findings.

For instance, they do not establish the precise nature of the relationships between entrepreneurship education and a wide range of entrepreneurial outcomes. Entrepreneurial outcomes are those phenomena – such as entrepreneurship awareness, entrepreneurial intentions, business skills development, entrepreneurial behaviour and new venture formation and management – which emerge by applying the knowledge and skills gained from exposure to entrepreneurship education.

6.2 ENTREPRENEURSHIP EDUCATION AND ENTREPRENEURIAL OUTCOMES

There is a mix of positive, negative and even ambiguous results in the literature regarding the nature of the relationship between entrepreneurship education and a

---

[15]See the report published by the Entrepreneurship 2020 Unit Directorate-General for Enterprise and Industry, European Commission entitled: Entrepreneurship Education: A Guide for Educators available via: https://www.schooleducationgateway.eu/en/pub/resources/publications/entrepreneurship-education—a.htm
[16]Fox et al. (2018, p. 62)
[17]Fayolle et al. (2016, p. 2)
[18]Neck and Corbett (2018)
[19]Nabi et al. (2017)
[20]Kuratko and Morris (2018)

range of entrepreneurial outcomes. Because of this, many researchers have taken a more cautious approach to exploring this relationship including meta-analyses of prior qualitative and quantitative studies in an attempt, at least, to understand the precise nature of the relationships between entrepreneurship education and different entrepreneurial outcomes. For example, a meta-analysis of 73 studies yielded mixed results with a significant, although a small, correlation between entrepreneurship education and entrepreneurial intentions.[21]

In contrast, some studies have reported a significant positive relationship with students' entrepreneurial intentions following analysis of entrepreneurship education projects in 400 higher education institutions across 70 countries including Africa.[22] Similarly, others believe that entrepreneurship education could have a strong positive effect on some students' attitudes towards entrepreneurial behaviour depending on their entrepreneurial experience or level of exposure and awareness of entrepreneurship education.[23] From an entrepreneurship standpoint, attitude refers to the extent to which an individual puts either a positive or a negative value on his or her ability to become an entrepreneur.

It relates to one's perception of having the attributes or capacity to fulfil firm-creation behaviours, which is similar to perceptions of self-efficacy originally mooted by Albert Bandura. Self-efficacy or self-regulation is an inherently persuasive psychological state that allows an individual to persist on a particular course of action he or she may deem as beneficial and advantageous, even in the face of challenges or obstacles.[24] Exposure to entrepreneurship education can enhance students' perceived entrepreneurial self-efficacy as they journey through higher education even under adverse conditions.

Students' self-efficacy acquired through knowledge and experience from exposure to entrepreneurship education can influence them to embrace entrepreneurship as a career choice, while also sensitising them to both the positive and the negative dimensions of becoming an entrepreneur. With self-efficacy linked to entrepreneurial attribute, the two important questions that then arise are what constitute entrepreneurial attributes? How are entrepreneurial attributes linked to entrepreneurship education, particularly in the context of Africa? In Tanzania, entrepreneurial attributes among higher education students exposed to entrepreneurship education have been associated with 'need for achievement', 'need for autonomy', 'creativity', 'risk taking', 'drive' and 'determination'.[25]

Notwithstanding, while exposure to entrepreneurship education seems to be associated with increased antecedents to entrepreneurial intentions and entrepreneurial attitudes, the success or failure in the process of new venture creation among students were not necessarily associated with entrepreneurship education.[26] As relevant, and as useful as these existing research studies may be, entrepreneurship education and the outcomes that it produces vary substantially from individual to individual, and across institutional levels and regional contexts. It thus makes it

---

[21]Bae et al. (2014)
[22]Venevenhoven and Liguori (2013)
[23]Fayolle et al. (2006)
[24]Bandura (1982; also see Bandura, 1997)
[25]Nyello et al. (2015)
[26]Athayde (2009)

difficult to precisely establish the nature of the relationship between entrepreneurship education and different entrepreneurial outcomes across multiple boundaries.

Establishing a precise relationship in any learning and business contexts tends to be difficult, and this depends on a range of different although related factors. For instance, one would need to consider how entrepreneurship education is taught in a particular educational setting; that is, whether by experiential or active mode – whereby business simulation including business accelerator programmes and incubation are used. Or by passive mode – whereby only theory and lectures are predominantly the norm. In addition, quality of the teaching personnel, the learning environment, and the assessed learning outcomes as well as the specific learning conditions under which individuals encounter entrepreneurship education may need to be considered.

If the teaching method is passive, whereby students encounter entrepreneurship education merely as a classroom experience, entrepreneurship education is unlikely to be beneficial. Thus, as earlier mentioned, adopting a practice-oriented learning approach whereby students learn 'by doing' will likely lead to more beneficial outcomes. In Africa, adopting a 'learning by doing' approach to entrepreneurship education delivery will likely serve a far more useful and functional purpose in terms of enabling students to become successful entrepreneurs after graduation.

From a human capital perspective, students who acquire entrepreneurial knowledge and skills through a 'learning by doing' approach are often better placed to prove and sustain the value of their entrepreneurship education experience through exhibiting increased entrepreneurial intention. If their entrepreneurial knowledge, skills and producivity were well harnessed, then ultimately, they are far more likely to display an effective entrepreneurial action through exhibiting firm-creation behaviours.

Whereas, if students only learnt theoretically and only in classroom settings without the experience of 'learning-by-doing', as currently the case in most higher education institutions in Africa, then the shallowness of their entrepreneurship education experience, coupled with the futility of their effort to own and control profitable venture, would sooner or later be revealed and potentially fizzle out.

6.3 ENTREPRENEURSHIP EDUCATION AS HUMAN CAPITAL

The notion that entrepreneurship education is an essential component of human capital is not a mere coincidence. It emerged from the empirical observation of human capital as resources for opportunity recognition and exploitation, which are important dimensions to the early stages of the entrepreneurial process. Opportunity recognition and exploitation are associated with human capital formation through the knowledge and skills acquired from exposure to entrepreneurship education and the experience gained from entrepreneurial training. Although research exploring the nature of this relationship is only now emerging, however, not many will dismiss the notion that knowledge and skills acquired from general education are the human capital attributes, which drive productivity and economic growth in a society.

Human capital constitutes those resources and assets possessed by an individual or a group (e.g. workforce) in form of skills, knowledge and experience acquired through education and training that makes them productive. Distinguished in terms of general and specific components, human capital was originally conceptualised by American Economist, Gary Becker, in the mid-1960s and formalised by the Labour Economist, Jacob Mincer, in the mid-1970s, as an estimate of an individual's productivity based on knowledge and skills acquired through education, training and experience.

Mincer further suggested that human capital activities involve 'not only the transmission and embodiment in people of available knowledge, but also the production of new knowledge, and that the diffusion of this knowledge produces individual (i.e. income) economic growth and its national equivalent as a factor of production.[27] General human capital involves overall practical experience and education, whereas specific human capital relates to 'education and experience limited to a particular activity or context'.[28] Entrepreneurship researchers borrowed the human capital concept to estimate the antecedents to entrepreneurial success.

The thinking is that human capital increases an individual's capability to discover and exploit opportunities that may not be visible to others,[29] helps to harmonise the strategic planning and marketing competencies required to exploit those opportunities,[30] and serves as a prerequisite for continuous learning essential to the efficient and effective management of an entrepreneurial activity. With emphasis on opportunity seeking and self-reliance, entrepreneurship education advocates the need for individual autonomy and proactive response to labour market demands through continuous training and skills development for self-employment.

Whereas general education may contribute to general human capital, entrepreneurship education contributes to both general and specific human capital. This is because entrepreneurial attribute and capability can be useful in any type of business situation that requires the use of generalist or specialist knowledge and skills to demonstrate entrepreneurial effectiveness. Entrepreneurship education provides the prerequisites for the acquisition of the competencies essential to achieve entrepreneurial effectiveness, which is the ability of an individual to behave or function in an entrepreneurial capacity.[31] Idea generation, innovation skills, envisioning opportunities, creativity and risk-taking are among several key entrepreneurial competencies essential to entrepreneurial effectiveness in any type of business environment.[32]

It is obvious that entrepreneurship researchers have long employed human capital to represent the combination and varying entrepreneurial competencies including knowledge, skills and experience acquired from education and training that can be used to create value through job creation.[33] As such, early-stage entrepreneurs exposed to entrepreneurship education have relied on their human capital attributes to eliminate the initial barriers to success including the Liability of Newness (LoN), which nascent entrepreneurs encounter due to lack of track record and legitimacy.[34] Specifically, formation of human capital attributes through the medium of

---

[27]Mincer (1984)
[28]Dimov and Shepherd (2005)
[29]Shane and Venkataraman (2000)
[30]Frese et al. (2007)
[31]Kuratko (2005)
[32]Mitchelmore and Rowley (2013)
[33]Marvel et al. (2016)
[34]Dimov (2010)

entrepreneurship education is believed to lead to success in the early stages of the entrepreneurial process.

From these perspectives, it seems entrepreneurship education, rather than TVET, can provide students and young people with greater levels of entrepreneurial competencies needed to successfully become self-employed and navigate the business environment. Therefore, there is little doubt that entrepreneurship education could offer a more meaningful solution to the persistent challenge of youth unemployment in Africa. As mentioned in the previous chapter, entrepreneurship education constitutes an important feature of general education, which is core to general human capital and employability skills. The priority then for many African countries struggling to tackle rising youth unemployment must be how to integrate entrepreneurship education into their wider general education system as a resource for human capital formation.

Integrating entrepreneurship education as a resource for human capital is essential to increase the stock of entrepreneurial knowledge and skills, which consequently could raise young people's productivity and ability to recognise and exploit opportunities for entrepreneurship. As a feature of human capital, entrepreneurship education has been used to establish the extent to which the accumulation of explicit knowledge and tacit knowledge, as well as the cognitive skills of nascent entrepreneurs were uniquely useful in opportunity recognition and exploitation in a way not immediately obvious to others.[35]

Explicit knowledge can be readily expressed, codified, stored and accessed, therefore easily transferable or shared with others. Whereas tacit or implicit knowledge includes those insights, intuitions, norms and beliefs that are entwined with experience that cannot be expressed or codified, therefore, difficult to transfer to others. We know that exposure to some form of education or training is necessary for an individual to be successful in exhibiting complex codified and uncodified knowledge and skills in the entrepreneurial process.

However, to recognise and exploit opportunities in a uniquely entrepreneurial manner, individuals must at least have a clear business goal, a deep insight into the dynamics of the business environment, and how to achieve this goal by deploying that insight in their response (or reaction) to different complex business situations. Thus, an intriguing question that arises is whether entrepreneurship education is sufficient to shape the cognitive and the intuitive abilities of an individual to specifically recognise and exploit opportunities in an entrepreneurially minded way. Exposure to entrepreneurship education and training merely in a classroom setting is insufficient to enable an individual to exhibit such complex business behaviour or even react to the complex changing dynamics of the business environment.

However, one could envision a situation in which individuals, through exposure to practice-oriented entrepreneurship education, could act in an entrepreneurially rational way by leveraging their explicit and tacit knowledge as well as use their entrepreneurial skills in decision-making. Consequently, while entrepreneurship education and training are relevant, entrepreneurs in fact require the experience and a clearsighted approach to dealing with the practical issues and opportunities related to

---

[35]Davidsson and Honig (2003)

entrepreneurship in today's modern economy. This entails using both explicit and tacit knowledge, including one's entrepreneurial acuity, which comes from knowledge, experience and practice of entrepreneurship.

As human capital components, knowledge and experience have been found to influence entrepreneurs' decision-making process when faced with different business situations as well their ability to recognise and exploit opportunities in different business contexts.[36] Also, from an empirical viewpoint, the skills and knowledge acquired from entrepreneurship education have been found to constitute the vital human capital resources, which individuals employ to make strategic business decisions for entrepreneurial success even in challenging business environments.[37] Thus, it means that the stock of human capital possessed by an individual in form of education, training, knowledge, skills and experience could be important resources for achieving an entrepreneurial success.

6.4 ENTREPRENEURSHIP EDUCATION AS HUMAN CAPITAL RESOURCE

In considering human capital as an entrepreneurial resource, the underpinning premise is that the greater the general human capital acquired through entrepreneurship education, the better the performance in undertaking an entrepreneurial task. The question is whether entrepreneurship education as a domain of general education provides the cognate knowledge and skills required to exhibit entrepreneurial attributes – for example, an accurate perception of risks and threats, and the ability to exploit opportunities for employment creation and economic development. Analysis of the literature revealed there are instances in which the knowledge and skills acquired from entrepreneurship education have influenced the ability of nascent entrepreneurs to accurate reognise and exploit opportunities as well as perceive risks associated with undertaking and entrepreneurship activity.

Before the recent focus on entrepreneurship education in Africa, the initial approach to human capital formation emphasised knowledge and skills development for paid employment. But in recent times, with rising unemployment, there has been a policy shift towards self-employment and job creation to tackle the persistently high rate of youth and graduate unemployment. Unlike TVET, with its focus on job-specific skills for paid employment, entrepreneurship education provides access to knowledge and skills needed to generate a business idea, incubate and commercialise that idea through identification and exploitation of opportunities including strategies to access start-up capital.

Thus, the effective use of such knowledge and skills at least guarantees social and economic benefits that come with livelihood access through entrepreneurship effectiveness and job creation, ultimately leading to economic growth. Empirical evaluation of an entrepreneurship education intervention programme piloted in higher education institutions in Africa showed that individuals can convert the knowledge and skills obtained from entrepreneurship education to livelihood opportunities. Indeed, there are many instances in developed and developing countries where students and young

---

[36]Martin et al. (2013)
[37]Anosike (2018)

people have converted the knowledge and skills acquired from entrepreneurship education to economic activity, which enabled them to participate in the labour market through job creation.

Job creation has wider social and economic benefits in terms of poverty alleviation, inclusive growth, and sustainable development. With exposure to entrepreneurship education, students can develop not just entrepreneurial intention and the knowledge and skills to initiate, start and run a new business, but also entrepreneurship awareness. Entrepreneurship awareness relates to attaining a state of knowledge and mindset that gives one the optimal direction towards achieving entrepreneurial effectiveness without the need to learn the full theory of entrepreneurship. Entrepreneurship awareness, entrepreneurial intentions, business skills development and starting a new business can be associated with exposure to entrepreneurship education.

However, with spiralling youth and graduate unemployment across Africa, and with more and more young people aspiring to obtain a higher education qualification, the fundamental question is how the higher education sector can use entrepreneurship education to influence youth entrepreneurship, thereby help to tackle high graduate unemployment. This challenge can easily be addressed by introducing a coherent model for entrepreneurship education. As shown in the previous chapter, even though the higher education sector has emerged as a key driver of economic development in a modern economy, unfortunately, Africa's higher education sector has not yet sufficiently developed the knowledge infrastructures and capabilities needed to make meaningful contribution to the region's economic growth including equipping students with knowledge and skills for job creation. The problem is that there is lack of a coherent model and approach to using entrepreneurship education to spur economic growth and economic development in the region.

Also, since the launch of the SDGs, there has been an increased focus on the vital role of higher education in economic development in a modern economy. Through knowledge and research commercialisation, employment creation, fostering growth, reducing poverty and boosting shared prosperity, the higher education sector plays an important role as a catalyst for economic development in a new economy. Also, by fostering high-quality and innovative research, scrutiny of the society, nurturing entrepreneurial skills through industry collaboration, the higher education sector has helped to develop local solutions to the global challenges that we face – from unemployment and food security to climate change and public health.

Besides, the important role of higher education in the knowledge economy has been reinforced at major regional (e.g. African Higher Education Summit, Dakar, Senegal) and international (e.g. UNESCO's World Conference on Higher Education) events.[38] These important developments have no doubt influenced the increased

---

[38]In 1988, following its annual conference on higher education, UNESCO declared among others that: 'developing entrepreneurial skills and initiative should become major concerns of higher education, in order to facilitate graduates' employability who will increasingly be called upon to be not only job seekers but also and above all to become job creators'. Subsequently, following a similar conference in 2009, it declared *inter alia*: 'Faced with the complexity of current and future global challenges, higher education has the social responsibility to advance our understanding of multifaceted issues, which involves social, economic, scientific and cultural dimensions and our ability to respond to them through their core functions (research, teaching and service to the community) contribute to sustainable development'.

uptake of higher education by young people across the world including Africa. For instance, official figures from the Department for Education (DfE) show that the proportion of young people in England (50.2 between 2017 and 2018) obtaining university education has passed the symbolic 50 percent envisioned twenty years ago when Tony Blair, the then British Prime Minister, called for half of young adults to obtain higher education qualification.

More recently, there is a big push by the current Tory government to reform further and higher education systems. Through the Skills and Post-16 Education Bill announced by Her Majesty in her 2021 Queen's Speech, the aim is to make is easier to provide vocational course at any age, as it is to acquire university education. Similarly, in Africa, there is a strong desire among young populations to obtain higher education, which has led to a significant growth in the sector. Between 1970 and 2008, the gross enrolment ratio for higher education grew by an average of 8.6 percent each year compared with a global average of 4.6 percent.[39]

In enrolment terms, this equates to a growth from 250,000 in 1970 to 2.25 million in year 2000, rising to 6.34 million in 2010. Today, the African Development Bank (AfDB) estimates that as many as 14 million young Africans, that is, about 14 percent of the youth population in SSA are in higher education. Even with this exponential growth, higher education enrolment in Africa remains significantly lower at 8.59 percent (2013 figures) than the global average of 34.5 percent led by North America (84.03 percent), Europe and Central Asia (62.07 percent), Latin America and Caribbean (43.3 percent) and the Middle East and North Africa (36.42 percent).[40]

Yet, with many higher education teachers still locked into a past where the emphasis was to prepare students for public sector employment, what is perhaps more worrying is that many higher education institutions in Africa do not yet have the capacity to deliver entrepreneurship education to support students and young people to become self-employed. Also, because of several challenges, researchers and practitioners have not been able to come up with evidence-based research to better guide policymakers and practitioners to develop a coherent approach to entrepreneurship education delivery. From a sub-Saharan African viewpoint, these challenges have two implications for achieving the SDGs.

Firstly, how can the role of the higher education sector be strengthened to educate and empower students to become self-employed? Secondly, how can higher education institutions use entrepreneurship education as an effective education and training mechanism to support young people's ability to contribute to economic development through employment creation in a globalising world? Answers to these questions cannot ignore the immediate social and economic challenges facing many African countries. With the region failing to meet the decent work target under the UN's SDGs agenda, and with many African governments struggling to address high youth unemployment and poverty amid a growing youth population, the priority must be on accelerating youth entrepreneurship.

One of the most effective ways to accelerate youth entrepreneurship in Africa is to introduce a coherent and integrated model of practice-oriented entrepreneurship

[39]Kigotho (2018)
[40]Roser and Ortiz-Ospina (2013)

education to support and empower ambitious higher education students interested in becoming self-employed and creating opportunities for others. Thus, if there is a serious commitment on the part of governments and education policymakers to promote and encourage youth entrepreneurship, then the way in which entrepreneurship education is taught in Africa's higher education institutions will have to be altered in a genuinely fundamental way.

6.5 TOWARDS A NEW MODEL OF ENTREPRENEURSHIP EDUCATION

If the higher education sector is to make any meaningful contribution to employment creation and economic growth in Africa, then there must be a robust and integrated model of entrepreneurship education curriculum that permits, encourages and enables students to experiment with their ideas, creativity and innovation in a collaborative and sustainable manner within an ecosystem framework. Students would be more willing and committed to pursue an entrepreneurship career if they were convinced that higher education systems, including the curricula, rules and regulations as well as financing and the business environments support and enable the realisation of their entrepreneurial ambitions.

Unfortunately, in a globalised world, the business environment is often entangled in a very complex web of competing social and economic dynamics that are sometimes outside the control of the individual, and even a country. These dynamics relate to the activities of human and non-human agents including inter and intra-organisational networks of public (e.g. business regulation) and private (e.g. employment creation) institutions, which can increase the complexity of an entrepreneurial ecosystem. However, entrepreneurial ecosystems can create value in the entrepreneurial process only if the agents within the ecosystem act in an interdependent manner. Value creation can be measured by start-up creation and success at individual and organisational levels.

In Africa, an important recent development in the entrepreneurial process is the heavy emphasis of entrepreneurship development programmes, which comprise setting up entrepreneurship centres and entrepreneurship or innovation hubs in higher education institutions. Within the higher education system, most entrepreneurship development programmes normally sit within business schools. With such arrangement, the overriding goal is to enable the conditions under which entrepreneurship can thrive among students, through that contribute to employment creation and economic development through programme design, pedagogy and practice.

As a general education curriculum, entrepreneurship education is open to most higher education students in Africa as part of their compulsory general studies course, particularly at undergraduate level. The core aim is to foster and instil in students and graduates an entrepreneurial mindset. That is, to influence a change from a culture of dependence in paid employment by influencing them to embrace creativity and innovation needed for self-employment. Self-employment requires the acquisition and use of core practical knowledge and some skills needed for entrepreneurship including problem or opportunity identification, ideation, incubation and access to market strategies essential to the early-stage process of venture formation.

In theory, by creating networking opportunities between established entrepreneurs and student entrepreneurs, and by investing in platforms that encourage academic–industry collaboration coupled with a quality classroom experience, practical knowledge and skills in entrepreneurship can be acquired. Academic–industry collaboration can be facilitated through business accelerator programmes, practice and research commercialisation, which can support and expand the talent pool of students with the potential to become successful entrepreneurs within a campus entrepreneurship or innovation hub. But higher education students in Africa expected to become entrepreneurs after graduation rarely have access to such integrated model of entrepreneurship education curriculum.

Analysis of the higher education landscape revealed that higher education institutions in Africa – except in a handful of top universities in South Africa, Nigeria, Kenya and Egypt, are struggling to introduce a coherent and integrated entrepreneurship education curriculum. Several reasons account for this situation. First, because Africa's higher education sector rarely has a strong linkage with the industry, most entrepreneurship education courses are designed by university professors and academics who themselves lack an industry experience, therefore have very little or no insight into the complexity and the changing dynamics of the labour market or the business environment.

Consequently, it is difficult to design an effective entrepreneurship education course that is able to alter students' mindsets and that also meets market expectations in a successful manner. These problems perhaps explain why students and graduates who have been exposed to entrepreneurship education lack knowledge of the basic principles of entrepreneurship, and how to launch an entrepreneurship career after graduation. Since the instructional materials including teaching and assessment techniques are often not-fit-for purpose. Secondly, apart from inadequate content and pedagogical issues, there is the related and wider problem of embracing the concept of entrepreneurial university by the higher education sector.

As an important constituency within the entrepreneurship ecosystem, the notion of entrepreneurial university denotes an institution that is in close connection with and provides 'entrepreneurship capital' for the benefit of its members including students and staff, as well as the wider society. Unfortunately, most higher education institutions in Africa have not yet fully connected with the concept of entrepreneurial university, neither have they figured out how to effectively transition into entrepreneurial entities as connected institutions rooted in their communities and the wider society – thereby, less dependent on inadequate government subsidies and students' tuition fees.

Thirdly, the ongoing global debate about what role higher education institutions should play as 'agents of change and innovation' in close interaction with the employability needs of students and the wider society is in fact not yet firmly rooted in the context of Africa. For the region, the immediate question should be what kind of political leverage higher education institutions should enjoy within a 'Triple Helix' framework in order to help drive economic development in a knowledge-based economy in which change is a constant phenomenon. The importance of being agile and responsive to change is even more evident in the current economic context of the COVID-19 pandemic.

With students' learning disrupted, we know that the health crisis has eaten away at the usual freedom, spontaneity, serendipity and the physical closeness that come with study life in high education institutions. Yet, unlike their global counterparts in Asia, Europe and elsewhere, most higher education students in Africa have been disproportionately affected due to the lack of digital infrastructure and knowhow in most African universities. Globally, the COVID-19 crisis has accelerated the debate about what higher education institutions should offer, to whom and how.

With most higher education institutions in Asia, Europe and North America embracing 'blended learning' as an immediate response to the crisis, the priority for Africa must go beyond what types of blended learning or online tools could be adapted to consider a more holistic and substantial conversation about reforming the sector. A key part of the reform process must ensure that higher education generates employment and delivers shared economic prosperity through an integrated model of entrepreneurship education that incorporates private sector expertise in programme design and assessment. In other parts of the world, such as in Europe and North America, where the higher education system is embedded in the industry and influenced by industry professionals, entrepreneurship education programmes have helped students to form and manage new businesses and employed others, thereby contributed to economic growth in a sustainable manner.

In Africa, entrepreneurship education courses are markedly different in that higher education curriculum simply does not exist on a scale capable of exposing students to a full-circle learning experience in entrepreneurship through strong academic-industry linkages. Apart from that, the outdated contents and poor quality of most programmes are symptomatic of the wider sector challenges of inadequate funding, inequality in higher education access, affordability and industry relevance. From employment creation and economic development standpoints, what is required is praxis, responsiveness and dialogue with all higher education stakeholders to develop an integrated framework for teaching entrepreneurship education in a more practical and meaningful way.

6.6 PRACTICE-ORIENTED ENTREPRENEURSHIP EDUCATION

The question of whether or not entrepreneurship can be taught and whether it empowers students to become entrepreneurs has for so long dogged entrepreneurship education researchers and practitioners. Higher education shapes students' post-study career intentions, and therefore can stimulate their interest in an entrepreneurship career. But higher education in Africa, which tends towards an individual-centred model of learning, is rather linear, and therefore proves counterproductive as a way to influence and nurture students' entrepreneurship career.

It is akin to what Allan Gibb referred to as a 'didactic model', whereby students receive knowledge and capabilities through a sequentially passive process and are then expected to start a new business soon after their graduation.[41] Also, there is a real risk that passive models of educating and training students may be generalising too much

---

[41] Gibb (1993); also see Gibb (2002)

and contextualising too little by, for example, paying little attention to the distinct composition and capabilities of individual students as potential entrepreneurs.[42] In a knowledge-driven economy, the increased role of higher education is, however, not merely focused on developing the distinct capabilities of individuals.

Attention has shifted towards how higher education can contribute to organisational productivity and wider societal development through the adoption of practice-oriented teaching and learning techniques. A linear and passive approach to teaching and learning entrepreneurship education is therefore clearly inadequate to stimulate entrepreneurship career, particularly in Africa where there is an urgent need to tackle widespread graduate unemployment. Thus, there is a need to transform the models through which higher education students and young people in schools are trained to become entrepreneurs. In fact, because entrepreneurship involves the actual formation of new ventures, there has to be a move towards adopting practice-oriented learning as part of a wider higher education reform.

The main concern is that the dominant form of rote teaching and passive learning limits the opportunity to leverage the synergies between the academia and the business community. In contrast, embracing practice-oriented entrepreneurship education will help to stimulate, influence and sustain students' entrepreneurial drive. From a psychosocial learning perspective, a practice-oriented learning mechanism puts human agency, rather than the curriculum or education provider, at the centre of education and training provision. The idea of agency is 'mediated' by 'the capacity to learn',[43] which can be experiential and/or collaborative in nature.

In this sense, learning or teaching may either occur in spontaneous ways involving a meaningful activity, or, in self-directed ways within 'a community of practice' whereby learners rely on role models to form and sometimes normalise their identity.[44] Education and training in such settings have been proven to trigger students' intention to act, more so than the transference of mere entrepreneurial knowledge in a classroom setting. Thus, similarly, practice-oriented entrepreneurship programme has been found to help in embedding the entrepreneurial competencies for success in a much more meaningful way for individual benefit,[45] which has in turn translated to employment creation and socioeconomic development.[46]

Similarly, entrepreneurial competencies (i.e. knowledge and skills) and entrepreneurial intentions can be triggered through observations. The use of observations to transfer entrepreneurial competencies suggests that the influence of role models (e.g. teachers, business owners, etc.) may be an important dimension to practice-oriented entrepreneurship education process.[47] The concept of role modelling as a means of practice-oriented entrepreneurship education delivery vis-à-vis a learner's perceived behavioural tendency, which involves the intentions, decisions and the drive to take an entrepreneurial action has been employed in entrepreneurship education research.

---

[42]Rasmussen and Sorheim (2006)
[43]Ahearn (2001, p. 112)
[44]Wenger (1998)
[45]Bauman and Lucy (2019)
[46]Premand et al. (2016)
[47]San-Martins et al. (2019)

With role models, the emphasis is on 'collective learning and reflection', which ensures that learning has a greater impact on an individual's mindset and orientation.[48]

As shown in Figure 6.1, practice-oriented entrepreneurship education strategies may include ideation, knowledge commercialisation, problem-solving and collaborative learning formats whereby successful business owners serve as influencers and the knowledge transfer agents in the entrepreneurial process involving higher education students, industry and the wider community. The opportunity to observe, reflect and learn from others, particularly business owners through role modelling, while not a common approach to entrepreneurship education delivery in Africa, can have a powerful effect on students' entrepreneurial ambition. After all, a learner can alter his or her aspiration and behaviour simply by being exposed to the success and mistakes of others including entrepreneurs. Also, by learning from one another, inspiring one another and by exercising leadership through role modelling and teamworking, students can acquire important survival tactics for a successful entrepreneurship career that may never form part of a theoretical classroom discussion.

Thus, in the higher education sector, practice-oriented learning techniques can be embedded in entrepreneurship education curriculum for the purpose of promoting and encouraging more student entrepreneurs. Ultimately, the aim is to shift students' post-study career mindset away from paid employment to self-employment. Although there is no 'one size fits all' approach to promoting practice-oriented entrepreneurship education, however, a platform that brings together higher education student's

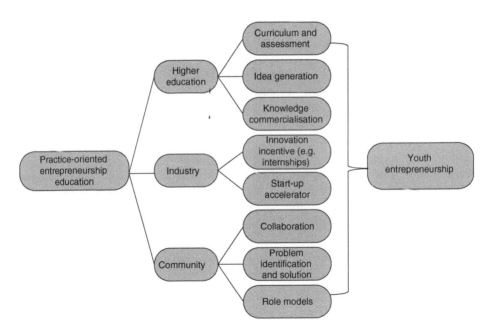

FIGURE 6.1 Typology of practice-oriented entrepreneurship education for graduate employment

[48]Fellnhofer (2017)

population, academics, business and community leaders for entrepreneurial action could offer an insight into how practice-oriented entrepreneurship education might work in reality. This principle underpins the ENACTUS project in Nigeria.

6.7 PRACTICE-ORIENTED ENTREPRENEURSHIP EDUCATION – ENACTUS PROJECT

ENACTUS Nigeria is a multi-stakeholder platform that brings together students, higher education institutions (HEIs), organisations, business groups and community leaders to identify and solve socioeconomic problems using creativity, risk-taking and innovation as catalysts for entrepreneurship in communities. Thus, under the platform, students studying entrepreneurship education as part of their core curriculum are challenged to exhibit entrepreneurial attributes and capabilities through competitions, which involve identifying and solving community-based problems.

By so doing, the students get an opportunity to work collaboratively alongside academics, business mentors, organisations, and community representatives. Working collaboratively enables students to hone their business skills, which better prepares them for their entrepreneurial journey after graduation. ENACTUS project exposes students to a wide range of real-life experiences enable them to exhibit and that enhance their entrepreneurial skills and capabilities in addition to academic qualifications. For instance, students can network and connect with prominent business leaders, learn how to communicate, and lead effective team effort by working with others to solve real-life problems.

Also, through such collaboration, students are exposed to other benefits and opportunities including internships, referrals as well as partnerships with companies seeking for entrepreneurially minded talents. Through a joined-up effort, real impact can emerge in the form of tangible solutions to specific organisational and community problems, formation of meaningful relationships and business networks. Thus, enabling students to improve their human and social capital beyond the classroom. Historically, ENACTUS Nigeria derived its inspiration from the US-based ENACTUS, which is committed to developing the next generation of young entrepreneurs and social innovators.

Established in 1975 to provide students and graduates with knowledge and skills for self-employment through an experiential learning process, ENACTUS was originally modelled on the vision of Students in Free Enterprise (SIFE). But ENACTUS Nigeria has been remodelled to reflect the contextual priorities of the Nigerian community while retaining the entrepreneurial spirit and transformative power of its founding vision. As a global movement, ENACTUS is represented in over 1,800 higher education institutions and boasts an annual membership of over 72,000 students and 550 corporate organisations and individual partners across 35 countries.

To date, the ENACTUS vision has directly impacted approximately two million people globally. The organisation is actively present in thirty HEIs in Nigeria with about 1,500 active student memberships. Altogether, its work in Nigeria has positively impacted about 1.5 million people directly and indirectly through various projects. Among others, students have worked on a wide range of community-led projects from converting plastic waste to wealth, enabling small businesses to scale using mobile technology, boosting farmers' yields and income more efficiently, transforming unused cabins and spaces into dignified spaces for the homeless, economic empowerment for widows, and created job opportunities for former prison inmates as well as helped to reduce environmental pollution.

Practice-oriented entrepreneurship education not only requires students to 'think outside the box' and work collaboratively in teams, but it also forces them to be creative and innovative in addressing community problems and wider societal challenges. From an environmental sustainability standpoint, a good example is an innovative project aimed at employing polyethylene terephthalate (PET City) bottles and nylons for other productive uses undertaken by the ENACTUS students' team at the Covenant University, Nigeria. PET is not bio-degradable, and in most cases, it is not properly recycled in Nigeria. Some end up in dump sites, while others are forced through drainages and sea, thereby affecting aquatic lives.

The negative effects on the environment are immense from environmental degradation to ecological disaster, which present serious health risks to both animals and humans. Motivated by a desire to reverse these environmental risks, and by working with various groups, the students spotted an opportunity to solve a particular problem within their community by initiating the PET city project. Coming from multidisciplinary backgrounds including the sciences, technology, arts and social sciences, the students initially encountered, but successfully navigated, several challenges before launching and completing their project.

With employment for themselves and ability to support their families, coupled with the underlying mission to keep the environment clean, the students and community members have now become energised behind a common cause as champions of the PET city project. The success of this project earned the team the position of national champions in the 2019 ENACTUS National Competition in Nigeria. The ENACTUS's case is just one example of how practice-oriented entrepreneurship can be implemented in schools. There are other ways in which higher education providers can introduce practice-oriented entrepreneurship education depending on their contextual priorities and resources. In conclusion, since different approaches to promoting and encouraging entrepreneurship among young people vary widely in scope and outcomes based on the quality, duration, resources and depth of a programme, an effective way to ensure the dissemination and diffusion of best practices is by assessing the impact of practice-oriented entrepreneurship education.

Thus, it is only by determining what works, what does not, and what lessons can be learnt, can the opportunity emerge for an improved practice, coupled with enhanced policy environment to embrace practice-oriented entrepreneurship education for employment creation and socioeconomic growth. Coincidentally, these views not only start to unpack how to address the thorny issue of high youth unemployment, but they also introduce a personal yet critical reflection on the wider context and meaning of employment in many countries across Africa. This relates to whether the nature of and access to entrepreneurship education programme which still forces as high as 90 percent of young Africans into the precarious informal sector with low productivity and income, can help to reduce high youth unemployment, thereby lead to social and economic transformation.

BIBLIOGRAPHY

Ahearn, L. M. (2001). Language and agency. *Annual Review of Anthropology*, 30, 109–137.

Anosike, P. U. (2018). Entrepreneurship as human capital: Implications for youth self-employment and conflict mitigation in sub-Saharan Africa. *Industry and Higher Education*, 33(1), 42–54.

Anosike, P. U. (2019). Entrepreneurship education as human capital: Implications for youth self-employment and conflict mitigation in Sub-Saharan Africa. *Industry and Higher Education*, 33(1), 42–54.

Athayde, R. (2009). Measuring enterprise potential in young people. *Entrepreneurship Theory and Practice*, 33(2), 481–500.

Bae, T. J., Qian, S., Miao, C., & Fiet, J. O. (2014). The relationship between entrepreneurship education and entrepreneurial intentions: A meta-analytic review. *Entrepreneurship: Theory & Practice*, 38(2), 217–254.

Bandura, A. (1982). Self-efficacy mechanism in human agency. *American Psychologist*, 37(2), 122–147.

Bauman, A., & Lucy, C. (2019). Enhancing entrepreneurial education: Developing competencies for success. *The International Journal of Management Education*, 19(1), 100293. doi:10.1016/j.ijme.2019.03.005

Béchard, J., & Grégoire, D. A. (2005). Entrepreneurship education research revisited: the case of higher education. *Academy of Management Learning and Education*, 4(1), 22–43.

Davidsson, P. (1995). Culture, structure and regional levels of entrepreneurship. *Entrepreneurship and Regional Development*, 7(1), 41–62.

Davidsson, P., & Honig, B. (2003). The role of social and human capital among nascent entrepreneurs. *Journal of Business Venturing*, 18(3), 301–331.

Dimov, D. (2010). Nascent entrepreneurs and venture emergence: Opportunity confidence, human capital, and early planning. *Journal of Management Studies*, 47(6), 1123–1153.

Dimov, D., & Shepherd, D. (2005). Human capital theory and venture capital firms: Exploring 'home runs' and 'strike outs'. *Journal of Business Venturing*, 20(1), 1–21.

Fayolle, A., Gailly, B., & Lassas-Clerc, N. (2006). Assessing the impact of entrepreneurship education programmes: A new methodology. *Journal of European Industrial Training*, 30(9), 701–720.

Fayolle, A., Verzat, C., & Wapshott, R. (2016). In quest of legitimacy: The theoretical and methodological foundations of entrepreneurship education research. *International Small Business Journal*, 34(7), 895–904.

Fayolle, A. (2018). *A research agenda for entrepreneurship education*, Cheltenham: Edward Elgar Publishing.

Fellnhofer, K. (2017). Entrepreneurship education revisited: Perceived entepreneurial role models increase perceived behavioral control. *International Journal of Learning and Change*, 9(3), 260–283.

Fox, J., Pittaway, L., & Uzuegbunam, I. (2018). Simulations in entrepreneurship education: Serious games and learning through play. *Entrepreneurship Education and Pedagogy*, 1(1), 61–89.

Frese, M., Krauss, S., Keith, N., Escher, S., Grabarkiewicz, R., Luneng, T., ..., Friedrich, C. (2007). Business owners' action planning and its relationship to business success in three African countries. *Journal of Applied Psychology*, 92(6), 1481–1498.

Garavan, T. N., & O'Cinneide, B. (1994). Entrepreneurship education and training programmes: A review and evaluation – Part 1. *Journal of European Industrial Training*, 18(8), 3–12.

Gibb, A. (1993). The enterprise culture and education: Understanding enterprise education and its links with small business entrepreneurship and wider educational goals. *International Small Business Journal*, 11(3): 11–34.

Gorlewicz, J. L., & Jayaram, S. (2020). Instilling curiosity, connections and creating value in entrepreneurial minded engineering: Concepts for a course sequence in dynamics and controls. *Entrepreneurship Education and Pedagogy*, 3, 60–85.

Huang-Saad, A., Bodnar, C., & Carberry, A. (2020). Examining current practices in engineering entrepreneurship education. *Entrepreneurship Education and Pedagogy*, 3(1), 4–13.

Kigotho, W. (2018). Higher education – caught in a double bind. *University World News*. Retrieved from https://www.universityworldnews.com/post.php?story=201803281625308 35. Accessed on 15 January 2021.

Kuratko, D. F. (2005). The emergence of entrepreneurship education: Development, trends, and challenges. *Entrepreneurship Theory and Practice*, 29(5), 577–598.

Kuratko, D., & Morris, H. (2018). Corporate entreprenuership: A critical challenge for educators and researchers. *Entreprenuership Education Pedagogy*, 1(1), 42–60.

Lindh, I., & Thorgren, S. (2016). Entrepreneurship education: The role of local business. *Entrepreneurship and Regional Development*, 28(5–6), 313–336.

Maresch, D., Harms, R., Kailer, N., & Wimmer-Wurm, B. (2016). The impact of entrepreneurship education on the entrepreneurial intentions of students in the science and engineering versus business studies university programs. *Technological Forecasting and Social Change*, 104, 172–179.

Martin, B. C., McNally, J. J., & Kay, M. J. (2013). Examining the formation of human capital in entreprenuership: A meta-analysis of entreprenuership education outcomes. *Journal of Business Venturing*, 28, 211–224.

Marvel, M. R., Davis, J. L., & Sproul, C. R. (2016). Human capital and entrepreneurship research: A critical review and future directions. *Entrepreneurship Theory and Practice*, 40(3), 599–626.

Mincer, J. (1984). Human capital and economic growth. *Economics of Education Review*, 3(3), 195–205.

Mitchelmore, S., & Rowley, J. (2013). Entrepreneurial competencies of women entrepreneurs pursuing business growth. *Journal of Small Business and Enterprise Development*, 20(1), 125–142.

Nabi, G., Liñán, F., Fayolle, A., Krueger, N., & Walmsley, A. (2017). The impact of entrepreneurship education in higher education: A systematic review and research agenda. *Academy of Management Learning & Education*, 16(2), 277–299.

Neck, H. M., & Corbett, A. C. (2018). The scholarship of teaching and learning entreprenuership. *Entrepreneurship Education Pedagogy*, 1(1), 8–41.

Nyello, R., Kalufya, N., Rengua, C., Nsolezi, M., & Ngirwa, C. (2015). Entreprenuership education on entrepreneurial behaviour: The case of graduates in the higher learning institutions in Tanzania. *Asian Journal of Business Management*, 7(2), 37–42.

Pittaway, L., & Cope, J. (2007). Entrepreneurship education: A systematic review of the evidence. *International Small Business Journal*, 25(5), 479–510.

Premand, P., Brodmann, S., Almeida, R., Grun, R., & Barouni, M. (2016). Entrepreneurship education and entry into self-employment among University Graduates. *World Development*, 77, 311–327.

Rasmussen, E. A., & Sorheim, R. (2006). Action-based entrepreneurship education. *Technovation*, 26(2), 185–194.

Roser, M., & Ortiz-Ospina, E. (2013). Tertairy education. Published online at OurWorldInData. org. Retrieved from https://ourworldindata.org/tertiary-education. Accessed on 15 January 2021.

San-Martins, P., Fernandez-Laviada, A., Perez, A., & Palazuelos, E. (2019). The teacher of entrepreneurship as a role model: Students' and teachers' perceptions. *The International Journal of Management Education*, 19(1), 100358. doi:10.1016/j.ijme.2019.100358

Shane, S., & Venkataramam, S. (2000). The promise of entreprenuership as a field of research. *Academy of Management Review*, 25(1), 217–226.

Vanevenhoven, J., & Liguori, E. (2013). The impact of entrepreneurship education: Introducing the entreprenuership education project. *Journal of Small Business Management*, 51(3), 315–328.

Wenger, E. (1998). *Communities of practice: Learning, meaning, and identity*. Cambridge: Cambridge Univesity Press.

ECONOMY AND INCOME OPPORTUNITY

7

The pace of global economic progress is losing momentum. Since the 2008 financial crisis, rising unemployment, poverty and starvation have depressed productivity growth, stagnated income, worsened inequality and in some cases triggered social tension. In addition, mounting debt has left many small businesses and households in a deteriorating financial distress. These problems, exacerbated by the economic fallout of the COVID-19 pandemic, have prompted fears that the global economy is heading towards a new decade of disappointing growth outcomes. Lack of global cooperation to tackle the COVID-19 pandemic and its varied mutations has discouraged investment and consumption, thereby creating uncertainty about a post-pandemic economic recovery.

Notwithstanding, early 2021 showed a strong economic rebound in emerging and developing economies (EMDEs) led mainly by China – the world's second largest economy. China's 2.3 percent annual economic growth in late 2020, although its weakest since the 1990s, makes it an outlier among other large economies in what has been a pandemic-ravaged year. By contrast, in 2020 alone, the United States economy might have contracted by as much as 3.6 percent, the Eurozone shrunk by 7.4 percent, while the global economy suffered an estimated 6.9 percent GDP contraction[1] – thereby resulting in a negative global economic growth of −4.9 percent.

Despite a seemingly positive economic outlook for EMDEs, for more than a quarter of African countries, the economic effects of the pandemic were likely to have wiped off a decade-long progress on per capita income gains. In sub-Saharan African (SSA), the disruptions to educational systems and business sectors have disproportionately slowed down human capital development and productivity growth and severely affected livelihoods and incomes. To compound matters, fiscal constraints and high debt burden hinder the ability of governments in SSA to provide the needed fiscal stimulus to kickstart their economies.

Without continuous fiscal stimulus, highly indebted African countries at the brink of economic collapse even before the pandemic cannot support their vulnerable workforce population and the struggling business sector to recover from the economic crisis arising from the pandemic. However, a further worsening of the situation could be avoided if

---

[1]World Bank (2021)

only policy makers could cease the opportunity to push for serious economic reforms targeting programmes that boost productivity and job creation, thereby raise incomes. Increased productivity and income are likely to spur spending and consumption, which are essential to kick-starting weak or failing economies. As an idea, productivity is typically expressed by the principle of output–input ratio. Thus, it is generally defined as the efficiency in production in terms of how much output is obtained from a given set of inputs.[2]

For so long, however, economists and researchers have struggled to measure or operationalise productivity levels based on the principle of input–output ratio. Measuring productivity can be a complex and elusive venture, especially where there are several outputs or inputs. This is often the case in relation to economic activities that occur within organisations and countries, with each having striking differences in their levels of productivity. Factors such as institutions, human capital, organisational structures, employees' skills level and social networks account for and influence the differences in levels of productivity within organisations and between countries. Even within narrowly defined business sectors, such as technological or engineering, differences in educational attainments and skill sets can also have a salutary effect on people's levels of productivity and income earning potential.

Differences in levels of productivity and income are in some cases determined by a combination of various factors beyond an individual's control. As such, if countries were to make proper investments in developing the human capital of their workforce population, then it would become far more easier to increase the productivity of their workforce, which in turn may translate into economic benefits and increased national prosperity. While the premise of these arguments may be acceptable, even desirable, they however also raise some important questions. One question is why do some countries have higher levels of human capital, productivity, income and economic growth than others? Explaining and disentangling the intricate nature of the relationship between productivity, income and economic growth can be problematic.

Notwithstanding, differences in institutional arrangements and government policies influence differences in educational attainment, human capital accumulation and consequently productivity. The differences in institutional arrangements also explain the large differences in income and economic growth between countries.[3] Differences in levels of productivity and institutonal arrangements also account for why some countries enjoy different or better standards of living, per capita income and economic prosperity than others. The world's most com-petitive and developed economies with high levels of productivity and per capita income, such as the United States and Germany, have strong institutional arrangements. Because of this, they are significantly more productive than even large EMDEs like India and Nigeria, where institutional arrangements may be weak, or even non-existent.

Also, the differences in institutional arrangements partly explain why productivity levels, per capita income and living standards in the United States and Germany are much higher at $US66,080 and $US57, 810 (2019 figures), compared to roughly $US6,920 in India and $US5,190 in Nigeria (2019 figures). Therefore, it seems strong institutions are the prerequisite for high productivity and economic prosperity. Also, productivity levels

---

[2]Syverson (2011)
[3]Hall and Jones (1999)

can determine whether one enjoys high or low levels of income, which has a positive or negative effect on their purchasing power and ability to contribute to the economy. For example, levels of educational achievements have either a favourable or unfavourable effect on people's income and productivity levels, which in turn affects their ability to enhance their personal well-being and contribute to societal growth.

Invariably, levels of productivity, income and economic growth are influenced by institutional arrangements within countries through the presence or lack of explicit formal 'rules of the game', such as laws and constitutions. With these perspectives, and from a narrowly defined economic standpoint, the pertinent question is how do institutional arrangements, whether formal or informal, overlap to determine differences in economic outcomes. Components of informal institutions, such as social networks, are not only linked with formal institutions, but also they overlap with economic activities which are deemed relevant to employment creation and GDP per capita income. In Africa, informal economic activities are as relevant to employment creation if not more than formal economic activities. Therefore, they overlap with formal and informal institutions to determine economic outcomes in a way core to the region's economic development.

7.1 FORMAL AND INFORMAL INSTITUTIONS

There is a misguided notion that economic activity, even a political process, is shaped primarily, if not exclusively, by formal 'rules of the game'. However, in reality, the political process and consequently economic outcomes of formal institutions within countries are often shaped and influenced by informal rules. As discussed in chapter two, institutions enable and constrain human activity. By so doing, they govern the prevailing 'rules of the game' that influence human behaviour as well as the political and social dynamics that define and shape economic outcomes. Less clear, however, is the distinction between these dynamics and how they interact within formal and informal institutions to determine economic outcomes for people, as well as the nature of the linkages that exist between them.

Some have attempted to distinguish formal institutions based on formal rules, which are regulated and enforced through a third party, usually the State. Whereas informal institutions have been defined based on informal norms within social networks that are self-regulating and self-enforcing.[4] The French Sociologist, Pierre Bourdieu, described the nature of these self-regulatory norms within informal institutions and their related benefits as a form of social capital accrued from 'mutual obligations, feelings of gratitude, respect, and friendship among network members'.[5]

Others have linked formal institutions to rules and procedures that are created, communicated and enforced through channels, such as constitutions, laws, regulations, courts, which are widely considered and accepted as official, whereas socially shared rules, usually unwritten, that are created, communicated and enforced outside of officially sanctioned channels have been associated with informal institutions.[6] Of course, the reality is that the outcomes of formal institutional arrangement in

---

[4]Knight (1992)
[5]Bourdieu (1986)
[6]Helmke and Levitsky (2004)

different areas of public (e.g. politics, legislation) and private (business, employment, career growth) life are shaped by 'unwritten' informal rules in a more or less visible way, as well as in a direct and indirect manner.

Across the world, there is a pervasive use of informal modes of exchange to 'create or strengthen the incentives to comply with formal rules'. Informal social networks – whose activities are enacted through 'clan-based norms', 'reciprocity', 'patri-monialism', 'clientelism' and 'corruption' – coexist with, and in some cases undermine formal State systems including political and economic activities within formal institutions.[7] In developed and developing countries, formal institutions that bind politics and the economy through legislative agenda are influenced by 'unwritten rules of the game', which are reified through personal relationships and social networks. This is the reality in many countries including the United States, United Kingdom, Russia, Japan and even in modern China with well-established formal institutions.

In these countries, human activity channeled through long-standing informal net-works shape and determine formal institutional outcomes for individuals and different groups. For instance, in the United States, basic social norms, such as reciprocity, constitutes the 'folkways' used by 'insiders' to influence patterns of legislative agenda and behaviour in the US Congress.[8] The 'folkways' underscores the fact that 'there are unwritten but generally accepted and informally enforced norms of conduct in the [US] chamber'.[9] Thus, it would seem that rather than 'explicit rules of the game' and moral principles, a blend of social norms and political expediency guide the legislative activities of 'insiders' (that is network members) to the exclusion, and even to the detriment, of 'outsiders'.

Similarly, in the United Kingdom, the 'old boys' club – an informal nepotistic social network of mainly middle-aged white men – has for several decades been a channel for and remains prone to 'gendered corruption' in political representation in the UK parliament.[10] Equally in Russia, the practice of *blat'* – the use of informal social networks to obtain favours and circumvent formal procedures – is used to facilitate preferential access to simple everyday needs, such as education and jobs and to enable actors to navigate and compensate for the rigid economic and politically complex and authoritarian systems of post-Soviet Russia.[11]

In Japan, the strict but unwritten rules of *amakudari* is a long-standing practice which ensures that elite officials of government agencies obtain employment in private companies upon retirement. This socially reciprocal practice not only allows private companies within the *amakudari* network to enjoy preferential treatment in obtaining government contracts, but it also enables them to avoid regulatory oversight. Thus, it raises concerns about the implicit patterns of collusion between the regulator and the regulated in the Japanese society.[12] Also, the practice of *jinmyaku* – an informal network involving superiors, subordinates and peers within an organisation and decision-makers in other organisations as well as with government officials – facilitates

---

[7]Lindberg (2003)
[8]Schneier (2010)
[9]Mathews (1959, p. 1)
[10]Stockemer et al. (2020)
[11]Ledeneva (2009)
[12]Mizoguchi and Van Quyen (2009)

informal exchanges and coordination of favours including jobs, career advancement and decision-making among members.[13]

Apart from the United States, United Kingdom, Russia and Japan, the inherently reciprocal nature of *guanxi* – which refers to a network of social connections that only manifests where there is something to be done – often blurs the boundary between personal and business relationships, as well as the relationship between State institutions and private businesses in today's China. As both an 'expressive' and 'instrumental' gesture, *guanxi* is a historically significant cultural practice that has for decades not only perplexed foreigners and outsiders alike, but it has also raised a serious ethical dilemma given its strong ties to Chinese political and socioeconomic systems.

Although an informal social practice, *guanxi* is very pervasive and effective in every aspect of personal and public life in China. Individuals and organisations with *guanxi* connections are known to enjoy huge political and economic advantage often achieved at the expense of others, which in turn creates significant disadvantages to parties outside the network. Historically seen as part of Confucian values, *guanxi* has today evolved into an institutionalised channel of corruption that often involves a complicated network between high-ranking government officials, businessmen, army or police and the mafia.[14] In each of these cases across different countries, to survive, informal social networks tend to rely on a utilitarian system of reciprocity and mutual solidarity among members. In Africa, by shaping the outcomes of formal institutions, the nature and dynamics of informal social networks are similar to those in other countries.

Membership of social networks is usually reserved for close professional associates, close friends, intimate friends, acquaintances and even family members. Social criteria, such as, ego, power and wealth are used to categorise or classify the level of influence, sway, benefits or even the level of favours or advantage network members can enjoy and leverage. Depending on their social standing, the frequency and intensity of the reciprocal exchange, individuals may move from one category or classification to another. Also, the scope of benefits that accrue to network members can be broad, ranging from job placements, preferential treatment in government contracts, regulatory waivers or lowering bureaucratic hurdles in obtaining formal documents, such as permits, licences, passports, identity cards and tax clearances.

In terms of *modus operandi*, social and personal interactions reinforce the 'unwritten rules', which is predominantly the hallmark of informal social networks. Network members often promote and advance their personal or group agenda through a social exchange process that confers on parties a mutually binding but implicit contract to honour the purpose of the exchange. In other words, the 'unwritten rules', whereby individuals requesting and offering a favour are always conscious and aware of future benefits that may accrue, prevent parties to the exchange from making the requirements of the contract explicit.

Yet, the requirement exists as a 'debt of honour' within the contract, which may be payable at any given time in different forms. Thus, reinforcing the 'chain of reciprocity' as an embedded norm in what is essentially a social process, the outcomes of

---

[13]Horak (2018)
[14]Fan (2002)

which influence the political process and economic prerogatives of formal institutions.[15] The nature and dynamics of the specific ways in which social networks operate in different countries clearly provide evidence that shows their activities influence political and economic outcomes of formal institutions. More pertinent, perhaps, is the extent to which informal economic ties shape formal economic activities within countries. Not much is known in the literature about the nature of this economic linkage, especially from the institutional context of informal economy.

7.2 INFORMAL ECONOMY

Against the backdrop of globalisation, shifting demographics, and weakening institutions that exists in many parts of Africa, the linkage between formal and informal economy (otherwise known as formal and informal sectors) has never been so pervasive. The nature of this linkage is so acute that old notions of Africa's informal economy as 'unorganised', 'backward', 'shadowy' and 'peripheral' to economic development have become meaningless. If anything, informal economic arrangements based on informal social ties and embedded formal institutional systems have entered into the heart of contemporary African countries through 'economic processes of subcontracting, transnational migration and diminished State involvement in employment'.[16]

By reinforcing the economic failures of formal institutions, the informal economy now functions as an intrinsic structure of contemporary African societies. As a result, the informal economy is widely seen as critical to the region's economic development in the same way as the formal economy, particularly in generating income opportunity for young people. Yet, economic activities in the informal economy largely remain outside the purview of State regulation. Because of the complexity and the controversy surrounding this subject, and the fact that informal economy as a phenomenon has failed to converge under a common economic theory even after several decades of research effort, it is important to first explain the historical context in which the informal economy may have gained the intellectual attention that it enjoys today.

The first emerged in the 1970s through the work of a renowned anthropologist, Professor Keith Hart. Hart's obsession with the patterns of economic life and the proliferation of casual labour and self-employment among poor urban migrants in Accra, Ghana, led to an investigation into the nature of income opportunity and economic activities that thrived outside the framework of official State institutions. Hart was initially interested in exploring 'whether the informal economic activities of the reserve army of the urban unemployed and the underemployed that make up a passive, exploited majority in Accra possess some autonomous capacity to generate income growth?'.[17] Although, his real and ultimate ambition was to unveil the basis of defining the concept of the informal economy.

---

[15]Lomnitz (1998)
[16]Meagher (2010)
[17]Hart (1973, p. 1)

However, after much effort, he conceded that any empirical attempt to define the informal economy was 'elusive'.[18] Perhaps, this elusiveness could be linked to the strong economic ties between formal and the informal economy. For Hart, the main distinguishing feature of informal economy relates to the fundamental question of the underlying motivation for engaging in work. That is, 'whether or not individuals seek to recruit labour on a permanent basis for a fixed reward'.[19]

Equally, this fundamental question explains why the issue of 'illegality' and 'legitimacy' of economic activities in the informal economy remain a highly contentious area of research interest. However, whereas enterprises in the formal economy are generally viewed to operate with a measure of permanence, structure and bureaucracy, which makes it possible to organise, determine, capture and count in official statistics – as such, widely seen to constitute the engine of the modern economy. The remainder are considered as informal economic activities. That is, enterprises that are variously grouped as 'the low-productivity urban sector', 'the reserve army of underemployed and unemployed', 'the urban traditional sector', which have quasi-permanence, little to no structure, difficult to determine – offer informal employment, therefore escapes official statistics and sanction.

The second source of intellectual impetus to informal economy emerged in 1972 through the World Employment Programme report of the International Labour Organisation (ILO) led by Cambridge Professor of Economics, Hans Singer. Singer, together with Fellows of the Institute of Development Studies (IDS) at the University of Sussex, United Kingdom, was one of the early economists employed by the United Nations (UN) shortly after the Second World War to investigate the nature of employment problems in developing regions of Africa, Asia and Latin America.

Launched as part of ILO's 50th anniversary, their mission was to develop sustainable policies and actions that would ultimately help to address employment problems in those regions. They found that Kenya had 'broad and fundamental' employment problems, which could have neither been understood nor addressed without a proper and broader analysis of the structure of the Kenyan economy and the trends in its development. Intriguingly, Singer and his ILO team had discovered that very great differences in 'incomes', 'productivity', 'access to resources' and 'government services' produced 'imbalances between the structure and location of the jobs in demands, and the type and location of available wage-earning opportunities'.

These imbalances were compounded by rapid population growth, coupled with the consequent growth in the urban population and school leavers, which far exceeded the growth of available wage-earning opportunities. This discovery led to several conclusions including the fact that 'the internal imbalances were linked to the extreme imbalances between the Kenyan economy and the world economy – in trade, technology and the conditions governing private foreign investment'.[20] Thus, both imbalances were deemed to have compounded and underlie Kenya's employment problems'. Therefore, they recommended far-reaching policy measures with huge implications for every sector and employment group of the Kenyan economy.

[18]Hart (1985, p. 1)
[19]Portes and Sassen-Koob (1987)
[20]Singer and Jolly (2012, p. 122)

Out of these recommendations came two approaches to defining the informal economy. The first notion was from the perspective of individual action, which inspired many sociological and anthropological studies in informal economy that we see today in much of Africa and Latin America. Particularly, it influenced the incorporation of the economic activities of the so-called marginalised workers into national labour force surveys on the basis of their income levels and connections with poverty. The second notion was enterprise-based, which informed the origin of numerous ILO studies in Africa through its Jobs and Skills Programme for Africa (JASPA); and in Latin America through its Regional Employment for Latin America and the Caribbean (PREALC); as well as in Asia, generally at urban city levels.

By all accounts, and given the inherently institutional barriers that prevented many private enterprises from flourishing, these two approaches held the State responsible as the root cause of informality and rise of the informal economy – a notion that heavily influenced the work of De Soto in Latin America. For the ILO, the conclusion was that the 'non-registration of the individual in the employment or social security registers, or non-registration of the enterprise in fiscal or commercial registers, was a basic criterion for defining the concept of informal economy'.[21] However, the definitional criteria put forward by both Hart and ILO were inadequate. They do not capture the full range of informal employment – *measured by the absence of the social protection including contract and benefits covered by labour legislation imposed on formal sector employment* – in both formal and informal economy.

Thus, for a definitional purpose, employment in the informal economy comprises all persons, regardless of their employment status, working in informal enterprises, plus all persons working informally in formal sectors of the economy including formal enterprises (e.g. households with paid employees, paid and unpaid domestic workers).[22] In fact, income arising from undertaking any of these employment activities can qualify as informal employment. Despite this, scholarly attempts to unify the informal economy under a common theoretical agenda remains elusive.

7.3 CONCEPTUALISING INFORMAL ECONOMY

Until now efforts to theorise the informal (or shadow economy) have narrowly focussed on the economic failures of mainly less developed economies. These failures relate to lack of human capital, poor economic planning and structural deficiencies in the economic systems of poor developing countries, their inability to transform and fully modernise their economies, deal with the socioeconomic fallouts of rural–urban migration as well as lack of the appropriate skilled and productive workforce to achieve national competitiveness. Such *ad hoc* understanding also meant that the presence of informal economy in much of developed economies has either been ignored or blamed almost entirely on the influx and economic activities of migrants from less developed economies who are believed to have imported economic survival strategies that were typical in their home countries. Whether or not these narrow view is true is beside

---

[21]Charmes (2012, p. 106)
[22]*Op. Cit.*

the point. Of interest, however, is the failure by modern economists and development theorists to fashion out a common theory of informal economy. Apart from the narrow focus on the structural deficiency in the economic systems of poor and developing countries, there are other different but important reasons why it has been difficult to theorise a common thinking on informal economy. Firstly, economic and development theories, whether propounded from a socialist, capitalist or post-modernist perspective, had neither foreseen nor signalled the inevitable emergence of the informal economy as a viable source of income for many people in developed economies. Even though such theories have made room for different shades of criminal activity in developed countries including income underreporting for tax avoidance as an inevitable response to State's imposition of a reliable tax system. Despite this, modern economists have yet to account for, or even fully explain the phenomenon of informal economy.

Secondly, economic theorists and development scholars have for so long under-estimated the significance of informal economy as a viable way to generate and grow income, especially in developing countries. Thirdly, and parallel to the second reason, is the notion that the underground or shadow economy[23] (e.g. drug trafficking, prostitution and smuggling), a core facet of informal economy found in most highly developed economies can only be linked to the presence of cheap immigrant labour from less developed economies. Thus, by implication, the presence of informal economy in highly developed economies, rather than associated with systems of their economic planning, was directly linked to the economic activities of migrants from less developed economies. This is not the case.

Historical accounts have in fact shown that immigrants from less developed economies, even though they form and cluster in their communities and tend to be mostly excluded from mainstream economic activities in developed economies – thus, more favourably disposed to take advantage of opportunities presented by informality – do not necessarily create opportunities for informal economy.[24] Also, a more recent analysis of aggregated data obtained from 158 capitalist economies including in developed and developing economies between 2009 and 2015 showed that economic activities in the shadow economy in these countries range from 24.94 percent in Estonia to 9.37 percent in Germany.[25]

At this scale, it would be hard to sustain the premise of the argument that economic activities in the informal economy in highly advanced countries are completely disconnected from their economic structures and systems. After all, the impact of

---

[23]Underground or shadow economy refers to those economic activities and income earned that circumvent government regulation, taxation or observation. More narrowly, these economic activities will include monetary and non-monetary transactions of a legal and illegal nature that would generally become taxable were they reported to State tax authorities. But they have been deliberately concealed from tax authorities to avoid payment of income, value-added (VAT), or other taxes and social security or natural insurance (NI) contributions, or to avoid compliance with certain legal labour obligations and standards, such as minimum wage, maximum working hours, safety standards or administrative procedures. Thus, shadow economy focuses on those productive economic activities that would normally be included in national accounts, but which remain hidden due to deliberate attempt to avoid tax and/or other regulatory burdens. For more on the size and nature of the global shadow economy see Medina and Schneider (2018) entitled: Shadow economies around the world: what did we learn over the last 20 years. IMF *Working Papers*.
[24]Sassen (1994)
[25]Medina and Schneider (2018)

advanced capitalism, which spurred the economic restructuring that has led to sharp decline of manufacturing and the rise of a service economy in mostly advanced and developed economies brought with it a new brand of informality in different sectors. Fourthly, and perhaps the most relevant reason is that the heterogeneous nature of informal economy in terms of the types of economic activities, types of firms, entrepreneurs and workers is so vast that it would almost certainly be pointless to theorise a standard notion of informal economy across the board.

For instance, in Latin America, and in economically more dynamic regions of Southeast Asia, the debate is focused on whether or not most actors in the informal economy are either 'constrained genuine entrepreneurs' or would they rather prefer to have a secure job. From an economic viewpoint, if one were to compare this situation to fewer dynamic regions of Africa where the debate is largely focused on the small groups of successful entrepreneurs and a much larger, ubiquitous survivalist group,[26] perhaps a clearer picture will emerge in relation to the heterogeneous nature, and also the difficulty in theorising a common thinking in informal economy. Of importance, although no less important than the elasticity of the informal economy, is the institutional deficiencies that incentivise the economic behaviour of actors, which is held together through economic linkages between formal and informal economy.

The nature of these linkages makes it difficult to distinguish the boundary between legality and illegality of economic activities in the informal economy. Analysis by the ILO has equally stressed the importance of these economic linkages for income opportunity, especially in Africa where there is a less pejorative view of informal economy.[27] Also, a core proposition of economic and employment literatures has been that informal and formal products and markets will always have an overlapping tendency, which may be competitive or complementary.[28]

A most common example of a complementary market would be when the informal sector promotes and sells formal sector products and services, as is often the case in different sectors of the African economy, particularly in the agricultural, household retail and mobile telecommunications sectors. Whereas in a competitive market, both sectors can compete within the same product and service market, and the informal sector may acquire market share by using informational advantage and lower pricing mechanism to attract lower-income consumers, thereby retain an overlapping customer base with the formal sector.[29]

Notwithstanding, theoretical explanations of informal economy have crystallised around four dominant competing themes, namely: dualist, legalist, voluntarist and structuralist schools of thought. As shown in Table 7.1, each of these themes subscribes to a very different causal theory of the root causes of informal economy. However, common among them is the fact that institutions and economic systems within countries play a key role in the existence and survival of the informal economy. If indeed, as the evidence suggests, then from a viewpoint of SSA a far more pertinent question will be how to build and sustain strong institutions to produce desirable social and economic outcomes for their citizens, such as high income, productivity and

---

[26]Grimm et al. (2012)
[27]Bangasser (2000)
[28]Xaba et al. (2002)
[29]Bohme and Thiele (2012)

TABLE 7.1 Theory of informal economy – different schools of thought

Dualist School	Proposed by early advocates (e.g. Hart; Singer and the ILO) who view informal economic activities as marginal, but which provide income opportunity mainly through self-employment to a large under-represented and poor segment of the population. The central argument of the dualist school is that these under-represented poor population operate in a distinct and largely disadvantaged segmented labour market, in which the key players are excluded from the main or formal economy. They blame the presence of informal economy on the structural imbalances (e.g. mismatch between people's skills and employment or economic opportunities) between population growth and economic opportunities in a modern economy. While advocates of the dualist school acknowledge there may be economic linkages between informal and formal economy, they pay little attention to the institutional factors, e.g. government regulation and how these could provide the incentive for informal enterprises.
Legalist School	The legalist school of thought focuses on how the formal regulatory environment, to the neglect of informal workers, serves as a catalyst for informal economic activities. The main argument is that institutional factors within a country, such as a hostile legal system, a rigid and/or bureaucratic business environment can be counterproductive for business creativity and innovation. This is because rigid legal systems can provide the incentive for individuals and groups to operate informally and set up their own distinct extra-legal norms and structures. This, perhaps, may have influenced the theoretical thinking of early writers about informal economy in Latin America, such as Hernando De Soto. In his thesis about Peruvian migrants who set up illegal markets in Pisa and systems to regulate and control the activities of its members, De Soto cited what he called 'mercantilist' interests that work within formal institutions to establish bureaucratic 'rules of the game', which in turn provide the incentive for informal economic activities. He advocates for a system that recognises and converts the creativity, innovation and assets owned by players in the informal economy into legally recognisable assets through simplifying the laws and removing bureaucratic hurdles.
Voluntarist School	The voluntarist school focuses on informal enterprises and the behaviour of informal entrepreneurs who deliberately avoid registration, regulation and taxation. Unlike the legalist, their behaviour is neither concerned nor motivated by the bureaucratic hurdles and challenges of regulatory constraints. Rather, there is a deliberate and conscious attempt to go into the informal economy after examining the benefits against the odds of formalising an enterprise. The central argument is that the economic activities in the informal economy undercut competition because they avoid tax and regulatory burdens as well as other factors of production. Therefore, the contention is that informal enterprises should be brought under the regulatory umbrella in order to increase government's tax base and revenue as well as reduce the unfair competition to formal enterprises.

(Continued)

TABLE 7.1   **Theory of informal economy – different schools of thought** (Continued)

Structuralist School	The structuralist school of thought is diametrically opposed to capitalism and views the informal economy as a distinct repository of subordinated micro-enterprises and alternative economic unit from which to recruit vibrant and cheap workers to reduce the labour costs, thereby raise the competitiveness of large enterprises in the formal economy. The central argument is that the institutional structures and systems of capitalism (e.g. organised labour, business laws, taxes) drives the informal economy. There is a strong connection between formal and informal economy, but the economic activities (e.g. informal workers, informal enterprises) are exploitative in that the latter is subordinated and more vulnerable to the systems of capitalism that drive the formal economy through the provision of cheap labour, products and services, as well as other business practices that spur global competition. The contention is that governments should develop robust regulatory systems and enact laws to strengthen employment protection for informal workers and offer informal enterprises that are economically linked with big capitalist corporations an easy way out to thrive independently.

shared prosperity within formal and informal institutional arrangements, and what are the consequences when they fail to do so?

The answers to these questions are best approached from structuralist and legalist schools of thought, particularly, focusing on the weaknesses of formal institutions, and how these weaknesses serve as the catalyst to informal sector economic activity. The informal sector may refer to the characteristics of all employment and work under-taken in which persons and the economic units and activities of the contracting parties lack legal status and obligation. Thus, for practical purpose, and to avoid confusion between the concepts of informal economy and informal sector, one may consider the informal sector as a component of the informal economy. Therefore, informal sector is the preferred terminology for the purpose of analysis.

7.4 WHY INFORMAL SECTOR EXISTS

In his widely acclaimed book, *The Other Path*, the Peruvian Economist, Hernando De Soto provides a powerfully vivid account of the political, social and economic factors that might give rise to informality within a country's economic system. Using his native Peru as a context, De Soto argues that economic activities in the informal sector flourish when the formal legal system imposes rules that far exceed the socially acceptable expectations, choices and preferences of those whom it has excluded within its framework, and when the State lacks the coercive force to restrain or legislate such activities. He observed that migrants in Lima city, the Peru capital, having migrated from villages to big cities in search of jobs and better economic opportunities were forced to occupy illegal settlements and to engage in illegal informal economic activities in order to survive. For De Soto, migrants' activities, such as erecting unauthorised settlements or starting a business, were not illegal or anti-social *per se*.

Rather, he believed that those migrants were motivated by a desire to achieve such essentially legal objectives needed for survival within an institutional system they felt had failed and excluded them.[30]

Even though De Soto's observations relate to the social and economic conditions of Peruvian migrants in Latin America, the migrants' social and economic experiences are similar to the socio-economic conditions of urban migrants in many African cities. This is because in the absence of strong formal institutions, as largely the case in many African countries, human behaviour including economic activities will inevitably be governed by informal institutional arrangements. Weak institutional arrangements may help to explain why the informal sector has emerged as and remains the main source of employment and income opportunity in Africa.

a) Size of Africa's informal sector

The actual size of Africa's informal sector is hard to estimate. However, recent events that have disrupted the global economy, such as, the 2008 financial crisis and the COVID-19 pandemic, offer sharply contrasting insights into the scope and significance of the region's informal sector. During the 2007–2008 global financial crisis, African economies performed comparably better than developed economies in terms of economic growth as a result of three key factors. Besides lower debt burden – which provided the much-need fiscal space to retain and pay public sector workers, higher commodity prices – which supported export earnings. But beyond these two reasons, the resiliency of the informal sector was crucial to the provision of employment for many people. The vibrant economic activities in the sector helped to sustain household income and consumption that somehow protected African economies from the full economic impact of the crisis.

With the current COVID-19 global pandemic, the conditions are starkly different. It is hard to say whether the informal sector can guarantee stable income for struggling African families affected by the economic fallout of the pandemic. Many informal sector workers, both in agricultural and non-agricultural sectors, have a grim prospect of surviving the devastating economic impact of the pandemic. The national and cross-border lockdowns and the consequent disruption to global supply chains have frozen regional and international trades, reduced global fiscal space, negatively affected commodities pricing and exports, and choked off domestic and foreign direct investments. Together, these compounding factors have led to a sudden drop in migrant remittances, which provide a main source of foreign direct investment in Africa.

Also, the disruption has caused severe shortage of food supply and products and reduced the ability of informal small traders who rely on buying and selling household consumables to generate income. It means that informal sector business owners, who were highly undercapitalised even before the crisis, are the least likely to bounce back given that they are ineligible to access government support schemes. If anything, the containment efforts implemented by many national governments disproportionately curb the ability of informal sector operators to earn income. Although the COVID-19 situation has threatened the livelihood of large swathes of African workers, informal sector operators are most at risk of exposure to the diseases and far more vulnerable to

---

[30]De Soto (1989)

the economic consequences of the diseases than any other workforce population group.

This is because, to earn income and survive, they must go out and mix with others from different households. Informal enterprises (e.g. shop owners, restaurant operators and retailers), which account for about 90 percent of all small businesses in Africa, and employ mainly undeclared and low skilled workers including unpaid family members, also share many of the vulnerabilities and precarious economic conditions of informal workers excluded from State-run financial support schemes.[31] Consequently, Africa's informal sector, home to the majority of the region's workforce population and micro-enterprises, may not deliver similar levels of economic buffer seen in 2008. Despite this, the informal sector – 'not the formal sector' – continues to drive economic growth in Africa. With informal employment being the main source of income opportunity, Africa has the highest share of informal labour globally compared to any other region.

The sector makes up micro and small-scale enterprises that generate employment and wealth of up to 60 percent of GDP in some African countries. The World Bank estimates that 86 percent of workers in SSA (2020 figures), that is, about 20 percent higher than in EMDEs, are employed in the informal sector, with 95 percent of younger and older persons classified as informal workers. In addition, the share of informal labour ranges from 98 percent in Democratic Republic of Congo, 95 percent in Mozambique, 90 percent in Tanzania, 88 percent in Ghana, 47 percent in Ethiopia to 43 percent in Gabon, with 77 percent of total employment in SSA found in the informal sector. By a close estimate, informal sector employment has exceeded formal sector employment in countries, such as, Uganda and Kenya.

b) Features of informal sector operators

Often described as 'unorganised', 'unregistered', 'backward', 'and 'shadowy' among others, the informal sector can be characterised both positively and negatively in terms of 'ease of entry', 'hidden from taxation', 'reliance on indigenous resources', 'labour intensity', 'low skill requirement' and 'under-employment', with lack of finance and access to markets seen as the two major entry barriers. In terms of composition, the sector is traditionally dominated by uneducated artisans and small-scale operators. But in recent times, it has increasingly attracted educated professionals who perceived their informal commercial activity as a means to supplement the income from their formal employment.

Similar shift in the composition of the operators has also been reported in Latin America where it is common for individuals operating a micro-enterprise to hold on to their formal sector jobs until the micro-enterprise is firmly established, thereby allowing them to effectively maintain different income sources.[32] In addition, there is an increasingly sophisticated informal sector operators that operate as clusters in large informal firms. Such operators are known to empower and provide 'skills of the trade' to aspiring new members through an organised system of apprenticeship schemes as

[31]Nguimkeu and Okou (2020)
[32]Maloney (2004)

well as through solid use of social networks of family and allies to enforce implicit contracts and insure risks.[33]

Such firms are prevalent in a variety of sectors in the African economy including, among others, in transport, music and the movie industry, as well as in wholesale and retail sectors. In terms of features, analysis of empirical studies reveals that the large informal clusters in the shoe and garment sectors in South-eastern Nigerian cities of Aba and Nnewi, for instance, employ tens of thousands of informal workers, and probably control a combined estimated annual turnover of more than US$1billion. Yet, most of these firms 'remain informal; unregistered, evade key taxes, and contravene basic labour regulations'.[34] Large informal firms are those that fulfil the criteria for a formal sector activity and sometimes pay the presumptive levy (local tax) to the authorities while making significant revenues beyond subsistence, yet choose to remain informal.[35]

However, even though some informal firms can be characterised as large as measured by their relative employee number, economic activities and corresponding turnover outputs, as well as their administrative structures are comparably weak. Formal firms of similar size usually have distinct departments and coherent internal structures that meet all the basic demands of a regulated sector. Whereas for the large informal firms, apart from the owner and a few permanent employees (usually family members and relatives), none of the usual formal organisational structures (e.g. marketing/sales, human resources, operations, finance/accounts) exist.

Another striking feature of informal sector in Africa is the vital role cash plays in the absence of financial support from banks. Many large informal sector businesses are self-financing. They are able to access finance as working capital or to purchase raw materials and labour through various informal but self-regulating credit system (e.g. *Esusu*) or micro-finance schemes. Access to finance has implications for growth and expansion for business operators. The increasing efficiency, turnover and size of large informal firms is a clear signal the sector has evolved and expanded under diverse economic circumstances. Hence, one can argue that some informal sector operators have clearly become efficient at generating job opportunities and household income in a way that goes beyond mere subsistence.

Less clear, however, is why owners of large informal firms with a sizeable work-force, turnover and income would prefer to remain informal and without State regulation and formal tax liabilities? Attempting to answer this question, especially from a legalistic and structuralist school of thought, raises even more problematic questions. From a legalist standpoint, it could be that actors participate simply by choice as a way to either resist or circumvent what they perceive as excessively formal legal requirements imposed by the State in relation to owning and running a business. From a structuralist perspective, there are two related possibilities. Firstly, it challenges the long and often held assumption that people are driven merely by survival and necessity to enter into the informal sector, rather than by an opportunity in an entrepreneurial sense. Secondly, it raises questions about the effectiveness of formal

[33]Brautigam (1997)
[34]Meagher (2009, p. 406)
[35]Benjamin and Mbaye (2012)

economic structures and ability of the State to generate sustainable employment, particularly in the formal sector.

Despite these possibilities, it is also possible that some informal sector operators in Africa are distinct in terms of their underlying motives and entrepreneurial capabilities. That is, there may be actors who enter the sector voluntarily, and therefore are better prepared and more creative at using their resources including skills, know-how and networks. Thus, such voluntary actors are intrinsically more capable of organising and managing their business than actors who might have been thrown involuntarily into the sector. In other words, it seems the main distinguishing feature of Africa's informal sector is the coexistence of different economic actors with different motives and distinct entrepreneurial capabilities, in the sense that such actors may be driven into the sector either by necessity or opportunity motives.[36]

With regards to actors with large informal enterprises who might have entered the sector voluntarily, it could also be that they felt that they would not necessarily be better off by operating within the formal sector. If indeed, then it could be that they were simply making the best choices open to them given their poor social and economic circumstances as a result of weaknesses in the institutional arrangements in their communities. These circumstances could relate to their low level of education, desire to operate outside the constraints of formal rules and obligations associated with formal institutional arrangements. If this is the case, then perhaps it makes sense to view Africa's informal sector as offering different channels of income opportunity to individuals beyond mere survival.

c) Institutions and the informal sector

Lack of strong institutions in any society is a recipe for alternative, often more restrictive and weak institutional arrangements. From an entrepreneurship viewpoint, while there are similarities in developed and developing economies related to the institutional arrangements that support entrepreneurship, there are also clear differences in areas as diverse as the underlying motives for business ownership, the process of new start-up creation including resource mobilisation, market entry, innovation and scaling of new ventures. However, in the absence of strong and supportive institutions, individuals, specifically entrepreneurs, are often forced to perform the difficult balancing act between satisfying their pressing economic needs and the regulatory requirements through entrepreneurship.

From the perspective of Africa, this raises several fundamental questions about how informal sector operators make decisions, mobilise resources, create ventures, act upon their survival instincts, develop and enact cognitive-behavioural norms in the absence of strong and supportive institutional arrangements. Perhaps, entrepreneurial resourcefulness, which broadly refers to ways in which entrepreneurs respond to difficulties and embrace opportunities in the midst of resource constraints,[37] may help to explain how informal sector operators mitigate limited institutional support (or lack thereof) by behaving and acting entrepreneurially.

---

[36]Maloney (2004)
[37]Powell and Baker (2014)

An important theme in the literature relevant to entrepreneurial resourcefulness is the emerging theory of entrepreneurial bricolage. Defined as 'making do by applying a combination of resources at hand to new problems and opportunities'.[38] Entrepreneurial bricolage offers a powerful lens through which to better understand how informal sector operators act amid environmental challenges. In an attempt to survive under conditions of substantial resource constraints, informal sector operators may exhibit acts of bricolage behaviour by improvising and effectuating their survival strategies, particularly when they perceive that State institutions and formal rules constrain and threaten their survival.

Although attempts have been made to distinguish bricolage behaviour from improvisation and effectuation,[39] it is important to remember that entrepreneurs often deploy a set of innovative tools and techniques at their disposal to make decisions and take action depending on the nature of the challenges they face and the available resources. Hence, it would seem restrictive, if not narrow, to consider bricolage behaviour merely in terms of how a combination of resources are used to respond to immediate challenges and opportunities.[40] Such a narrow view excludes other possibilities and innovative ways through which entrepreneurs 'make do with whatever is at hand'. Across Africa, entrepreneurs not only demonstrate high levels of resourcefulness, but they have also improvised and succeeded in the midst of environmental challenges and scarce resources.

In Kenya, for instance, the notion of *jua kali* (Swahili meaning for hot sun) is used to refer to the informal traders and artisans who 'make do' and 'improvise' as a means to survive under severe resource constraints. Acts of improvisation in the midst of environmental challenges and resource constraints is not limited to Africa. In Southern Asia, the idea of *jugaad*, which describes practices of 'jury-rigging', 'making do' and 'improvising under constraints' is also used to characterise the adaptive mode of urban governance prevalent in cities across India, where a large share of economic activities take place outside State regulation.[41] Thus, entrepreneurs, especially in the informal sector, often deploy whatever means necessary to either respond to challenges and opportunities or to accomplish their ambition, especially under conditions of lack and unsupportive institutional arrangements.

Broadly speaking, bricolage behaviour embodies acts of resourcefulness, adaptiveness, improvisation and persistence that entrepreneurial actors exhibit as they seek ultimately to accomplish (i.e. effectuate) their entrepreneurial ambition. These acts uniquely serve, and, in most cases, enable entrepreneurial actors 'to make do with whatever is at hand' when taking entrepreneurial action in resource poor and constrained environments. In resource-poor developing economies, most entrepreneurship activities in the informal sector are a product of necessity, desperation and in some cases seen as an act of defiance in response to unsupportive, weak, or inadequate State institutions.

This contrasts with the notion of entrepreneurship in the formal sector in rich developed Western economies where there is more emphasis on innovation and capital

---

[38]Baker and Nelson (2005, p. 333)
[39]Baker et al. (2003)
[40]Davidsson et al. (2017)
[41]Chattaraj (2017, p. 1)

accumulation for business growth. However, the substantial poor informal entrepreneurs across Africa exhibit entrepreneurial behaviour in a survivalist, rather than in an innovative sense of raising capital.[42] For them, entrepreneurship represents a route out of poverty, a means by which to earn a living and survive given that they have little capital, education or even experience.[43] Notwithstanding, bricolage behaviour not only enables entrepreneurship actors to considerably mobilise resources, but it also allows them to recombine resources and practices to bring about positive institutional change.[44]

In other words, it is not just the mere fact of starting or making do with whatever is available, but there is a transformative process that occurs when the resource-constrained entrepreneur draws upon and combines the freely and cheaply accumulated resources and convert these resources into wealth. From an employment generation standpoint, the behaviour of Africa's large informal sector firms has a transformative effect on the wider institutional environment in that they act as 'double agents' who neither exists nor survives merely by 'mobilising' and 'repurposing' resources. Through their actions and behaviour, they in fact have the capacity to instigate a process of what some have referred to as an 'actor-initiated institutional change'.[45] Whereby, the ability to mobilise and reuse resources means that any legitimacy associated with the resources may equally be repurposed through three channels of institutional legitimacy – moral, cognitive and pragmatism.[46]

In Africa, the institutional legitimacy accorded to informal sector firms emerges in form of economic linkages with the formal sector. It is through this linkage, that bricolage entrepreneurship behaviour survives confrontation with formal institutional arrangements and the legal environment. Collectively, the transformative process that occurs through bricolage helps to normalise what others have referred to as 'institutional deviance'. The concept of deviance is emblematic of a much larger institutionalised problems of 'making do' and 'improvisation' as means of survival under 'resource lack and constraints, which is seen as central to the legitimacy and survival of informal sector.[47]

With these perspectives, it is possible that an actor-initiated change inevitably would be directed towards a consciously motivated effort to protect the business from an institutional arrangement that is perceived as both constraining and hostile. From a standpoint of African informal sector operators, and because of others institutional and economic problems, the only practical way to protect the business is to remain illegal and not pay tax. This situation is analogous to the particular behaviour of those actors with large informal firms in south-eastern Nigeria who are reluctant to operate within the formal sector, thereby shouldering their own fair share of the tax burden. Yet, in a different way, their reluctance could be seen as a deliberate act of defiance towards a formal institutional structure they perceived has constrained and excluded them – similar to the behaviour of Peruvian migrants in Lima city.

Arguably, owners of such large informal firms deserve credit for their entrepreneurial ingenuity and resilience amid the institutional and environmental challenges

---

[42]Banerjee and Duflo (2007, p. 151)
[43]Baumol et al. (2007, p. 3)
[44]Desa (2012, p. 730)
[45]Campbell (2004, p. 74)
[46]Suchman (1995)
[47]Webb et al. (2009)

they have encountered. Equally, it is important to remember that in such contexts, entrepreneurial talents could be diverted and used as an unproductive or destructive asset. This is important, especially in the context of the economic linkages between the informal and the formal sector in which the latter has to shoulder tax liabilities. Various forms of forward and backward economic linkages exist between business operators in the informal and the formal sectors. The enablers of backward linkages include flow of raw materials, equipment, finance and consumer goods from the formal to the informal sector, while forward linkages are twofold – on the one hand are sub-contracting agreements between informal sector operators and public and private entities in the formal sector, and on the other hand through the supply of consumer goods from informal sector enterprises to the formal sector.[48]

Also, firms in the formal sector purchase inputs from those produced in the informal sector (i.e. forward linkages). Equally, formal sector firms supply inputs to firms (or even individuals) in the informal sector (backward linkages). Other forms of linkages include technology – where there is transference of technology from one sector to another, and financing – where there are vertical and horizontal linkages between formal and informal sectors in the provision of credit facilities. Under horizontal linkages, banks might compete directly with informal money lenders in provision of credit, whereas under vertical linkage, informal lenders have access to formal lenders, such as banks.

These economic linkages are not just limited to the informal sector in SSA. In Southeast Asia, for instance, vertical and horizontal linkages have long been in existence between formal and informal lending institutions. For instance, in the Philippines, banks are known to extend formal credits to informal lenders in the hope that the practice will improve loan conditions for informal business owners shut out of the formal sector.[49] However, the nature of economic linkages between formal and informal sector in Africa can sometimes be exploitative. In the sense that formal sector firms including multinationals seeking market entry and dominance in rural Africa may sometimes exploit their relationship with informal sector networks.

Notwithstanding, the underlying nature of the economic linkages between informal and formal sector is such that the capitalist forces that might have unravelled the vitality and employment-creation potential of the formal sector have simultaneously and inevitably forced the explosion of the informal sector.[50] Emerging from the nature of these economic linkages is a strong argument and question about the *illegality* of economic activities in the informal sector.

7.5 ILLEGALITY AND LEGITIMACY OF THE INFORMAL SECTOR

The issue of illegality and legitimacy of economic activities in the informal sector has been and remains a highly controversial subject. The legal–illegal debate is informed

---

[48]Arimah (2001, p. 114)
[49]Floro and Ray (1997)
[50]Potts (2008, p. 157)

primarily by prescriptions that guide economic activities that have been formalised and codified in laws and regulations within a State. Whereas the legitimate–illegitimate debate more narrowly captures prescriptions for social acceptability based on only norms, values and beliefs of a large population segment within the society that have the propensity to disregard prescriptions of laws and regulations.[51] As a result, these debates have given rise to three distinct sectors of the economy, namely, formal sector, the informal sector and the renegade sector.[52]

In the formal sector, operators exploit legal and legitimate means to produce legal and legitimate ends regardless of the constraints, whereas the renegade sector refers to the types of activities taken to exploit illegal and illegitimate opportunities (e.g. child trafficking/prostitution and tax evasion) which lack social acceptability. However, the informal sector emerged as a result of the barriers and the costs of achieving a legal status as well as incongruities and weak enforcements of laws and regulations. The informal sector combines illegality (e.g. use of undocumented workers) and legitimacy (e.g. manufactured products, farm produce) to exploit income opportunities that may be socially acceptable in different societies.

The use of undocumented workers to manufacture products or to harvest agricultural produce (e.g. cocoa, potatoes) come into this category. For example, Tables 7.2 and 7.3 provide an illustration of legitimate and illegitimate sources of income in the formal and informal sectors. Essentially, to operate in the formal sector requires legalising one's business enterprise through registration and meeting all tax obligations. Unlike in the informal sector, where operators are unregistered, and therefore outside the State's tax net. In definitional terms, achieving legality for any informal commercial enterprise would require satisfying two legally binding obligations – becoming part of the regulated formal sector through registration of the enterprise and secondly, sustaining that registered status by fulfilling certain legally binding requirements including tax obligations. This entails compliance with a number of registration processes as a way of sanctioning the legal existence of the enterprise, and the continuity of its legal status as an economic entity permitted to operate in legitimately determined activities (e.g. trade) and subject to tax liabilities.

To understand why individuals, particularly informal sector operators in Africa, might be put off about legalising their business, one needs to consider the length of time and the requirements for legalising a new business. Across the world, the length of time it takes to register a commercial entity and through that assume a fully legal status varies from a few hours to several days into more than a month depending on where the business is domiciled and how easy it is to register and start a new business in that country. Out of 190 countries that the World Bank surveyed in 2019 for ease of doing business, the average regional rank for countries in SSA was 51.61 percent. The World Bank's measure for starting a business considers several regulatory procedures, time, cost and paid-in minimum capital requirement for a small-to-medium sized limited-liability company to formally start up and operate as a legal entity.

Reflected on a scale from 0 to 100, where 0 represents the lowest and 100 represents the best performance, the ease of doing business scale captures the gap of each country from the best regulatory performance as it applies to local firms observed in

---

[51]Lagos (1995)
[52]Webb et al. (2009)

TABLE 7.2 Comparative illustration of legitimate and illegitimate formal and informal income opportunities in sub-Saharan Africa

Formal income opportunities		Informal income opportunities	
Legitimate	*Illegitimate*	*Legitimate*	*Illegitimate*
Private sector and public wage/salary employees	Bribery	Herbalists or traditional healers	Prostitution
Christian churches clergy and staff	Networking	Pentecostal churches	
Non-governmental organisation (NGO) employees	Influencing	Bar and restaurants operators	Money doubling
Private education professionals	Fraud	Barbers and hairdressers	Smuggling
Hotel industry and travel agents	Scams (a.k.a 419)	Shoe shiners and shoe menders	Black market currency exchange
Manufacturers and industrialist	Cronyism	Drivers, handcrafts, tailors	Drugs peddling
Self-employed professionals and their staff including: Physicians/nurses/midwives	Corruption	Domestic workers (house maids)	Armed robbery
Other, e.g. pharmacists and laboratory technicians/lawyers/engineers/architects/accountants/auditors	Embezzlement	Retail trading/kiosk operators	
Telecommunication Operators	Smuggling	Manufacturers, e.g. garment, shoes	
Contractors		Street vendors, e.g. food, telecoms	
		Repair and maintenance services, e.g. auto mechanics, household	
		Goods, mobile phones	
		Farmers, bakers, food processors	
		Entertainment, e.g. music, movie, traditional dancers	

TABLE 7.3 Informal sector activities in sub-Saharan Africa

Informal productive sector	Informal service sector
• Agricultural production	• Dressmaking
• Mining and quarrying	• Hairdressing
• Small/large-scale manufacturing (*Ethnic clusters*)	• Repair and maintenance of small household goods
• Building and construction	• Television repairs
• Arts and craft (*Ethnic clusters*)	• Engine repairs
• Entertainment (*Ethnic clusters*)	• Vehicle repairs
Manifested in	• Panel beating
• Food production	• Electrical installation
• Furniture making	• Carpentry
• Garment/shoemaking (*Ethnic clusters*)	
• Welding and ironworks	**Informal health services**
• Brick laying, draughtsmanship	• Traditional birth attendants
• Craftsmanship, weaving (*Ethnic clusters*)	• Herbalists
• Movie-making (*Ethnic clusters*)	• Traditional spiritualists
• Music, traditional dancing	• Medical practitioners (Chemists/pharmaceuticals)
• Traders, e.g. textiles (*Ethnic clusters*)	

Informal credit/lending sector

• Informal money lending (Isusu, Esusu)

• Foreign exchange (*Ethnic clusters*)

each of the indicators across all ranked countries.[53] Indicators range from starting a business, getting credit, paying taxes, enforcing contracts, cross-border trading, access to electricity, registering a property to resolving insolvency and protecting minority investors. Nigeria, Africa's largest economy, ranked 146 out of 190 countries surveyed compared to the region's second largest economy, South Africa, which ranked 82. In Africa, Mauritius was regarded as the best country to start a business and access business support (20/190), followed by Rwanda (29/190).

In terms of how individuals or entrepreneurs find it easy to start a business, the regional average for SSA is 78.52. At 82.97, Nigeria ranked 120 out of 190 countries surveyed, slightly above the regional average but well short of the region's best performers like Burundi, which ranked 17/190 globally with a performance score of 94.84, followed by Mauritius which ranked 21/190 with a performance score of 94.34.

---

[53]World Bank (2020)

Nigeria's ranking for starting a business is particularly interesting. It has one of the largest networks of informal sector businesses and cluster of informal employment globally.

Of the major obstacles to legalising and sustaining the legality of an enterprise in Nigeria, business registration and financing are the most cited barriers. It takes on average about 32 days and multiple procedures to legally register a new small-to-medium sized commercial enterprise. From checking the availability of company's name, preparation of the requisite incorporation documents, to tax registrations and local government inspections, the procedure seems to be daunting and onerous, therefore inefficient. There are two main legal hurdles to establishing and sustaining a new bona fide commercial enterprise in Nigeria – the actual registration of the enterprise and the procedure related to fees and taxation. As shown in Figure 7.1, both hurdles can take anywhere between thirty-one and thirty-four days to complete, depending on one's personal contact with authorities and the personnel.

FIGURE 7.1 Stages of legally incorporating a small-to-medium sized enterprise in Nigeria

In some cases, if an elected politician is involved, then the process could be fast-tracked to anywhere between 10 and 15 days. Even so, each of these hurdles entails different degrees of complexity and burden that present enormous challenges to an intending business owner and the low-skilled civil servants responsible for implementing government policies in relation to business registration. However, Nigeria's business registration process could be transformed to make the system more agile and efficient. For instance, integrating the number of days for registering a new commercial enterprise with the Corporate Affairs Commission[54] (CAC) and the Federal Board of Inland Revenue (FBIR), which altogether currently takes about fifteen days, could help to reduce the number of days and make the registration process less burdensome and lengthy.

It requires the use of modern and reliable technologies to create a one-stop online shop to reduce waste, speed up the process and generate savings from reduced overheads and better turnaround. Achieving this deppends on addressing a host of other infrastructural challenges including the poor electricity supply in Nigeria. Disruption to electricity supply presents a very serious logistical challenge for business owners most of whom lack the means of supplying their own electricity. As a result, most small business owners mainly rely on generators to supply electricity, which means that they mostly operate under unwholesome conditions. These conditions have been blamed for the reluctance on the part of informal sector operators to comply with certain aspects of the Nigerian labour and tax laws.

Thus, there is a need to sensitise multiple stakeholders including government officials, the relevant Trade Unions and the representatives of informal sector operators about the relationships and the benefits of tax payment, improved infrastructures and better working conditions. Part of a sensitisation programme needs to introduce a framework that simplifies the process of incorporating a new business as well as introduce sustainable government-backed incentives (e.g. access to finance, permanent location with generous lease terms and tax relief) to recognise the value of economic activities in the sector, thereby encourage operators to register their businesses.

Having a robust and reliable online business registration system including a database of company names currently registered with CAC, as well as improved working conditions, could significantly reduce the red tape by as much as 15–20 days. A much leaner and more efficient business registration process, coupled with improved accountability about taxation and government expenditure, could encourage owners of large informal firms to register and remain legal. Also, the savings from reduced overheads could be put towards reskilling or up-skilling CAC's employees to cope with the demands of a much leaner and efficient new business registration processes.

7.6 RECOGNISING THE VALUE OF THE INFORMAL SECTOR

It is not the case that all individuals who enter the informal sector primarily to earn a living and survive do so illegally. There are several related factors why people may

---

[54]The Nigerian government department with the statutory responsibility for the formation, regulation and the management of legal companies in Nigeria.

choose to enter the informal sector. These range from weak institutional arrangements that constrain their ability to legitimately enter and earn a living within the formal sector, such as excessive regulation, high cost of entry, high unemployment, low income levels in the formal sector and poor infrastructure, to practices such as corruption and a culture of low tax compliance. Apart from these factors, others including some affluent owners of large informal firms voluntarily opt to remain in the informal sector because of the potential to accumulate wealth without financial tax obligations.

Owners of large informal firms prefer to avoid the financial obligations that come with a registered enterprise, hence they find operating their business informally more attractive. Put off by what they perceive as the prohibitive costs of sustaining a legal status, informal sector actors in some cases are motivated by a desire to accumulate and multiply wealth by avoiding the financial obligations of maintaining legality. In fact, a large proportion of informal sector operators, as high as 60–70 percent in Latin America, who entered the sector voluntarily are known to have generated substantially more revenue and income than those who fulfil the legal obligations of owning a business.[55] Thus, it appears that significant percentage of economic activities in the informal sector are voluntary.

If this is the case – and given that the informal sector largely operates based on membership of clusters, and in most cases have a common cultural and ethnic identity – then from a policy viewpoint, it makes sense to rethink the regulatory burdens, such as onerous business registration process that excludes such a large population segment. Within informal sector environments, there is a large cluster of business owners who share similar norms, values and behaviours and tend to engage in a particular trade, with their identity extending to race, ethnicity and cultural background.[56] In Nigeria, for instance, there is a cluster of voluntary informal sector operators with the same ethnic backgrounds in South-eastern Nigerian cities of Aba, Onitsha and Nnewi.

Also, in *sabon gari* (meaning strangers' quarters) regions of Kano and Kaduna States in northern Nigeria, ethnic clusters serve the needs of both their immediate and the wider communities. In addition, a large swathe of ethnic Yoruba women that trade mainly in textile materials at the Balogun market in South-western Nigerian city of Lagos 'make do', while negotiating their survival through Nigeria's patriarchal informal sector contexts. Also, as a way to mobilise collective action, informal sector operators form common identities with potential stakeholders including investors, suppliers, employees and customers through discourse including stories, conversations and shared experiences.[57]

Individuals that enjoy shared or common identity often co-operate with each other, and, as a way of demonstrating a strong commitment may be motivated to act in support of one another even in the face of personal risks. We see this commitment demonstrated through schemes, such as, the *Isusu* or *Esusu* – which is an informal system of credit finance very common in Africa whereby individuals make contributions for the purpose of assisting members financially. Two major factors explain the 'cycle of informality' in Africa's business environment. Apart from the orientation to

---

[55]Maloney (2004)
[56]Schartz (1984)
[57]Horn (2005)

avoid the financial implications and the bureaucratic procedures for legally establishing a commercial enterprise, business operators are also motivated to operate
informally due to the related pressure of the tax obligations that become immediately binding as the commercial enterprise starts to operate legally.

As Figure 7.1 shows, a registered commercial enterprise in Nigeria is subject to two
mandatory tax obligations – the payment and declaration of income tax and value-
added tax (VAT) based on income and profits. However, large informal firms whose
economic activities are comparable to firms in the formal sector in terms of income
and outputs end up without tax liabilities as a result of weak institutional arrangements. Like many countries in Africa that operate a cash-based economy, business
transaction in Nigeria's informal sector is conducted in cash. It means that large
informal firms can conceal third-party transactions, turnover and taxable profits.

There is also the issue of capacity constraints on the part of authorities to capture
data and administer tax effectively, particularly in relation to census and proper
documentation of the largely untaxed informal sector operators. This is compounded
by lack of accurate business records and the incentives to encourage many disillusioned informal sector operators to embrace the system of tax administration and
governance applicable to the formal sector. In addition, lack of up-to-date and
accurate records of business accounts including revenues and expenditure make it
difficult for the authorities to undertake any meaningful tax assessment to establish
proportionate levels of tax liability for informal sector operators. Apart from these,
there is the wider problem of complicated tax structure in most African countries.

For instance, Nigeria's taxation mechanism imposes excessive administrative burden
on business owners. Formal sector firms invest nearly 940 hours per year to file statutory tax returns. Compared to Botswana (140 hours), New Zealand (70 hours) and the
United Kingdom (2–5 hours), Nigeria has one of the highest rates of tax return globally.
Since its adoption in 1993, and subsequent implementation in 1994, a number of
serious and complex challenges have hampered the effective administration of the value
added tax (VAT) system in Nigeria. Some of these challenges include limited skills
among tax officials to handle tax administration, lack of appropriate knowledge of VAT
operations, underutilisation due to high rate of tax evasion, lack of record keeping
by business owners and low VAT education among the general public and VAT-able
organisations.

Apart from these problems, there are other related challenges, such as, the key
features of the VAT system that deter informal sector operators from sustaining their
legal obligations even after they have registered their businesses. Thus, without a
simplified taxation mechanism, many owners of small business will be unable to
comply with tax obligations and simply take the view that they are better off
remaining outside the tax system. Evidence suggests that informal operators perceive
the system of taxation and the self-policing mechanism as costs to the business and
unnecessary burden on their profits,[58] although in reality this is not the case. Technically speaking, VAT is transferred to finished goods, which means that the consumer
is the one who ultimately pays for VAT.

---

[58]Aruwa (2008)

But the lack of awareness and appropriate knowledge of VAT operations means that informal sector operators believe that they would end up absorbing these costs. To change behaviour and encourage a sustainable culture of tax compliance among all business owners, policy around greater education and awareness of taxation system and adjusting the VAT rate to accommodate economic activities in the informal sector could be a vital incentive. Besides challenges related to taxation, employment obligations including employment contracts with minimum wage and compliance with other legal obligations present informal sector firms with an insurmountable barrier to register and formalise their enterprise.

Although, arguably, informal firms may be exempt from taxation because of low levels of profitability, employment obligations represent fixed costs, and informal firms might find these costs a bit difficult to absorb. This is because most informal sector commercial activities including employment relationships and wage arrangements are usually without worker protection or contractual obligations on the part of the employing firm or individual. As such, devising separate employment relationships contracts for the informal sector to embrace their actual capabilities, without undermining employment rights and protection, could be one way of addressing some of the challenges associated with employment obligations.

More broadly, a mutual dialogue between government agencies and representatives of informal sector workers, whereby the latter act as proxies in employment matters, will likely change perceptions, attitudes and behaviour towards employment obligations. A key part of this policy must encourage informal sector representatives to take an active role in drafting new forms of employment relationships including collective bargaining, employment rights and responsibilities, new codes of behaviour, forging greater relationships between the formal sector and the informal sector as well as creating formal channels for dispute resolution among members.[59]

An important but very rarely considered area in which informal sector actors in Africa may benefit, and ultimately be supported to move towards the mainstream of formal institutions, is through an inclusive policy of education in taxation affairs and entrepreneurship education. Both entail the provision of practical skills for establishing and managing a small firm in a sustainable manner, as well as create awareness about the socioeconomic benefits of tax payment. A sustained and well-targeted education programme including intensive sensitisation effort championed by informal sector representatives is likely to lead to attitudinal and cultural shift, and eventually compliance.

Entrepreneurship education can raise the creativity and entrepreneurial dynamism of informal sector actors by providing them with the basic knowledge and skills they need in order to manage their business in a more profitable manner. But to incentivise and encourage a buy-in and compliance in tax payment, there also needs to be increased transparency and accountability on the part of the government and the tax authorities, who many informal sector operators perceive as corrupt. Through the provision of increased access to reliable information about tax expenditures, delivery of public services and infrastructures particularly in health, education, accessible roads

---

[59]ILO (2002)

and electricity, this perception may begin to change, and consequently improve tax compliance behaviour.

In conclusion, given the scale of economic activities of informal firms and the social acceptability that they enjoy across Africa, especially through strong economic linkages with the formal sector, it is difficult to sustain the argument about the illegality of their economic activities. From a policy standpoint, what might be more helpful, as others have argued, is perhaps to: (1) mitigate the disadvantages and marginalisation the sector suffers, (2) increase the absorption capacity of players (e.g. urban poor and migrants), (3) improve their productivity and income as well as (4) the working conditions of its workers.[60]

BIBLIOGRAPHY

Arimah, B. C. (2001). *Nature and determinants of the linkages between informal and formal sector enterprises in Nigeria*. Oxford: Blackwell Publishers.

Aruwa, A. S. (2008). The administration and problems of value added tax in Nigeria. *Finance and Accounting Research Monitor*, 2(2), 1–18.

Baker, T., Miner, A., & Eesley, D. (2003). Improvising firms: Bricolage, account giving and improvisational competences in the founding process. *Research Policy*, 32(2), 255–276.

Baker, T., & Nelson, R. E. (2005). Creating something from nothing: Resource construction through entrepreneurial Bricolage. *Adminstrative Science Quarterly*, 50(3), 329–366.

Banerjee, A., & Duflo, E. (2007). The economic lives of the poor. *The Journal of Economic Perspectives*, 21(1), 141–167.

Bangasser, P. E. (2000). *The ILO and the informal sector: An institutional history*. Geneva: International Labour Organisation Publications.

Baumol, W., Litan, R. E., & Schramm, C. (2007), *Good capitalism, bad capitalism and the economies of growth and prosperity*. New Haven, CT: Yale University Press.

Benjamin, N. C., & Mbaye, A. A. (2012). The informal sector, productivity, and enforcement in West Africa: A firm-level analysis. *Review of Development Economics*, 16(4), 664–680.

Bohme, M., & Thiele, R. (2012). Is the informal sector constrained from the Demand Side? Evidence for six West African Capitals. *World Development*, 40(7), 1369–1381.

Bourdieu, P. (1986). The forms of capital. In Richardson, J. (ed.), *Handbook of theory and research for the sociology of education* (pp. 241–258). Westport, CT: Greenwood.

Brautigam, D. (1997). Substituting for the state: Institutions and industrial development in eastern Nigeria. *World Development*, 25(7), 1063–1080.

Campbell, J. (2004). *Institutional change and globalization*. Princeton, NJ: Princeton University Press.

Charmes, J. (2012). The informal economy worldwide: Trends and characteristics. *Margin – The Journal of Applied Economic Research*, 6(2), 103–132.

Chattaraj, S. (2017). Governing informality: how urban governance works in India. Oxford Review of Economic Policy, Working Papers, 10th May 2019. Retrieved from https://cprindia.org/people/shahana-chattaraj

Davidsson, P., Baker, T., & Senyard, M. (2017). A measure of entrepreneurial bricolage behavior. *International Journal of Entrepreneurial Behavior and Research*, 23(1), 114–135.

De Soto, H. (1989). *The other path – the economic answer to terrorism*. New York, NY: Basic Books.

---

[60]Papola (1980)

Desa, G. (2012). Resource mobilization in international social entrepreneurship: Bricolage as mechanism of institutional transformation. *Entrepreneurship Theory and Practice*, 36(4), 727–751.

Fan, Y. (2002). Guanxi's consequence: Personal gains at social cost. *Journal of Business Ethics*, 38(4), 371–380.

Floro, M., & Ray, D. (1997). Vertical links between formal and informal financial institutions. *Review of Development Economics*, 1(1), 34–56.

Grimm, M., Knorringa, P., & Lay, J. (2012). Constrained Gazelles: High potentials in West Africa's informal economy. *World Development*, 40(7), 1352–1368.

Hall, R., & Jones, C. (1999). Why do some countries produce so much more output per worker than others? *The Quarterly Journal of Economics*, 114(1), 83–116.

Hart, K. (1973). Informal economic opportunity and urban employment in Ghana, *The Journal of Modern African Studies*, 11(1), 61–89.

Hart, K. (1985). The informal economy. *The Cambridge Journal of Anthropology*, 10(2), 54–58.

Helmke, G., & Levitsky, S. (2004). Informal institutions and comparative politics: A research agenda. *Perspectives on Politics*, 2(4), 725–740.

Horak, S. (2018). Construct definition: Jinmyaku (Japan). In Ledeneva (Ed.), *The global encyclopaedia of informality* (Vol. 1, pp. 94–96). London: University College London Press.

Horn, P. (2005). New forms of collective bargaining: Adapting to the informal economy and new forms of work. *Labour, Capital and Society*, 38(1&2), 209–224.

International Labor Organisation (2002). *Supporting workers in the informal economy: A policy framework*. Working Paper on the Informal Economy. Geneva: ILO.

Knight, J. (1992). *Institutions and social conflict*. New York, NY: Cambridge University Press.

Lagos, R. A. (1995). Formalizing the informal sector: Barriers and costs. *Development and Change*, 26(1), 111–131.

Ledeneva, A. (2009). From Russia with "Blat": Can informal networks help modernise Russia? *Social Research*. 76(1), 257–288.

Lindberg, S. I. (2003). It's our time to chop: Do elections in Africa feed net-patrimonialism rather than counteract it? *Democratization*, 10(2), 121–140.

Lomnitz, L. (1998). Informal exchange networks in formal systems: A theoretical model. *American Anthropologist*, 90(1), 42–55.

Maloney, F. W. (2004). Informality revisited. *World Development*, 32(7), 1159–1178.

Mathews, D. (1959). The folkways of the United States Senate: Conformity to group norms and legislative effectiveness. *The American Political Science Review*, 53(4), 1064–1089.

Meagher, K. (2009) Trading on faith: Religious movements and informal economic governance in Nigeria. *Journal of Modern African Studies*, 47(3), 397–423.

Meagher, K. (2010). *Identity economics: Social networks and informal economy in Nigeria*. Woodbridge, Suffolk; Rochester, NY: Boydell & Brewer.

Medina, L., & Schneider, F. (2018). *Shadow economies around the world: What did we learn over the last 20 years?* IMF Working Papers, No. WP/18/17, African Department, Washington D.C., IMF Publications.

Mizoguchi, T., & Van Quyen, N. (2009). Amakudari: The post-retirement employment of elite bureaucrats in Japan. *Journal of Public Economic Theory*, 14(5), 813–847.

Nguimkeu, P., & Okou, C. (2020). A tale of Africa today: Balancing the lives and livelihoods of informal workers during the COVID-19 pandemic, *Policy Brief*, 1(3), Office of the Chief Economist, Africa Region, World Bank Group.

Papola, T. S. (1980). Informal sector: Concept and policy. *Economic and Political Weekly*, 15(18), 817–824.

Portes, A., & Sassen-Koob, S. (1987) Making it underground: Comparative material on the urban informal economy in Western Economies. *American Journal of Sociology*, 93(1), 30–61.

Potts, D. (2008). The urban informal sector in Sub-Saharan Africa: From bad to good (and back again?). *Development Southern Africa*, 25(2), 151–167.

Powell, E., & Baker, T. (2014). It's what you make of it: Founder identity and enacting strategic responses to adversity. *Academy of Management Journal*, 5(5), 1406–1433.

Sassen, S. (1994). Informal economy: Between new developments and old regulations. *Yale Law Journal*, 103(8), 2289–2304.

Schartz, S. (1984). Pirate capitalism and the inert economy of Nigeria. *Journal of Modern African Studies*, 22(1), 45–57.

Schneier, E. (2010). Norms and folkways in congress: How much has actually changed? *Congress & the Presidency*, 15(2), 117–138.

Singer, H. W., & Jolly, R. (2012). Employment, incomes and equality: Lessons of the ILO employment strategy Mission to Kenya. In: Jolly, R.. (Ed.), *Milestones and turning points in development thinking. (IDS Companions to Development)*. London: Palgrave Macmillan.

Stockemer, D., Wigginton, M. & Sundstrom, A. (2020). Boys\club or good ol' boys club? Corruption and the parliamentary representation of young and old men and women. *Parliamentary Affairs*, 74(2), 314–332. gsaa004, doi:10.1093/pa/gsaa004

Suchman, M. (1995). Managing legitimacy: Strategic and institutional approaches. *Academy of Management Review*, 20(3), 571–611.

Syverson, C. (2011). What determines productivity? *Journal of Economic Literature*, 49(2), 326–365.

Webb, J. W., Tihanyi, L., Ireland, R. D., & Sirmon, D. G. (2009). You say illegal, I say legitimate: Entrepreneurship in the informal economy. *The Academy of Management Review*, 34(3), 492–510.

World Bank (2020). Doing Business 2019. Comparing Business Regulation for Domestic Firms in 190 Economies. Retrieved from https://www.doingbusiness.org/content/dam/doingBusiness/media/Profiles/Regional/DB2019/SSA.pdf. Accessed on 02 April 2021.

World Bank (2021). Global economic prospects. Retrieved from https://www.worldbank.org/en/publication/global-economic-prospects. Accessed on 01 February 2021.

Xaba, J., Horn, P., & Motala, S. (2002). *The informal sectors in Sub-Saharan Africa ILO Working Paper (No. 848) on the Informal Economy, Employment Sector*, Geneva: International Labour Organisation.

CONCLUSION

8

This book has focused on three different sets of interrelated goals. The first goal was mainly directed at the sustainable development challenges Africa faces despite the significant socioeconomic progress seen in the region over the last three decades. The second was to establish more firmly the institutional contexts that might have given rise to these challenges. The third was mainly substantive. It examined the related issues that have evolved while writing this book in the context of the economic fallout of the COVID-19 pandemic and how the region can cease the opportunity to re-build. By providing the occasion to go beyond mere academic discussion to delve into details about the realities of sustainable development challenges in Africa, this book, of course, bridges research insights and practice. Through that it offers the granularity that will help policymakers, development experts and governments to chart a different but bold direction.

Thus, the first set of these objectives is concerned with an over-optimism that understates the social, political and economic realities of many Africans in our modern economy. With several African countries growing rapidly, amid the sluggish global recovery from the 2008 financial crisis and the compounding economic effects of the COVID-19 pandemic, it would seem the region's darkest hour is behind. Yet, in these contexts, it is important to come to grips with the economic consequences of Africa's reliance on foreign aid, and the threat that presents to gaining economic independence in the same way the region gained political independence in the 1960s. This threat, coupled with the wider contemporary issues of population growth, urbanisation, infrastructure, mass unemployment and brain drain, has serious repercussions for other related although more recent challenges, such as climate-related risks, food insecurity and the disruption brought about by the Fourth Industrial Revolution (4IR).

The second set of objectives relates to institutional dysfunctions and their implications for socioeconomic development in an age of globalisation and the 4IR. Although I began at a micro level by looking at how institutions enhance and constrain people's life chances through access (or lack) to education, income and health, much of the book has been devoted to the macro contexts of the efficacy and the transformational impact of functional institutions, their benefits, particularly in access to quality education and healthcare as a pathway to achieving high human development and economic growth outcomes in Africa. Other related arguments are that the stunted socioeconomic growth and human development we see in Africa today has been as a direct result of poor institutional arrangements and their associated dysfunction. Among others, corruption, governance failure, rent-seeking and resource plunder were of particular concern. These factors, which stem from institutional dysfunctionality, are the root causes of prevalent social and economic deprivation we see in the region today. In many instances, but particularly in relation to Africa's demographic challenge, I have argued that institutional dysfunction is the difference between either demographic dividend or demographic time bomb.

This reflects my long-held concern, although shared by others, that lack of accountability and misuse of Africa's abundant natural resources limit the ability to build the strong foundations for sustainable development through reform and investment in quality entrepreneurship education and training for young people. A reformed general education and training system, particularly moving away from a didactic model toward a more practice-oriented education, will also address poor human capital, young people's employment needs, thereby reduce rising youth unemployment. With these concerns, coupled with significant challenges imposed by the COVID-19 economic crisis, come the need to recognise more widely people's growing appetite for change at all levels of the institutions that govern their political, social and consequently economic lives. Particularly, by creating the conditions that enable young people to occupy political leadership, there is a high probability of realising the dream of a more politically stable Africa under the African Union's new vision of the '*Africa We Want*'. One that is anchored on an inclusive, egalitarian, peaceful and economically prosperous Africa.

But when I go back in history, coupled with the acute institutional failures seen in the current social, political and economic situation in countries like Egypt, Ethiopia, Kenya, Nigeria and South Africa, perhaps I am more wary than optimistic about whether Africa can realise this new vision in my lifetime. Since the same leaders who got the region into its current precarious socioeconomic state still hold political and economic power. If anything, they are still pursuing broadly similar policies without any sign that these will help to reduce the deepening inequality and poverty that many Africans suffer. Yet, if I cast aside my pessimism, perhaps, there is a reason for optimism. But only by having in place the proper institutional structures for effective political and economic governance. As such, to achieve this new vision, this book makes a powerful case for building more efficient and inclusive social, political and economic institutions. The analyses and perspectives draw attention to different but interrelated ways through which African governments have approached, in a rather less holistic manner, their development policies and how they can build politically strong and economically resilient societies.

In a nutshell, by revisiting the ubiquity of 'Africa Rising', a notion that has been frequently used in public discourse about Africa's economic progress, I have tried to unpick the paradox by giving social, political and economic contexts to how Africa can emerge from a dire state of political hubris and economic stagnation to forge ahead as a more productive and self-sufficient region in a changing world. Particularly, as the region begins to re-build following the devastating impact of the COVID-19 pandemic, achieving economic self-sufficiency through regional integration is vital. Also, I have gone on to examine the institutional contexts of Africa's demographic challenges. The issues that concern me the most relate to low human development, youth unemployment, and poor education and training; especially emphasising through the analysis of entrepreneurship education and human capital the implications of these demographic challenges for income opportunity in the informal economy. In this concluding chapter, my focus is to synthesise the key points that have emerged from the preceding pages, particularly the interrelations between the three goals.

8.1 ON AFRICA'S ECONOMIC SUCCESS

In Chapter 1, I argued that Africa's recent economic progress, while unprecedented, is often celebrated in ways that mask the social and economic realities of many ordinary people in the region. There is no denying that since the millennium most African countries have maintained a double-digit economic growth unlike in many parts of the world. But what is worrying, perhaps even puzzling, is that over the same period, in addition to exponential increase in mass unemployment and poverty, as high as one-third of African countries that have benefitted from massive debt relief are now either in or at a high risk of debt distress. Given the extensive debt relief, increased inter-national partnerships that have seen record foreign direct investments – controversially led by China, the counter-intuitive situation in which unemployment and poverty have increased in the region over the same period defies logic and under-standing. It raises the question about the sustainability of Africa's development model, which is largely tied to foreign debt and aid.

As I have argued, there are, of course, conditions (e.g. to recover from natural disaster or unforeseen global economic shock) that may warrant the necessity of foreign aid assistance. But the cycle of unending aid programme to Africa simply cannot be in the best service of the region's ability to achieve economic self-sufficiency. Unfortunately, well-known efforts to address this challenge have been trial and error due to corrupt practices in both donor and aid-recipient countries. Particularly, many aid-recipient poor African countries have been misled to believe that real socioeconomic transformation and progress can emerge from Official Development Assistance (ODA) or foreign aid. But this is not true.

In fact, those African countries that receive the largest share of ODA year on year, such as, Ethiopia, Egypt and Nigeria (which I cited as case studies), continue to experience long periods of extreme poverty and political fragility. Also, overwhelming evidence has shown that donor countries often use aid to introduce, induce and in most cases advance a variety of their own political agenda and economic interest including as a weapon to maintain a colonial and strategic geopolitical stronghold. If anything, as the 'big elephant in the room', aid has been shown to slow the pace of economic progress. By disrupting the ability of aid-dependent African countries to achieve political and economic equilibrium in governance and accountability, aid has in reality harmed democratic institutions in those countries. My point in raising these uncomfortable realities stems from the fact that it is only by a better understanding of the sheer scale of these challenges can one truly acknowledge and begin to compre-hend the full extent of the fragility of Africa's economic success story over the intervening period.

In hindsight, one could argue that Africa's problems have not always been entirely of its own making. Many of the region's intractable socioeconomic problems have been traced, at least in part, to different activities orchestrated by outsiders aimed at dispossessing the region of its wealth. The sheer scale of plunder of the region's natural wealth through commercial activities may never be accurately measured or fully known. Aggregated data from various sources of financial outflows and inflows, however, provide a snapshot of the financial deficit Africa may have historically suffered, and perhaps continues to suffer through various commercial activities with the rest of the world.

In 2015, Mark Curtis, a former Research Fellow at the London-based Royal Institute of International Affairs (a.k.a. Chatham House), attempted to give some context to this financial deficit. In his view, sub-Saharan African (SSA) countries collectively received $161.6 billion mainly through loans, personal remittances and aid from outsiders. Whereas, in the same year, about $203 billion was drained out of the region either through illicit financial outflows, repatriation of profits by big corporations, debt servicing, brain drain and through the imposition of climate change costs. Thus, making SSA a 'net creditor to the rest of the world in the region of more than $41 billion'. Mark's conclusions are also shared by the Global Financial Integrity (GFI), a Washington-based not-for-profit research and advisory organisation.

GFI reported that illicit financial outflows (e.g. deliberate misinvoicing in trade and leakages in the balance of payments) from developing and emerging economies was about $1 trillion in 2014, 'with SSA experiencing a ratio between 5.3 percent and 9.9 percent of fraudulent misinvoicing higher than any other geographic region' in that year. If one were to use these measures to compute the financial deficits Africa may have suffered to 2020, then the net financial loss to Africa would more than quadruple. Yet, by comparison, the region retains the highest ratio of debt including foreign governments that dictate the activities of big multinationals and international financial institutions, such as the World Bank and the International Monetary Fund (IMF). Apart from the movement of illicit and illegal monies, there are other ways in which the rest of the world may have extracted and perhaps continues to extract heavy financial resources from Africa.

The extractive industries (e.g. oil, gas, minerals), where Africa has the least human capacities and the institutional mechanisms to compete, and perverse World Trade Organisation (WTO) rules, which allow richer and more powerful members to negotiate and erect arbitrary and insurmountable trade policies that present a barrier to export the agricultural produce of many African countries equate to a neo-colonial system of foreign aid administration. Yet, curiously, and perhaps strikingly, lack of conditions for inward investment and overdependence on foreign aid cannot be blamed on outsiders alone. There are many reasons why one may justify holding Africa's political leaders responsible for many of Africa's social and economic problems. Africa's political leaders, in compliance with international development partners and donor countries, have an abysmal record of using aid as a powerful weapon to distort the socioeconomic realities in many African countries. Thus, this distortion has for several decades ensured that Africa remains an unrivaled magnet for foreign aid.

Given the controversy surrounding the subject of foreign aid, I have argued that the basis for providing aid to Africa should be based on similar principles that governed the European Recovery Programme (ERP), also known as The Marshall Plan, in the aftermath of the Second World War. I have explained in practical detail how this could work in the context of Africa and for the benefit of donor and recipient countries. Thus, regardless of how aid programmes are packaged and presented, if the proper institutional mechanisms for effective governance and accountability that limit the need for the endless cycle of foreign aid are missing, then aid is ever unlikely to contribute to human development and real economic growth in Africa.

8.2 ON HUMAN DEVELOPMENT AND ECONOMIC GROWTH

Addressing the challenges of human development and economic growth can take different forms. Measured by three distinct although related indicators, namely, *standard of living* (measured by income), *level of knowledge* (measured by access to quality education) and *long and healthy life* (measured by life expectancy at birth), most African countries rank very low on the global Human Development Index (HDI) compared to the rest of the world. Their poor ranking is directly attributed to institutional factors including inadequate investment in basic infrastructures of education and health.

Although the implications of poor human development outcomes for economic growth have been extensively discussed in the preceding chapters, the scale of the challenge becomes daunting when one considers Africa's largest economy and its most populous – Nigeria. Out of the 189 countries surveyed in 2018, the latest year when cross-country HDI results were publicly available, Nigeria ranked low at 157 in the HDI. Nigeria suffers from a protracted deficiency in energy and electricity supply, which is critical to support the country's failing educational systems, enterprise and health sectors. To compound matters, at a mean of 60 years old (59 for males and 63 for females), life expectancy is significantly less than the global average of nearly 73 years old.

In fact, other African countries with large population including Ethiopia and Democratic Republic of the Congo equally have low human development outcomes, ranking 173 and 176, respectively. The HDI score (0.532) for the SSA region has repeatedly been low since records began, only improving slightly from 0.398 in 1990 to 0.537 in 2017 compared with the global average of 0.728.[1] To achieve a higher HDI, Nigeria and other African countries must at least overcome three distinct although related hurdles. Firstly, they must create the conditions that improve people's quality and length of life (i.e. life expectancy index). Secondly, they must provide access to knowledge and skills for secure employment (i.e. education index). Finally, they must put in place concrete measures that guarantee decent standard of living for their citizens (i.e. GNI index measured by income per capita – PPP$).

As such, components of institutions, such as education and health, play a vital role in enhancing human development outcome and ultimately economic growth. Unfortunately, across Africa, the quality and access to all levels of education have seen a steady decline since the mid-1990s because of several interrelated factors. Among these are infrastructural challenges and funding crisis, which have led to overcrowding, dilapidation, poor learning quality and productivity outcomes. Quality of learning is poor across all age groups because most classrooms are short of modern textbooks, learning materials and lack the relevant technologies, teaching personnel and digital space needed for effective learning in the twenty-first century.

Apart from infrastructural challenges, social factors, such as cultural norms and patriarchal tendencies, whereby emphasis is placed on male education, create a

---

[1] UNDP (2019)

gender bias in access to education. This makes learning and education inaccessible for mostly young girls, thereby hinders individual and societal growth. Gender bias in access to education is particularly prevalent in two of the most populous countries in Africa – Nigeria and Ethiopia. UNESCO's latest analysis (2015 records) of Nigeria's education sector shows that there is a significant variation between male literacy at 71.26 percent and at 52.66 percent, the low level of female literacy is particularly more acute in northern Nigeria. Among 15–24-year-olds, male literacy is 81.58 percent compared to the female literacy rate of 68.29 percent, which is significantly lower than the median average of 75.03 percent for this population group globally.

Similarly, in terms of educationally disadvantaged countries even by African standards, Ethiopia presents one of the most striking examples of how patriarchal practices limit women's access to education. In Ethiopia, there is a very high school drop-out rate and low attainment rate among females. On the World Bank's educational attainment sub-index which captures the gap between males and females' access to education from primary to tertiary education, Ethiopia holds the tenth bottom spot ranking 134 out of 144 countries ranked globally. For example, compared to 10.8% for males, about 17.16% of females of primary school age are out of school. Also, the country has a 14.21% attainment level for females compared to 37.28% for males. At 44%, girls are disproportionately burdened with household chores than boys, which is estimated at 22%. As a result, girls are twice more likely to abandon school than boys.

Lack of access to education impacts women's life chances. At a wider level, it reduces their ability to become independent, break the glass ceiling and make informed choices for themselves, their children and their families. As a social determinant of access to quality healthcare, education provides a very important social ladder and economic benefit for girls, particularly in the areas of reproductive health and in the reduction of infant and child mortality. As a powerful driver of human development, education is also one of the strongest instruments for spurring high productivity, economic growth, improved health outcomes, gender equality, peace and stability in any society. Yet, with the education sector in crisis and with increasing household poverty in many African countries, many school-age girls from poorer backgrounds are forced to contribute to household income through street-vending and early marriage. Thus, girls from poor households make up the growing number of young populations that are learning the least, particularly during national lockdowns due to the COVID-19 global pandemic.

To compound matters, Africa's education sector is underserved due to poorly qualified teachers, low pay and poor training, which have led to low morale among the teaching personnel. Coupled with these factors is work intensification, which have implications for under-capacity, underperformance and lack of innovation at all levels of the education value chain. Also, attracting and retaining highly qualified personnel in the education sector has been and continues to be a major challenge in many African countries, particularly in rural communities. In most cases, highly qualified teachers emigrate to either urban areas or abroad where working conditions appear to be more favourable. Combined with these challenges are budgetary constraints. While countries in Asia, Central America and Europe are investing massively in the upskilling of their teaching personnel and innovation of their educational sectors, adequate budgetary allocation to the education sector across Africa has stagnated if not in declined in real terms.

By allocating on average only 7 percent of annual total budget to education, well below the 26 percent recommended by the United Nations, most African countries are failing to prioritise and make adequate investments that would enable them to suffi-ciently educate their rapidly rising illiterate populations. As ingredients of human development, education and literacy are vital to employment and employment crea-tion needed for economic growth. Illiteracy adversely affects the ability of individuals to provide for and protect themselves. Illiterate people are far more likely than literate people to disproportionately face a lifetime of poverty and social vulnerability that comes with being poor including in health choices and understanding the importance of their civic duties and responsibility. In economic terms, illiteracy and poor health reduce workplace productivity. Together, these conditions adversely affect a country's GDP, economic growth prospects and consequently national competitiveness.

As such, eradicating the root causes of poor human development outcomes requires more than just adequate investment in education and health infrastruc-tures. Attention must be shifted towards reversing the main sources of State revenue and wealth African governments have relied on for so long. Notably, foreign aid and natural resources revenues mainly from the extractive industry, rather than agricultural, manufacturing or even the services sector. To expand the revenue base, thereby support measures and national programmes that improve human devel-opment, there is a need to diversify their economies. But economic diversification cannot be beneficial in a context in which institutional arrangements are dysfunc-tional, deficient or inadequate in their set-up. Institutional barriers limit the ability of the State to invest in and support individuals to access the relevant education and training, which is essential to human capital formation, livelihood access and pro-ductivity, and consequently high human development outcomes. Absence of human capital and productivity hinders creativity and innovation needed for entrepre-neurship and economic growth to thrive through employment creation. One crucial example of how institutional barriers have hindered human capital, productivity and economic growth in Africa can be seen in the context of natural resource governance. Analysis of the forces driving these institutional barriers and ways in which to tackle and reverse their economic impacts were the primary focus of chapter three.

8.3 ON NATURAL RESOURCE GOVERNANCE

One of the most controversial subjects in development discourse is the notion that the pace of economic development in resource-rich countries of the Global South is much slower than in resource-scarce countries of the Global North. It is a well-known fact that the commercial value of Africa's enormous natural resources including oil, natural gas and minerals is unquantifiable. From small resource-poor countries, such as Burundi, Eswatini and Guinea-Bissau, to resource-rich and large countries like Nigeria, Democratic Republic of Congo and Angola, Africa is home to large swathes of untapped rich natural and mineral resources. Yet, the region is comparably home to the world's poorest with more than a third of the population living in precarious socioeconomic conditions.

Many decades of natural resources revenues derived from commercial activities initiated by African governments in partnership with big multinationals have neither boosted shared prosperity nor helped to reduce the prevalence of economic deprivation in the region. Measured in terms of natural resource capital per person, Gabon with its 2.1 million people should logically be one of the richest countries in the world given that the country is rich in diamond, gold, natural gas and petroleum as well as uranium and iron ore. Yet, with nearly 40 percent of its working-age population unemployed, and with an estimated 60–70 percent of Gabonese only marginally surviving on less than $1 per day, it is obvious that poverty presents natural resource-rich African countries with enormous social and economic challenges. Weak institutional arrangements hinder the ability of resource-rich African countries to transition away from overdependence on natural resources as their main source of export earnings.

Notably, the prevalence of poverty and economic deprivation in countries such as Nigeria and Angola – Africa's largest petroleum exporters – can be traced to their overdependence on export earnings from oil. Worse, most commercial activities in their oil sectors have mainly benefited and continue to play to the advantage of large multinational oil companies over local competitors. This situation often leads to all sorts of other social vices including political and civil unrest – as is the case in Nigeria's oil-rich Niger Delta region. The problem is that Nigeria and Angola, despite more than 50 years of oil discovery on their shores, have little to no human capacity and the institutional mechanisms to effectively regulate and optimise upstream and downstream deep-water oil and natural gas productions. As a result, their natural resource sectors are highly prone to weak natural resource governance, corruption, oil revenue mismanagement and plunder.

Because of weak natural resource governance, multinational oil companies operating in both countries often engage in capital flight through a yearly cycle of underpaid taxes and profit repatriation. Capital flight occurs when significant financial and non-financial assets are taken out of a country, mostly during periods of economic distress and political uncertainty. Other factors that could trigger capital flight are doubts about the stability of a country's financial health and institutions, as well as in cases where corruption is perceived to be endemic. The economic cost of capital flight is hard to estimate. Coupled with corruption and weak natural resource governance, capital flight however contributes to the prevalence of resource curse and Dutch disease in African countries, which in turn hinder economic development. Over time, as these problems persist, they become institutionalised – thereby, leading to political instability and poor economic growth outcomes.

Weak governance of natural resource wealth makes it very difficult if not impossible to achieve better economic outcomes. Thus, to address the challenges of resource curse and Dutch disease, natural resource-rich African countries must consider the following measures. Firstly, they must build and maintain strong institutions and diversify and liberalise their economies through the implementation of market-led policies. Secondly, they must raise people's confidence in the management of revenues and funds from natural resources through increased accountability and publication of natural resource revenue inflows and outflows held in SWF in form of national savings. Finally, they must ensure that the regulatory framework including natural resource governance and all oil-related commercial activities have a national legislative oversight and, at least, are benchmarked against international norms and standards for natural resource governance and management.

8.4 ON ACHIEVING DEMOGRAPHIC DIVIDEND

Chapter four focused on the challenges, prospects as well as the social and economic imperatives of achieving demographic dividend in Africa. Amidst the challenges that shape the lives of many young people across the world, the economic fallout of the COVID-19 pandemic has more badly affected young people in Africa than in any other region. Millions of school age population at all levels have been kept out of education and training by the economic crisis and disruption arising from the pandemic. Particularly in locations not served by digital and ICT infrastructures. Because of this, young Africans, more than any population group, are now at a greater risk of being left much further behind in unmet educational attainment, unemployment and poverty, and in access to healthcare and economic opportunities than their global counterparts. With no education, employment and training (NEET), it means that they are twice more likely than their older counterparts to have a NEET status.

Even before the onset of the COVID-19 pandemic, young Africans were more prone to engage in crime, political violence and social unrest as a result of lack of livelihood opportunities and disaffection with the political and economic conditions in their countries. Also, because of institutionalised patriarchal norms and narrow definitions of a woman's place in the African society, young women are more likely to have a NEET status. With no educational and employment prospects, women's only chance of income and economic stability is mainly through a male partner. This puts them at a much higher risk of domestic abuse and violence, which spiked during the COVID-19 pandemic due to global and national lockdowns to contain the diseases. NEET status among any population group ready to enter the workforce have widespread implications for high unemployment and intergenerational poverty. It diminishes the prospects for shared prosperity and societal growth.

For those young people in employment including graduates, they have low productivity and income because they are mainly in the informal sector without adequate social and economic protections of secure employment. As a negative outcome of informal employment, in-work poverty is more prevalent in Africa (96 percent of employed youths are thought to be in poverty) where between 50 and 70 percent of young people are in informal employment, thus, poor. The International Labour Organisation (ILO) estimates that out of the 429 million young informal sector workers globally, around 55 million, about 13 percent, are extremely poor – that is, they live on an income below $1.90 per day, while 71 million, or 17 percent are moderately poor and live on an income below $3.20 per day. Also, because of limited scope for training, there is no career advancement for workers in the informal sector unlike those in the formal sector.

In-work poverty persists in Africa because young people are denied access to quality education and relevant work-based training, which can provide them with access to secure livelihoods with decent wages. Lack of access to livelihoods and decent income leads to emigration among mostly young Africans aged 24–35 years old. Mass emigration of young talents leads to brain drain, which is the net negative effect of emigration of highly trained and educated Africans to other parts of the world. As a negative phenomenon, it presents Africa with a considerable social and economic challenge in terms of human capital flight. By its nature, it impedes economic progress, and thereby limits the prospect of achieving demographic dividend. Because of these interrelated demographic challenges, I have argued that by placing greater emphasis on youth employability, integrating young people's ideas and priorities with national economic planning and by leveraging the four key themes of Education, Entrepreneurship, Employment and Engagement, it may be possible to curtail and possibly reverse the incidence of brain drain, increase workforce productivity and consequently spur economic growth.

8.5 ON YOUTH EMPLOYABILITY

This book has tried to explain with broadly different yet related themes how strong and inclusive institutions can be used to create the conditions that support youth employability. In particular, the demands of employability skills and productivity can be understood in the institutional contexts of education and training provision versus labour market needs. The issue is not just that education and training provisions in Africa are disconnected from labour market needs, but also, there is the ironic situation in which Africa has the least productive and skilled workforce globally even though it has the youngest population. This situation presents a significant development and demographic challenge for the region, particularly in terms of prevalence and rising youth unemployment.

With only about 3 million out of 10–11 million youths that enter the labour market annually after school obtaining decent jobs, there is a danger that a significant percentage of Africa's young population may be condemned to a lifetime of unemployment and poverty unless serious steps are taken to reverse this situation. Because of this, providing young Africans with employability skills to thrive and prosper is vital to achieve demographic dividend. The main challenge is targeting education and training provision to fully deliver those skills needed by young people to obtain and survive in employment in our globalised knowledge economy. Work-based skills, such as learning, critical thinking, teamwork, communication and problem-solving skills, creativity and initiative, ICT literacy and digital skills, are essential to work and effective collaboration in the knowledge economy. Unfortunately, despite massive investments by various African governments in work-based and vocational training programmes, such as, TVET, youth unemployment remains very high and growing.

As a work-based programme, TVET curriculum is widely perceived as inadequate to meet labour market needs in today's knowledge economy. Because of this, young people and employers are often reluctant to invest in TVET graduates. The problem is that TVET structures including delivery patterns and outcomes are fragmented, coupled with the fact that evaluation of TVET programme has proven far more problematic than issues related to the inadequacy of its contents and pedagogies.

Apart from this, there is no credit transfer framework to help providers and employers to harmonise and evaluate TVET's learning outcomes. This limits its portability across Africa, especially between Anglophone and Francophone countries. Unlike the experience in other parts of the world, where by, for example, the

European Credit Transfer System (ECTS) supports portability of learning outcomes, which increases the appeal of vocational education and training programmes through mobility and access to jobs across different regions and countries. This is also the case in Asia and Latin America, respectively, where the Latin American Reference Credit (CLAR), The ASEAN University Network (AUN) and ASEAN Credit Transfer System (ACTS) are the instruments used to evaluate the workload completed by students in different subject interests.

The lack of a harmonised system of assessing the quality of TVET learning outcomes arises from several issues related to its current strategy and implementation. Several years after adopting TVET followed by a series of reforms, many African countries still view it merely as a mechanism to supply skilled labour to employers in specific sectors of the traditional economy, such as manufacturing, agriculture and engineering. Because of this, many providers have been slow and reluctant to align its strategy, format and delivery with labour market needs of a fast-changing globalised knowledge economy in which new 4IR technologies are disrupting the ways in which individuals work and organisations behave. As such, this central point was highlighted in chapter five with analysis of technical vocational education and training (TVET) and entrepreneurship education, and how both could be combined as part of general education strategy to benefit the region.

General education across most African countries provides a standardised system of assessing attained learning outcomes in any education and training in ways that have been difficult to achieve through TVET. Integrating TVET into general education system in a new strategy would not only require that governments, employers and education providers work collaboratively to develop relevant and coherent legislation, pedagogies and contents. But it also demands that in measuring TVET's learning outcomes that more emphasis be placed on human capital development, digital skills, entrepreneurship and self-employment. As shown in chapter six, entrepreneurship education constitutes an important feature of general education, which is core to accessing the human capital ingredients needed for self-employment.

8.6 ON ENTREPRENEURSHIP EDUCATION AS HUMAN CAPITAL

Knowledge and skills for self-employment foster entrepreneurship, which eases labour market constraints, and ultimately contributes to job creation and economic growth. But the major challenge for African governments and policymakers has been what type of education can be used to effectively support young people to become self-employed. Across the region, like the rest of the world, there has been policy shift towards the importance of entrepreneurship education in schools to encourage students and graduates to develop entrepreneurial competences to enable them to become self-employed or entrepreneurs. Some large economies in Africa, such as Nigeria and South Africa, have national policies on entrepreneurship education geared towards encouraging and empowering students and graduates to become job creators rather than job seekers.

However, educators lack the capacity to deliver entrepreneurship education beyond the classroom environment. Because of this, the effect of entrepreneurship education on student's entrepreneurial intention and behaviour has been at best marginal and has not been felt as widely as envisaged. In today's knowledge-based economy, entrepreneurship education cannot be limited to a classroom experience. Exposure to entrepreneurship education merely as an academic exercise in a classroom environment is insufficient to prepare and enable one to make complex business decisions or deal with the complexities and the changing dynamics of the business environment. Thus, for the positive effect of entrepreneurship education to be felt, then educators, especially higher education providers, must embrace and use practice-oriented strategies to teach entrepreneurship beyond the classroom in a more holistic manner. By boosting opportunities for practice-oriented entrepreneurship education, it is possible to create the levers that will enable students and graduates to acquire entrepreneurial knowledge and skills for self-employment.

For this to happen, higher education providers must widen their entrepreneurship education net by investing in campus innovation hubs, academic–industry collaboration and technological transfer offices (TTOs). This will help to expose students to the practice and experience of entrepreneurship, encourage and enable them to experiment with their ideas and use their creativity and innovation beyond the classroom. By so doing, they are more likely to be adequately prepared and equipped to successfully deal with the complexities and challenges of the business environment as nascent entrepreneurs. Thus, in this sense, entrepreneurship education becomes a proxy for human capital formation which students need to become successful nascent entrepreneurs. From a research perspective, although hard evidence to support the association between entrepreneurship education and human capital is limited and scarce, especially in the context of Africa, the theoretical premise that underlies this viewpoint and its implications for entrepreneurial success is useful and intuitively compelling.

Human capital constitutes the resources and assets an individual or a group (e.g. workforce) has in form of skills, knowledge and experience acquired through education and training that makes them productive. By the same token, entrepreneurial knowledge and skills are resources for opportunity recognition and exploitation, which are important dimensions to the early stages of the entrepreneurial process. Opportunity recognition and exploitation has been associated with human capital formation through knowledge and skills acquired from exposure to entrepreneurship education and the experience gained from entrepreneurial training. The thinking is that human capital increases an individual's capability to discover and exploit opportunities in a way that may not be visible to others,[2] helps to harmonise the strategic planning and marketing competencies required to exploit those opportunities[3] and thereby serves as a prerequisite to the efficient and effective management of entrepreneurship activity even in unstable business environments of Africa.[4]

---

[2]Shane and Venkataraman (2000)
[3]Frese et al. (2007)
[4]Anosike (2018)

With emphasis on opportunity seeking and self-reliance, entrepreneurship education advocates individual autonomy and proactive response to labour market demands through training and skills development for self-employment. Entrepreneurship education provides the prerequisites for those competencies essential to achieving entrepreneurial effectiveness, which is the ability of an individual to behave or function in an entrepreneurial capacity.[5] Idea generation, innovation skills, envisioning opportunities, product innovation, creativity, risk-taking propensity and scanning environments for initial opportunities are among several key entrepreneurial competencies that are essential to entrepreneurial effectiveness in any type of business environment.[6] As such, formation of human capital attributes through the medium of entrepreneurship education is believed to lead to success in the early stages of an entrepreneurship career. Specifically, early-stage entrepreneurs exposed to entrepreneurship education have relied on their human capital attributes to eliminate initial success barriers including the Liability of Newness (LoN), which nascent entrepreneurs encounter due to lack of track record and legitimacy.[7]

With these empirical perspectives, human capital has come to represent a combination and varying entrepreneurial competencies including knowledge, skills and experience acquired from entrepreneurship education and training that can be used to create value through job creation.[8] Through education programmes that enhance the ability to identify and exploit opportunities for entrepreneurial activity, human capital is essential to knowledge creation, skills acquisition and consequently raising young people's productivity. Positioned as a component of human capital, knowledge and skills acquired from entrepreneurship education can be a very useful tool to navigate any business environment. Some have found that entrepreneurship education can be used to establish the extent to which explicit knowledge and tacit knowledge, as well as the cognitive skills of nascent entrepreneurs are well adjusted, thus, uniquely useful in opportunity recognition and exploitation in a way not immediately obvious to others.[9]

Explicit knowledge can be readily expressed, codified, stored and accessed, therefore easily transferable or shared with others. In contrast, implicit or tacit knowledge cannot be shared with others. They include those insights, intuitions, norms and beliefs that are entwined with experience that cannot be expressed or codified, therefore difficult to transfer to others. For individuals to be able to exhibit complex codified and uncodified knowledge and skills in the entrepreneurial process, some form of education and training is necessary. This is where entrepreneurship education becomes useful. However, to recognise and exploit opportunities in a uniquely entrepreneurial manner, individuals must at least have a clear business goal and plan, have a deep insight into the dynamics of the business environment through exposure to practice-oriented entrepreneurship education and how to achieve this goal by deploying that insight in the entrepreneurial process, especially in their reaction to different complex business situations and contexts.

---

[5]Kuratko (2005)
[6]Mitchelmore and Rowley (2013)
[7]Dimov (2010)
[8]Marvel et al. (2016)
[9]Davidsson and Honig (2003)

Individuals who possess greater levels of entrepreneurial knowledge and skills, as well as experience through exposure to entrepreneurship education arguably are likely to have and thus able to exhibit a unique ability to recognise and exploit opportunities for entrepreneurial success. Therefore, the intriguing question is whether entrepreneurship education, in and of itself, is sufficient to shape the cognitive and intuitive abilities of individuals to specifically recognise and exploit opportunities in an entrepreneurially minded way. Thus, for many African countries seeking to use entrepreneurship education to influence higher education students' and young people's entrepreneurial intention and behaviour, the pressing priority must be how to use more effective delivery strategies to ensure that entrepreneurship education delivers the resources needed for entrepreneurial success. Yet, research has neither fully explored nor explained the intricacies of entrepreneurship education as a resource for entrepreneurial success.

Thus, with these perspectives come the need for Africa's education sector, particularly higher education, to address two critical challenges, which have implications for sustainable development. Firstly, how can the role of the higher education sector be strengthened to accelerate youth entrepreneurship? Secondly, how can higher education institutions specifically use entrepreneurship education as an effective mechanism to support students at their early-stage entrepreneurship journey? Answers to these questions inevitably cannot ignore the wider context of the institutional challenges facing many African countries. Various conceptualisations of institutions in the literature have shown that institutions play a vital role in defining and shaping educational outcomes for individuals. Educational outcomes have implications for success in the entrepreneurial process through knowledge and skills needed for creativity, accurate perception of risk, opportunity recognition and opportunity exploitation.

As systems of established rules that enable shared patterns of thought, expectation and action by imposing 'form' and 'consistency' on human activities,[10] institutions play an important role in shaping an entrepreneurial process by constraining and enabling entrepreneurial behaviour in any society. However, the linkage between institutions, laws and regulations implies that governments can intervene and influence 'the rules of the game'.[11] Such intervention can be useful to the extent governments also recognise and have adequate and accurate perception of existing formal and informal institutional arrangements that govern human entrepreneurial behaviour and economic activity within specific business contexts.

Formal institutional arrangements involve 'universal and transferable rules of the game' including constitution, laws, by-laws, edicts, charters and regulations that encompass elements, such as property rights and contracts.[12] By contrast, informal institutional arrangement embraces tacit values, attitudes and norms of a society, which are enacted and reified through social conventions, interpersonal contacts and relationships.[13] In most societies, the human and non-human activities that constitute formal and informal institutional arrangements do not exist in isolation, or,

---

[10]Hodgson (2006, p. 2)
[11]Van Arkadie (1989)
[12]North (1990)
[13]Fukuyama (2000)

independent of each other. Thus, as shown in the previous chapter, formal and informal institutions in fact act interdependently. Through a symbiotic relationship process, formal and informal institutional arrangements influence and shape economic linkages between formal and informal economy in significantly diverse ways.

8.7 ON AFRICA'S INFORMAL ECONOMY

Examining the fluxes driving Africa's booming informal economy, the vast income opportunity it offers to millions of Africans, the motivation of the actors and how to make the sector to work more efficiently and effectively were my primary focus in chapter seven. What seems to be the priority for many African governments, and perhaps even challenging, is how best to bring large informal firms into their tax net. But challenge goes beyond the issue of taxation. African governments face a trade-off between taxing informal firms and not taxing them altogether. In any case, they face a dilemma in that there is a risk that undermines the credibility and the legality of their tax systems. This dilemma, perhaps, helps to explain why economists and development experts have for so long been dogged by the controversy surrounding the central question of legitimacy and the legality of economic activities in the informal economy.

Some have argued that if the barriers to achieving legality were mitigated, such as, by lowering registration burden and tax obligations, then informal firms are likely to register their business, pay tax and take advantage of the benefits that come with an official status. However, lowering the registration burden and tax obligations for informal firms is not without their challenges. Although lower taxation might incentivise informal sector operators to regularise their economic activities with State authorities, there is no evidence that informal sector activities would suddenly or completely disappear if lower taxation was introduced. There are two main reasons why lower taxation may not entirely solve the problems associated with economic activities in the informal economy including the issue of tax evasion prevalent among informal firms.

Firstly, even if lower tax burden leads to registration of existing informal firms, it may not prevent the entry of new ones because of the inherent structural weaknesses in the economic system of many African countries. Secondly, financial incentives may not be sufficient to reverse the economic rationale strongly held by many informal sector operators who perceive that the costs and benefits of operating informally far outweigh the costs and benefits of operating formally within the tax net. In both cases, there is very little to show that lowering the financial burden of registration and taxation would lead to a significant change in behaviour within and outside the sector. Financial incentives, important though they are, cannot guarantee that informal sector operators would not choose to pursue other courses of action that satisfy their own personal agenda, such as, by remaining informal at the expense of the State. Thus, there are no easy options.

Notwithstanding, chapter seven laid out a much simpler process of easing the unnecessary bureaucratic burden of new business registration across Africa to bring these legal requirements for business ownership in line with best practices in other regions across the world. It also proposed more sustainable schemes that could be used to mitigate the financial burden of being a legal business entity in the region. African governments must prioritise investment in developing strong and sustainable business support systems across the board, not just for informal sector operators. The main goal must be to ensure there is a level playing field with effective ways of enhancing the ability of all the actors in the small business and enterprise (SME) sector to flourish within a structured and a well-regulated framework that offers individuals and businesses the flexibility to thrive, and thereby contribute to economic growth.

From a policy perspective, growth strategies that focus on promoting measures that seek to level the playing field for small business owners including enabling business operators in the informal and formal sectors to co-exist alongside their distinct capabilities could help to change perceptions and to some extent attitudes and behaviour within the informal sector. A key part of any incentive should particularly focus on helping informal sector workers to improve their business practices, devise mechanisms of representation (e.g. through accreditation or election of representatives) and enhance their capabilities to lobby public and private agencies for better bargaining rights and improved labour market conditions that retain the flexibility of the informal environment. The importance of new forms of employment relationships for the informal sector in India's informal sector has proven to be vital to achieving levels of work ethos and employment practices consistent with the core labour standards set out by the ILO.

Also, the provision of financial and management advisory services can be a very powerful way of addressing the current knowledge and skills gap in Africa's informal sector, particularly in the areas of bookkeeping, separating personal and business expenditures and record keeping, which are requirements to access formal finance from mainstream lenders. It is not unrelated that one of the major factors inhibiting growth of small businesses in Africa, particularly informal firms, is lack of access to finance. To grow, small businesses need access to finance and credit to fund medium- to long-term investments. But because of poor business practices, including in some cases absence of book-keeping records, access to finance remains a major barrier to growth for small business operators. To put the situation into perspective, only between five and ten per cent of informal sector businesses have access to formal loans, usually through proxies and representatives. Good business practices and proper accounting practices could help informal sector operators to track and use their assets as collateral to access finance, lack of which is the greatest obstacle and threat to the viability and sustainability of Africa's SME sector.

Research and policy should also focus on understanding how to standardise the criteria that support small businesses to access finance through effective regulation and monitoring. More finance can help informal micro-enterprise operators to increase their economic activity, employ more workers, expand and grow their businesses, and thereby enhance their ability to contribute to economic growth and sustainable development. As a condition to access finance and capacity-building initiatives as well as access to representation in employment matters, owners of informal firms must therefore demonstrate evidence of their registration status, at least. Alongside, it also requires that the economic apparatuses of government, institutions and the business environment must be such that encourage not stifle the creativity and ingenuity of small business operators in the formal and informal sectors.

BIBLIOGRAPHY

Anosike, P. (2018). Entrepreneurship as human capital: Implications for youth self-employment and conflict mitigation in sub-Saharan Africa. *Industry and Higher Education*, 33(1), 42–54.

Davidsson, P., & Honig, B. (2003). The role of social and human capital among nascent entrepreneurs. *Journal of Business Venturing*, 18(3), 301–331.

Dimov, D. (2010). Nascent entrepreneurs and venture emergence: Opportunity confidence, human capital, and early planning. *Journal of Management Studies*, 47(6), 1123–1153.

Frese, M., Krauss, S., Keith, N., Escher, S., Grabarkiewicz, R., Luneng, T., …, Friedrich, C. (2007). Business owners' action planning and its relationship to business success in three African countries. *Journal of Applied Psychology*, 92(6), 1481–1498.

Fukuyama, F. (2000), *Social capital and the civil society*. IMF Working Paper No. 74. Washington DC: International Monetary Fund (IMF). Retrieved from https://www.imf.org/external/pubs/ft/wp/2000/wp0074.pdf

Hodgson, G. (2006). What are institutions? *Journal of Economic Issues*, 40(1), 1–25.

Kuratko, D. F. (2005). The emergence of entrepreneurship education: Development, trends, and challenges. *Entrepreneurship Theory and Practice*, 29(5), 577–598.

Marvel, M. R., Davis, J. L., & Sproul, C. R. (2016). Human capital and entrepreneurship research: A critical review and future directions. *Entrepreneurship Theory and Practice*, 40(3), 599–626.

Mitchelmore, S., & Rowley, J. (2013). Entrepreneurial competencies of women entrepreneurs pursuing business growth. *Journal of Small Business and Enterprise Development*, 20(1), 125–142.

North, D. (1990). *Institutions, institutional change and economic performance*, New York, NY: Cambridge University Press.

Shane, S., & Venkataramam, S. (2000). The promise of entreprenuership as a field of research. *Academy of Management Review*, 25(1), 217–226.

United Nations Development Programme (2019). *Human development report 2019 beyond income, beyond averages, beyond today: Inequalities in human development in the 21st century*. New York, NY: UNDP. Retrieved from http://hdr.undp.org/sites/default/files/hdr2019.pdf

Van Arkadie, B. (1989). *The role of institutions in development (English)*. Washington, DC: The World Bank. Retrieved form http://documents.worldbank.org/curated/en/575481468740986684/The-role-of-institutions-in-development

INDEX

Page numbers followed by f, t indicate figures and tables, respectively